The Dynamics
of Korean
Economic Development

CHO SOON

The Dynamics
of Korean
Economic Development

Institute for International Economics
Washington, DC
March 1994

Cho Soon, a Visiting Fellow at the Institute during 1987, has served as Deputy Prime Minister of the Republic of Korea (1988–90) and, until recently, as Governor of the Bank of Korea. He was Professor of Economics prior to joining the Korean government. He is a member of the Korean Academy of Sciences and has written widely on the problems of development and on Korea.

INSTITUTE FOR INTERNATIONAL ECONOMICS
11 Dupont Circle, NW
Washington, DC 20036-1207
(202) 328-9000   FAX: (202) 328-5432

C. Fred Bergsten, *Director*
Christine F. Lowry, *Director of Publications*

Cover design by Naylor Design, Inc.

Printed in the United States of America
97 96 95 94   5 4 3 2

Library of Congress Cataloging-in-Publication Data

Cho Soon, 1928–
  The dynamics of Korean economic development / Cho Soon.
    p.   cm
  Includes bibliographical references and index.
  1. Korea (South)—Economic conditions—1960- 2. Korea (South)—Economic policy—1960- 3. Industrial promotion—Korea (South)
  I. Title.
  HC467.C41564   1994
  338.95195—dc20   93-42822
                                                CIP

    ISBN 0-88132-162-1

Marketed and Distributed outside the USA and Canada by Longman Group UK Limited, London

The views expressed in this publication are those of the author. This publication is part of the overall program of the Institute, as endorsed by its Board of Directors, but does not necessarily reflect the views of individual members of the Board or the Advisory Committee.

Contents

Preface

The Institute has conducted a series of projects related to Korea, which has rapidly become one of the world's leading economies. In early 1993, we published *Korea in the World Economy* by former Finance Minister Il SaKong. In 1990, we published a revised version of *Adjusting to Success: Balance of Payments Policy in the East Asian NICs* by Bela Balassa and John Williamson that included a substantial section on Korea. In 1989, we published a volume of papers on *Economic Relations Between the US and Korea: Conflict and Cooperation?* edited by Thomas O. Bayard and Soo-Gil Young.

In addition, Korea was one of the *Pacific Basin Developing Countries* analyzed by Marcus Noland in 1990. The possibility of a US-Korea Free Trade Area was considered by Yung Chul Park and Jung Ho Yoo in *Free Trade Areas and US Trade Policy*, edited by Jeffrey J. Schott in 1989. In February 1994, the Institute hosted the first meeting of the new Korea–United States 21st Century Council in an effort to further strengthen the economic relationship between the two countries.

This new volume provides a further intensive analysis of the Korean economic experience and its future outlook. It is written by Dr. Cho Soon, a former Deputy Prime Minister of Korea and Governor of the Bank of Korea. Dr. Cho was previously Professor of Economics at Seoul National University and spent 1987 at the Institute, as one of our Third World Visiting Fellows sponsored by the Ford Foundation. He brings a unique combination of academic and practical experiences to this analysis, which we feel will make a major contribution to further understanding of the "Korean economic miracle" and where it may be headed now.

The Institute for International Economics is a private nonprofit institution for the study and discussion of international economic policy. Its purpose is to analyze important issues in that area, and to develop and communicate practical new approaches for dealing with them. The Institute is completely nonpartisan.

The Institute is funded largely by philanthropic foundations. Major institutional grants are now being received from the German Marshall Fund of the United States, which created the Institute with a generous commitment of funds in 1981, and from the Ford Foundation, the William and Flora Hewlett Foundation, the William M. Keck, Jr. Foundation, the C. V. Starr Foundation, and the United States–Japan Foundation. A number of other foundations and private corporations also contribute to the highly diversified financial resources of the Institute. About 16 percent of the Institute's resources in our latest fiscal year were provided by contributors outside the United States, including about 7 percent from Japan.

The Board of Directors bears overall responsibility for the Institute and gives general guidance and approval to its research program— including identification of topics that are likely to become important to international economic policymakers over the medium run (generally, one to three years), and which thus should be addressed by the Institute. The Director, working closely with the staff and outside Advisory Committee, is responsible for the development of particular projects and makes the final decision to publish an individual study.

The Institute hopes that its studies and other activities will contribute to building a stronger foundation for international economic policy around the world. We invite readers of these publications to let us know how they think we can best accomplish this objective.

C. FRED BERGSTEN
Director
February 1994

Acknowledgments

In 1987, I was offered a visiting fellowship at the Institute for International Economics, which allowed me to spend a year in Washington. The days with the Institute were extremely rewarding; the weekly discussions were stimulating and instructive. The Institute was then, as it is now, engaged in provocative policy-oriented research that included Korean issues.

The atmosphere at the Institute stimulated me to write a short book on Korea. My views on the Korean economy, I thought, might be a useful addition to the literature on the Korean economy. I managed to complete nearly the entire manuscript by the time I joined the Korean government, and my tenure there covered one of the tumultuous periods in Korean history: the democratic movement, accompanied by eruption of labor disputes and great wage and price inflation. I was subsequently released from the government and then was appointed governor of the Bank of Korea.

Now I am back in the private sector and have decided to complete the book. So many things have happened in Korea and elsewhere. I find it impossible to incorporate all these developments, but I have updated the figures and tables and added passages on many recent developments.

The Korean economy is, as economies of most other countries in East Asia, in a state of transition. The Korean government is taking a hard look at what is to be done. The perspectives expressed in this book, I hope, provide a useful point of reference.

I have to thank most sincerely the Institute for International Economics, especially C. Fred Bergsten and the fellows at the Institute, for their assistance and patience. I would also like to thank Professor Sung Kwack of Howard University, Dr. Jong Park at the Federal Reserve Board, and Dr. Yoon-je Cho at the World Bank for the generous assistance they rendered while I was in Washington. Dr. Kye-sik Lee at the Korea Development Institute, my assistant at the Economic Planning Board, did his best in encouraging me to complete the work. Economists of the Research Department, Bank of Korea, read the manuscript and prepared figures and tables. I have to single out Mr. Chul Park and Mr. Sang-hun Lee, specifically for their most valuable contributions in supplying data and materials on recent developments. I sincerely thank Valerie Norville for her excellent and thorough editing of my manuscript. Thanks are also due to Miss Ji-hee Kim, my able secretary, for her patient assistance. Of course, the shortcomings of the book are entirely my own.

The Dynamics
of Korean
Economic Development

1

Introduction

Objective of the Study

The economic performance of Korea during the last four decades has been almost universally acclaimed. No other developing countries, except for the other Asian newly industrializing economies (NIEs), have matched its vigorous growth. To those familiar with the Korean socioeconomic situation at the time of liberation from Japanese rule in 1945, the speed of industrialization is little short of a miracle. The country was among the poorest in the world; within a span of four decades, it has transformed itself into an industrial country.

In the southern half of the Korean peninsula, the political chaos and economic breakdown following the liberation was truly forbidding. Whatever survived was destroyed by the savage war of 1950–53, and until the end of the decade the country barely managed to subsist. Hardly anyone would have imagined that such a country could become an industrial force to be reckoned with in the international economic sphere. Korea appears to be among the few examples of economic success in the developing world, and this fact alone makes the Korean performance appear remarkable to students of economic development.

Much has been written on the Korean economy: its success story has been retold many times. Yet I feel compelled to write this book because I think that the nature of its success is inadequately understood in the rest of the world as well as in Korea. In addition, recent changes in the domestic and international environments are forcing Korea into the process of far-reaching readjustment, and therefore new perspectives on its development are required. The country is about to head for a new phase in its development, and the old perspectives that guided development in the past are fast becoming obsolete.

The purpose of this study is to present new perspectives on Korea's economic development in the light of recent changes in both the domestic and international spheres. I will assess the dynamics of Korean economic growth during the last three decades and analyze the new constraints and prospects the country will face in the decades to come. I will also suggest new policy directions to overcome the constraints and to take advantage of new opportunities. By tracing the ways in which government, businesses, and workers have shaped economic development, I hope to highlight the uniqueness of Korea's development pattern and offer my own interpretations of the reasons for Korea's success and probable consequences of this success.

The Korean experience deserves a careful analysis for several reasons. First, Korea has been following a development path that has enough in common with those of other successful developing countries so that careful study would help economists formulate a fruitful general view on the development processes in contemporary developing economies. Second, whether the country can eventually become an economically advanced country remains an interesting issue for the students of economic development. In the 19th century, Japan was the only non-European country that succeeded in modernizing. The Japanese experience has provided social scientists with an enduring source of interest. During the post–World War II period, Korea and the other Asian NIEs have been experiencing similar transformations. Whether, how, and how soon Korea can join the group of developed countries will be extremely interesting to the students of social studies, and the saga of its ongoing transformation will likely be no less significant to world economic history than the Japanese experience.

Perspectives on the Past Growth

Condensed Growth

As will be shown in the next chapter, the rate of growth of GNP in Korea was rather slow until 1961, but it has accelerated since 1962, when the first Five-Year Economic Development Plan was launched. Few developing countries have shown such high rates of growth, except for Taiwan.[1]

---

1. Hong Kong and Singapore also showed comparable rates of growth. But these two countries are city-states, and it is in many ways difficult to compare them with Korea and Taiwan.

The rates of growth of Korea and Taiwan during the 1960s and 1970s surpassed those of all advanced countries during their commensurate period of development. The highest average annual growth rate among advanced countries between 1886 and 1913 was attained by the United States at 4.3 percent; the corresponding figure during the interwar period (1913–38) was Japan's 4.5 percent (Shinohara 1961, 6).[2] The growth record of Japan between the Meiji Restoration of 1868 and the outbreak of World War II, certainly one of the most sustained and rapid, failed to compare with that of Korea and Taiwan during the 1960s and 1970s. It was only during the post–World War II period that Japan achieved growth rates comparable to those of Korea and Taiwan. The annual average rate of growth of Japan during the 1950–70 period was approximately 10 percent, surpassing any other records in history.

During the last three decades, Korea and Taiwan managed to transform from traditional agricultural economies to industrial ones. The great transformation that these two countries achieved was comparable to what advanced countries achieved over the course of a hundred years—that is, Korea and Taiwan condensed a century's worth of growth into three decades.

Similarly, Japan, whose per capita income was only about 17 percent of that of the United States at the end of World War II, succeeded in transforming itself in the postwar period from an economically and technologically backward country to an advanced country. Japan also condensed the usually long and slow process of economic maturity into only several decades (though, as will be explained later in this chapter, the Japanese growth process did in some respects differ from the typical and simple condensing process found in Korea and Taiwan).

Several interesting phenomena stand out. First, it was the three East Asian countries with similar factor endowments that achieved the condensed growth. Second, they achieved this growth during roughly the same period after World War II. These two facts suggest that the similarity in the experiences of these three countries cannot be a chance occurrence. There must be some common factors accounting for the condensed growth of all three.

First and foremost, one can point out the similarity in resource endowments. Korea has limited supplies of coal, iron, tungsten, limestone, and kaolin, while other resources are scarce or nonexistent. Even resources for agricultural development are not plentiful. Arable land accounts for just 20 percent of total land; climate, soil, rainfall, and temperature are all unfavorable for agricultural production. The natural resources of Taiwan and Japan are not significantly better than those of Korea. Because of their poor natural resources, the three countries have to import most raw

---

2. Myohei Shinohara, *Nihon-Kei-Zai no Seicho to Jung-Kang (The Growth and Cycles of the Japanese Economy)*, Tokyo, Sobunsha, 1961, p. 6.

materials for their industries. Even though the agricultural productivity per unit of land in these countries is among the highest in the world, all import significant quantities of agricultural products.

In contrast with its poor endowment of natural resources, Korea is favored with human resources. In 1992 the population of Korea was 43.7 million, a twofold increase over the early 1950s. Korea is among the most densely populated countries in the world, with 440 people per square kilometer. With the exception of city-states, Bangladesh has the highest population density (699 people per square kilometer); Korea is third after Taiwan (553 people per square kilometer).[3]

With a large population in a small area, Korea had widespread surplus labor at its initial phase of development. The wage rate, determined primarily by that prevailing in the agricultural sector, was at subsistence levels. In fact, at the beginning of Korean economic development there was widespread hidden unemployment in the rural areas and open unemployment in the urban areas. The possibility of developing these areas lay in making effective use of the surplus labor in manufacturing. To be sure, not all countries with surplus labor can develop manufacturing industries effectively. The labor force has to be equipped with those attributes required for modern industrial activities: for example, a minimum standard of literacy, discipline, and a desire to "get ahead." Furthermore, there has to be vigorous entrepreneurship, administrative skill, and efficiency in government.

In this respect, Korean people were well-equipped for manufacturing. Years of subsisting on scarce land have nurtured strong survival traits, such as tenacity and pragmatism. The potential labor force was largely literate and ready to work long hours for low wages. Many entrepreneurs with a "can do" spirit emerged; they took advantage of the government policy encouraging investment with favorable bank loans and allocation of foreign exchange.

Most economists agree that the source of Korea's success lies in the adoption of an export-led growth strategy. But this raises two questions: why have other developing countries not adopted the same export-led growth strategy, and why have some countries that have adopted this strategy not been as successful as Korea? Korea was able to adopt this strategy more readily and more successfully than, for example, the Latin American countries for two reasons. First, Korea's comparative advantage in the initial stage of development more clearly lay in labor-intensive manufacturing industries than in most other developing countries.

---

3. The population growth rate of Korea in the 1950s was over 3 percent. Recently, the rate decelerated sharply to 0.91 percent. If this trend continues, the population growth rate is expected to reach as low as 0.8 percent by the end of the century (National Statistical Office, 1992, *Social Indicators in Korea*).

Second, an export-led growth strategy enabled the country to exploit its comparative advantage. The strategy also made it possible for Korea to fully employ the redundant factor (i.e., labor) and to remove the constraints posed by the shortage of other factors (i.e., natural resources). Seen in this way, the export-led growth strategy in Korea in the early 1960s was a policy choice the Koreans were led to make in order to remove inherent constraints.[4] This strategy was blessed by the favorable international environment prevailing during the 1960s.

Factors Accounting for Condensed Growth

The East Asian postwar labor-surplus countries are much more able to develop manufacturing industries than other developing countries. It may be recalled that Alexander Gerschenkron (1962, 8) argued that the speed of industrialization in an underdeveloped country is usually much faster than that of advanced countries, mainly because it can take advantage of a backlog of technological innovations developed in the more advanced country. In other words, the backward country, to use the expression employed in this book, can "condense" the process through which technological innovations are developed and applied.[5] The experiences of Korea, Taiwan, and, to a lesser extent, Japan seem to confirm the Gerschenkron thesis, although these East Asian countries have been favored by many other factors as well.

First, not only technology but also capital can be much more easily imported today than for countries developing in the 19th century. In the case of present-day developed countries, capital and technology historically were mostly generated within national boundaries. Capital had to be accumulated through the efforts of many generations, and technology had to be improved through a painstaking learning process. The

---

4. For Latin American countries such as Brazil, Argentina, and Mexico, comparative advantage lay, at the initial stage of development at least, not in manufacturing industries but in primary industries. The pattern of resource endowment, along with the large sizes of these countries, was not fully compatible with the export-led growth strategy, and one might say that this led these countries to adopt import substitution policies during the postwar period. The pattern of resource endowment thus seems to be part of the reason these countries have not been able to exploit fully the latecomer's advantage in achieving rapid growth.

5. Professor Kazushi Ohkawa characterized the rapid development of Asian developing countries as "compressed growth." See his *Keizai Hatten to Nippon no Keiken (Economic Development and Experiences of Japan)*, Tokyo, Daimei-do, 1970, p. 33. I prefer the expression "condensed" because the rapid growth of developing countries does not simply compress the whole process of normal development into a smaller volume or a shorter time but abridges the normal development process by omitting or delaying the adjustments that accompany economic growth.

contemporary developing countries, however, can dispense with this process at the initial stage of development; they can now import both and thus eliminate obstacles to export-led growth.

Second, a small domestic market is not the constraint for today's developing countries that it once was. According to traditional trade theory, an exporting country normally has to produce for the local market before exploring overseas markets in order to gather information on people's preferences and to cultivate consumers' taste for their products. The isolated domestic market is expanded *pari passu* with the increase in income, which is necessarily a slow process. The "big-push" model of economic development in vogue in the 1950s was intended to defeat this particular bottleneck through a "big push" in investment.

But during the postwar era, the almost-unlimited markets in advanced countries have been readily available to the exporters of labor-intensive goods, as has information on these markets. Furthermore, developing countries' export goods are usually standardized ones for which advanced-country demand is virtually assured. Consequently, the contemporary developing countries no longer need, at the initial stage of development, to develop local markets before exporting to overseas markets. They can export goods even before the local population develops a taste for their products.

There is a third, very important benefit for resource-poor countries of today in the pattern of postwar technological development. Resource-saving technologies have been developed with great speed, and the resource content of manufactured goods thus has been constantly and drastically reduced, to the great relief of resource-poor economies. There has recently been an infinite variety of resource-saving technological improvements, as best exemplified by those related to energy. Thus, resources are becoming less important constraints than in the pre–World War II days, and the law of diminishing returns is becoming less of a scourge for labor-surplus developing countries.

Last but not least, today's world is not dominated by imperialism, as was the case a century ago. According to the traditional notion, only the more advanced and the stronger of the traders benefits from free trade. This actually was the case in the 19th century; advanced countries invariably forced the less advanced countries to open their ports. During that period, the advanced countries' commercial fleets were more often than not equipped with guns. But today the less advanced countries often stand to gain from trade with advanced countries. Adam Smith wrote in his *Wealth of Nations* ([1776] 1950) that trade between a rich country and a poor country would benefit both but benefit the latter relatively more than the former, provided that the former does not use military power. Smith's prophecy is partly being borne out today.

We have thus far discussed factors that have contributed to the "condensed" growth of Korea and Taiwan during the last three decades and of Japan during the 1955–73 period—factors that are more or less common to all three. It is, however, both interesting and important that the three countries reveal so many differences with respect to the thrust of development strategy and the style of economic management. These differences are likely to account for the inevitable divergence in their economic performances and social environments. It is the task of economists and social scientists to ascertain not only those factors held in common but also dissimilarities in patterns of development.

The Role of Government

By and large, the government has promoted Korean economic development much more directly and actively than is the case in either Taiwan or Japan, with the result that Korean development has been marked by greater unevenness in income growth, prices, trade, and in the pattern of structural change.

Here again, the Gerschenkron thesis offers a basic frame of reference. He suggests that a developing country tends to establish its industrial structure differently from the advanced countries and that the higher the degree of backwardness, the stronger will be the role of the government and the more discontinuous and uneven development is likely to be, the degree of these differences depending upon the degree of backwardness. The experiences of Korea and Taiwan may not fall in neatly with the Gerschenkron thesis (1962, 7 and 45), but it does have some bearing. The unevenness of Korean development is in fact due to the active and direct role of the Korean government, which in turn is due to a sense of urgency on the part of the Korean populace.

The condensed growth pushed by the government was achieved at the cost of retarded development of social structure and institutions. For the past 30 years, the government made many major decisions regarding the management of the Korean economy. This is not to say that economic development would have been impossible without government involvement. Indeed, there were instances where the momentum of development was kept alive only by the remarkable endurance of the workers and people and despite mistakes made by the top decision makers in the government. Nor is it true that the Korean government gave due regard to the importance of human and institutional factors in its development effort. Rather, the government in the 1960s and 1970s, absorbed by the prospect of an early catch-up with advanced countries, failed to heed the importance of human and institutional factors as determinants of long-term development, leaving as its inheritance a peculiarly unbalanced structural pattern. What is emphasized here is that the Korean government unleashed the already-present prodevelopment spirit of the people and set the tone for development, giving it a unique Korean flavor. All the structural characteristics of the Korean economy, the unbalanced relationship between conglomerates and small enterprises, the labor-management relationship, the structure of the financial industry, and the like can be understood only in the context of the government's policies.

Another way to view Korean development is through the relatively extensive, versus intensive, character of its growth. The condensed growth of Korea over the last three decades has been a variant of an extensive-growth model: that is, it has been derived mainly from the use of existing domestic and imported resources and technologies. As the country exhausts the resources of extensive growth—e.g., raw materials, labor force, and machinery—its growth must take on an increasingly intensive character. This means that, in order to continue vigorous growth, the country must cultivate sources of intensive growth: those that enhance the productivity of existing resources through indigenously generated innovation and reforms. On the microeconomic level, these enhancements may include establishment of a corporate culture that encourages technological and managerial innovations and promotion of more harmonious labor-management relations, among others. On the macroeconomic level, they would consist of improvements in the efficiency of the competitive market system, industrial restructuring for greater balance in the economy, and reforms in government organizational management. These may be properly called the "software" of the economic society as opposed to its "hardware," which consists, for example, of plants and equipment at the micro level and the legal and regulatory framework at the macro level. Condensed growth is based largely on hardware, but the intensive growth of the future should be based more on software.

The major difference between economic hardware and software is that the former can be imported, but the latter cannot. Plants and equipment can be imported, and so can technology. But innovations in management and indigenous technology cannot. The legal and regulatory framework and government organizational reform may be easily modeled after those of other countries, but the practices and ways in which they operate cannot be so easily duplicated.

A developing economy, even in the course of condensed growth, should prepare itself for the day when the sources of condensed growth are exhausted by cultivating the sources of intensive growth. If an economy is properly prepared, it will continue to grow; if it is not, condensed growth will not be succeeded by a more normal and intensive growth process. A prime example of condensed growth that was transformed into intensive growth is the experience of Japan during 1955–73. During this period, the Japanese economy achieved a sort of condensed growth, but at the same time, it succeeded in cultivating the sources of intensive growth by enhancing technological capability and by improving corporate culture and industrial relations. In the Korean economy, the sources of intensive growth have not yet been satisfactorily cultivated, and current economic difficulties have their origins in this fact.

Scope of the Study

In this study, the story of development will be told with emphasis on the role of the government, in contrast to other related works that concentrate mainly on the analysis of economic variables. Without this focus, it would be difficult to understand the ways in which resources are allocated in Korea, to comprehend the importance of institutions in establishing the structure of the economy, and to formulate economic policy directions. As this study focuses on government's role, it therefore will emphasize of political economy.

The questions I address are not all quantitative ones, and accordingly, answers cannot all be given in quantitative terms. Indeed, these questions are not purely economic ones; they pertain as well to sociocultural matters. The questions examined here are precisely those that preclude the exactness associated with quantitative analysis. This book, therefore, will assume the style of historical and political-economy discourse. I will base my argument on factual observations while making liberal use of my own judgment.

This study consists of eight chapters. Chapters 2 and 3 provide an overview of Korea's development during the last 40 years. I will highlight developments in terms of a few macroeconomic indicators. I will also discuss the main points of Korea's development strategy as formulated by the Korean government in the early 1960s and will trace the ways in which they have been applied during the successive five-year plans.

The basic development strategies, as discussed in chapters 2 and 3, have contributed to condensed economic growth but at the same time have spawned several intractable structural problems. These problems will occupy the remainder of the book. Specifically, chapter 4 will deal with entrepreneurship, conglomerates, and small and medium enterprises. The chapter will address the quality of entrepreneurship in Korea, the problems of concentration of economic power, and policies to alleviate it. Chapter 5 examines labor-related problems, including the recent labor-management disputes, rapidly rising wages, and the main features of labor unions. Chapter 6 will be devoted to problems concerning finance, including development of banks, nonbanking financial institutions, and capital markets. Chapter 7 discusses problems of foreign trade, the position of the Korean economy in the world, and Korea-US trade relations. Chapter 8 summarizes my own views on the prospects of the Korean economy. Each chapter will conclude with discussions on policy implications.

2

Korean Economic Development in the 1950s and 1960s

Overview of Development

After liberation from Japanese rule in 1945, Korea experienced tremendous political, social, and economic turmoil, the severity of which was beyond description. The government, established in August 1948, made great efforts to restore production facilities and to arrest inflation, and it had achieved a certain degree of success before the Korean War broke out in June 1950. The savage war lasted three years, costing the tottering nation two-thirds of its production facilities and nearly 1.5 million lives. After the cease-fire in 1953, recovery from war damage proceeded rapidly with the help of US economic aid. Reconstruction was largely completed by 1956, and the near hyperinflation was brought under control.[1] However, the economy heavily depended upon US economic aid and lacked a plan for establishing sustained long-term growth. It was not until the early 1960s, when the military government launched the first five-year economic development plan, that the Korean economy found the path to high growth rates. Thus, the success story of Korea's development usually begins here.

Development and Economic Policies in the 1950s

Highlights of Development

The 1950s are generally considered merely a period of economic stagnation, and the government is thought not to have done much to promote

---

1. Inflation rates in the 1950s, on a WPI basis, were 25 percent in 1953, 80.5 percent in 1955, and 16.1 percent in 1957.

long-term economic development. Throughout the decade, the government became increasingly autocratic and ineffective, and economic management was plagued by waste and inefficiency. However, the country did achieve a few important policy objectives during the 1950s that became the basis of more rapid growth during the 1960s. Thus, the 1950s were in some sense a period of preparation for the next and subsequent decades. It is impossible to describe all important aspects of development during this period in detail; a few of the more important achievements are emphasized here.

The first was farmland reform, officially announced in 1950 and carried out in 1954. After liberation in 1945, the right and the left intensely debated the principles governing land reform in an atmosphere of divided public opinion. The right-wing government finally adopted a policy of reforming the ownership system of farmland based on "confiscation with payment" and "distribution with payment." The government purchased farmland from landowners and distributed it to the tilling farmers. As a result, the economic basis of landowning gentry in rural communities collapsed, and many independent farmers emerged. The traditional sharecropper farming system was replaced by a tenant farming system, and the productivity of the agriculture sector has since continuously increased.[2]

The Korean government had hoped that the former landowners would be induced to start businesses with the compensation paid by the government and eventually become industrial capitalists. This expectation was not borne out; the landowners simply lost their land. Part of the reason was that the landowners were not paid with money but with securities of five-year maturity to be redeemed in five equal installments in the course of five years. The real value of these securities fell rapidly due to hyperinflation that was raging during the redemption period,[3] and sometimes even annual payments were not paid on time. In effect, the land was virtually confiscated from the landowners without much compensation. Most of the landowners completely lost their livelihood, and they did not become industrial capitalists.

Another notable development was the sale of Japanese-owned enterprises and properties taken over by the US military government after liberation. These enterprises numbered about 600, and their employees amounted to 48.3 percent of the total in manufacturing industries in 1948 (Federation of Korean Industries 1986, 755). The sale of these enterprises was a significant policy innovation at that time. It reflected the

---

2. It is noteworthy that Korea, Taiwan, and Japan were the noncommunist Asian countries that had land reform.

3. The expectation of inflation caused the prices of these securities to plummet, and the landowners were induced to sell them to urban speculators at much-depreciated prices.

basic policy line pursued ever since by the Korean government—to maintain the free enterprise system.

According to the provisions of the first constitution, enacted in 1948, the Republic of Korea was to become a welfare state, like the one envisaged by the Weimar Republic constitution during the interwar period in Germany. It stipulated nationalization of natural resources, state ownership of key industries, and laborers' right to share in profits. It also emphasized social justice and balanced economic development. This welfare state–oriented constitution was amended in November 1954 to allow a greater role to the private sector, and the Korean economic system subsequently assumed a more free-market character. The most impending task for Korean industrial policy, in keeping with the direction in economic policy envisaged by the new constitution, was to sell the property and production facilities formerly owned and operated by the Japanese to prospective entrepreneurs. This the government did on a large scale; most of the former Japanese properties were sold to private individuals, with the exception of commercial banks and some public utilities.

Those who acquired these properties reaped windfall capital gains because the properties were sold at a price significantly below market value. The beneficiaries were either former employees or those who had prior connections with the enterprises. Many became successful businessmen and have since become leaders in the Korean business community. They were the core of a class of important businessmen that emerged and began to accumulate capital.

After the armistice in July 1953 and with economic aid from the United States, light industries were established. Among the most important were food, cement, plate glass, chemical fertilizers, textiles, and paper. Electrical facilities were expanded, and considerable infrastructural investments were made in transportation, communication, education, and housing. These investments provided the foundation for the industrial development of the 1960s.

The most notable feature of the Korean economy during the 1950s was its dependence on US economic aid. Before the Korean War, US assistance consisted mostly of food and relief supplies. But after the war, it included raw materials and capital goods for industrial use. The total aid from both US and international organizations reached approximately $3 billion during this period. International assistance reached its peak in 1957 and 1958, began to decrease slowly in 1959, and ended at the end of the 1960s. In the latter half of the 1950s, US aid accounted for almost 80 percent of total imports.

Before and after the Korean War, Korea was among the poorest countries in the world. At the beginning of economic reconstruction, most of the gross saving was financed by US aid; the portion of gross saving from domestic sources was extremely low. In the 1950s, gross domestic investment was 12 percent of gross national disposable income, and most of the investments in social overhead capital (infrastructure) and production facilities were eventually made possible by US aid.

Many articles have been written on the effects of US aid on the Korean economy. According to some economists, US aid did not contribute significantly to the development of the Korean economy. Not many Koreans believed economic assistance to be effective. Even the US aid authorities seem not to have evaluated the results of economic assistance very positively. Many believed US aid did not contribute to capital formation in Korea, since it was heavily tilted toward consumer goods. Yet only 14 percent of the aid was in capital goods, and the balance was in consumer goods (Steinberg 1985, 26). The US and Korean critics also thought that because aid was primarily in the form of surplus agricultural products and consumer goods, it hindered the development of Korean agriculture and the emergence of domestic industries. Besides, many believed that the US aid primarily served to sustain the authoritarian Syngman Rhee regime. Moreover, US aid authorities felt that the Korean government was interested only in maximizing the receipt of the US aid and that they thus neglected to establish policies for achieving long-term development (Steinberg 1985, 21). These evaluations partly reflect the prevailing sense of frustration in the 1950s about the Korean political and economic situation.

In all fairness, one may concede that US aid did make an important contribution. Although this aid was heavily biased toward the short-term objective of economic stabilization, it tided the country over during a difficult period and allowed it to make many important investments that formed the basis for subsequent development.

For example, the Counterpart Fund, established with the proceeds, in Korean currency, from the sale of aid materials, financed a considerable portion of the Korean government's budget and investments in social infrastructure and key industries. This fund also became a major source of money for loans from the Korean Reconstruction Bank, established in 1954 to finance basis industries. Furthermore, US aid helped enable Koreans to invest in educational institutions—investment in human capital during this period being a major factor in Korea's development in the ensuing decades.

Major Economic Policies

The Korean government was unable to establish a consistent development policy in the 1950s. As noted earlier, economic life, as well as the government budget, was largely sustained by US aid. Everything was in shortage, and the government was too preoccupied with day-to-day affairs to conceive programs for long-term development. Developing a long-term economic outlook was beyond the government's means; the immediate problem was to achieve price stability by increasing the supply of daily necessities. To achieve these ends, the Korean government consistently maintained a policy of "three lows":[4] low grain prices, low interest rates, and a low exchange rate (i.e., an overvalued domestic currency).

Grains, and particularly rice, were at the center of Korean economic life during the 1950s. The price of rice was the single most important determinant of inflation, and it was very important for the government to maintain the lowest possible price. This was accomplished by importing surplus US agricultural products. Grain prices declined sharply as grain imports from the United States accelerated, and the sharp drop in grain prices decreased the domestic farmers' incentive to produce grains. Despite the harm to farmers, the government continued to import surplus US grains to placate the politically strong urban population.

During the decade, the commercial banks were owned and operated by the government, and interest rates on bank loans were kept consistently low in order to aid business. Even during the hyperinflation period before and after the Korean War, interest rates were fixed very low in accordance with the Maximum Interest Rate Act, which imposed maximum nominal loan rates at 20 percent. Real interest rates were always considerably negative throughout this period, in effect giving subsidies to borrowers. The interest rates applied to loans for financing priority projects were even lower. Despite the advice of the Monetary Board, the decision-making body of the Bank of Korea, the Maximum Interest Rate Act was not abolished during this period. Those who had purchased the former Japanese-owned plants and facilities added the special benefit of low-interest loans to their windfall profits.

The implied subsidy to borrowers came at the expense of savers. Thus, the low interest-rate policy was a strong deterrent to the long-term development of banking institutions. Interest rates in the private money market, outside institutional finance, were very high, so as to maintain the positive rates of interest in the unorganized money market. As people shunned formal financial institutions, the bulk of the financial resources of the country flowed through the informal money market, perpetuating a dual market structure. Low interest rates in the institutional financial sector discouraged the emergence of small and medium enterprises, since they were largely denied access to the banks and had to borrow from the unorganized money market at high nominal interest rates.

The last of the three "lows" was the policy of keeping the domestic currency overvalued (i.e, a low won-dollar exchange rate); this policy maximized the receipt of dollars from the US armed forces, which was then the major source of supply for dollars. The policy also was thought

---

4. The Korean government never expressed in so many words that it would pursue these policies. But, these policies were certainly very consistently maintained, throughout the 1950s, marking the most outstanding characteristics in the whole gamut of economic policies during the decade.

to be necessary in order to supply foreign exchange to the "end users" (i.e., business) at low prices in domestic currency terms and to help stabilize the price level. The exchange rate system the government adopted at that time was a variant of a multiple exchange-rate system; there were complicated sets of exchange rates, which differed according to the sources and uses of the foreign exchange. In general, the government kept all exchange rates as low as possible. The overvaluation of the domestic currency was a source of windfall profit for those enterprises that had been allocated aid materials. It worked well for those enterprises producing goods primarily for domestic demand. The result was to encourage what are now referred to as import-substitution industries, a term that would not have been familiar to Koreans at that time.

Many people characterize the Korean industrial policy during the 1950s as one focused on import substitution. If one defines import-substitution industries as those that produce and sell for the domestic market, the Korean industries established during the 1950s were, for the most part, import-substitution industries. In the face of an absolute lack of materials, industries that were initiated during this period were most likely to cater to domestic demand. It was only later that they were labeled import-substitution industries. Korean policymakers then made no clear dis-tinction between import substitution and export industries; these activities merely took place in sequence. Industries that at first produced to meet domestic demand—that is, played the role of import substitution—in a later period made the transition to producing for overseas markets.

Overview of Development Since the Early 1960s

The remainder of this chapter will present highlights of Korea's development since 1962 in terms of a few basic macroeconomic indicators. Since it is impossible to give a detailed account of every aspect of development in this book, a brief summary of Korean economic performance will suffice. Korea's development, as far as is visible through macroeconomic indicators, can be characterized by high growth rates of GNP and per capita income, high inflation rates in the 1960s and 1970s, declining unemployment rates, rapid structural transformation (i.e., rapid expansion of the manufacturing sector at the expense of the primary sector), and rapid increases in exports and imports.[5] A brief account of each of these aspects follows, along with corresponding data on Taiwan, which provides an international comparison between the two economies that are the most similar.

---

5. These characteristics, except for inflation, show that the Korean economic development had a resemblance to what Simon Kuznets (1966) called modern economic growth.

Figure 2.1 Korea, Taiwan: GNP growth rates, 1962–91

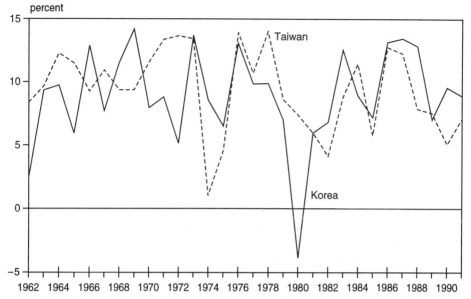

Sources: Bank of Korea, *Economic Statistics Yearbook,* 1991 and 1992; *National Accounts,* 1990; Director-General of Budget, Accounting and Statistics, Executive Yuan, *National Income in Taiwan Area of the Republic of China,* 1991.

GNP Growth

Figure 2.1 gives the average annual rates of GNP growth for Korea and Taiwan during the period under study. Korea's GNP growth rate during the 1950s, at about 4 percent per annum, was not impressive, but it leaped in the 1962–66 plan period to 7.8 percent per annum. The annual average GNP growth rate in 1967–71 and 1972–76 rose to 9.7 percent and 9.1 percent, respectively, but decelerated to 5.7 percent in 1977–81 due to the second oil crisis and the political unrest in 1980. Between 1986 and 1988, the Korean economy showed unprecedented double-digit GNP growth rates for three consecutive years, thanks, among other things, to the rapid appreciation of the Japanese yen, which gave rise to the big export boom for Korea, low international interest rates that mitigated the debt service burden, and low oil prices that reduced costs for import materials.

The sustained high growth rates Korea experienced are almost without precedent in the developing world, except for Taiwan and other Asian NIEs.

Inflation Rate

Until the early 1980s, Korea experienced galloping inflation, as shown in figure 2.2. Inflation rates were almost always in double-digit figures

Figure 2.2a Korea: inflation rates and money growth rates, 1962–92

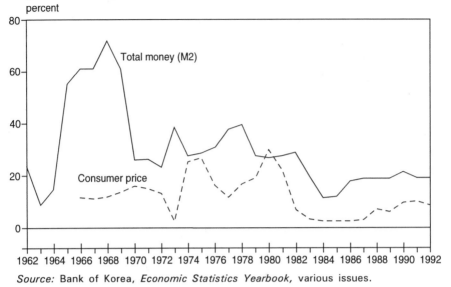

Source: Bank of Korea, *Economic Statistics Yearbook*, various issues.

Figure 2.2b Taiwan: inflation rates and money growth rates, 1962–92

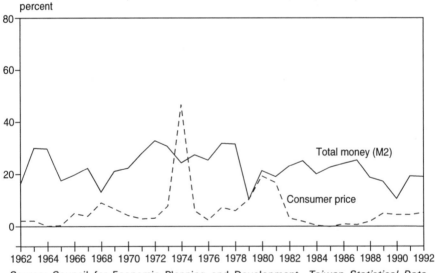

Source: Council for Economic Planning and Development, *Taiwan Statistical Data Book*, Republic of China, 1992.

throughout the high-growth periods. This is due, among other things, to the inflationary financing of investment, which caused a rapid uninterrupted increase in the money supply. Note that inflation was particularly severe in the 1970s, when the government made an all-out effort to foster heavy and chemical industries. By the mid-1980s, however, infla-

Table 2.1 Unemployment rate, 1962–91 (percentages)

Year	Unemployment rate	Year	Unemployment rate
1962	n.a.	1977	3.8
1963	8.2	1978	3.2
1964	7.7	1979	3.8
1965	7.4	1980	5.2
1966	7.1	1981	4.5
1967	6.2	1982	4.4
1968	5.1	1983	4.1
1969	4.8	1984	3.8
1970	4.5	1985	4.0
1971	4.5	1986	3.8
1972	4.5	1987	3.1
1973	4.0	1988	2.5
1974	4.1	1989	2.6
1975	4.1	1990	2.4
1976	3.9	1991	2.4

n.a. = not available.

Source: Bank of Korea, *Economic Statistics Yearbook*, 1992.

tion had largely subsided, with the increase in money supply visibly reduced. The inflation record for the last several decades and the behavior of prices during the last several years suggest that the Korean economy has an inflation-prone structure.

Unemployment

The steady but rapid growth of manufacturing industries has been accompanied by a steady decline in the unemployment rate. The unemployment figures of Korea, given in table 2.1, may somewhat understate the unemployment problem in the early phase of economic development, in that they fail to reveal the widespread hidden unemployment that prevailed in the 1960s. At any rate, it is undeniable that unemployment has been steadily declining, and in recent years the unemployment rate has been below 3 percent.

Saving and Investment

One of the remarkable aspects of Korea's development can be found in the behavior of saving and investment, which is shown in figure 2.3. Two aspects deserve particular attention. One is that, in the 1950s, the ratio of gross saving to gross national disposable income was around 12 percent,[6] but it has been increasing with astounding speed; in 1988 it

---

6. During the 1950s, current transfers from the rest of the world (mostly from the United States in the form of economic aid) accounted for a substantial portion of the gross savings shown in the table. Therefore, the saving ratios, excluding the current transfers during the 1950s, were much lower than shown in the table.

Figure 2.3 Korea: saving, investment, and net lending shares in GNP, 1962–91

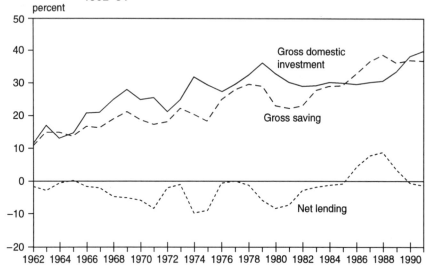

Sources: Bank of Korea, *National Income in Korea,* 1982; *National Accounts,* 1990; *Economic Statistics Yearbook,* 1991 and 1992.

reached 38 percent. One may enumerate many factors responsible for this significant rise in the propensity to save, but the rapid rise in GNP itself originating from the rapid increase in exports is the single most important factor. Saving and investment ratios for Taiwan are presented in figure 2.4.

The other remarkable fact is that, until the very recent past, gross investment far exceeded gross saving. The excess of investment over saving was, of course, financed by borrowed foreign saving after the termination of US aid in the early 1960s. In 1986, however, saving significantly exceeded investment, and in 1987 and 1988, the excess of saving over investment expanded further. Corresponding to this turn of events was the appearance in that year of the balance of payments surplus, which was brought about by the great increase in exports as described earlier.

Structural Change

The rapid growth of GNP and employment has been accompanied by a substantial structural transformation in the economy. Table 2.2 shows that Korea was a predominantly agricultural country in the 1950s; the agriculture and fishery share of GDP between 1953 and 1961 was about 40 percent, as compared with 13 percent for manufacturing. The share of agriculture and fisheries has rapidly shrunk since the early 1960s to

Figure 2.4 Taiwan: saving, investment, and net lending shares in GNP, 1962–90

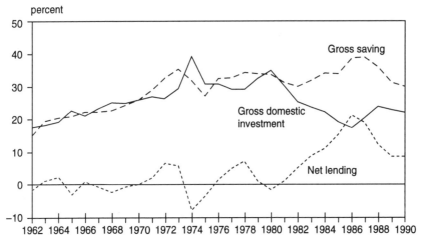

percent

Source: Director-General of Budget, Accounting and Statistics, Executive Yuan, *National Income in Taiwan Area of the Republic of China*, 1991.

about 9 percent in recent years. At the same time, the manufacturing sector increased from 13 percent in the 1950s to 30 percent in recent years. Public utilities such as gas, electricity, water, and construction also registered considerable gains, while services expanded their share of GNP from 41 to 46 percent.

The structure of manufacturing industries itself has undergone a tremendous change during this period. Although mainly labor-intensive light industries were established in the 1950s and in the early 1960s, the government started fostering heavy and chemical industries toward the late 1960s and accelerated investment in the 1970s in electronics, machinery, steel and iron, shipbuilding, and chemical industries. As a result of the policy emphasizing heavy and chemical industries since then, the proportion of these industries in the total manufacturing sector has increased to approximately 60 percent in recent years. Figures 2.5 and 2.6 illustrate the structural changes of both Korea and Taiwan.

Foreign Trade

The most remarkable aspect of Korea's development is the phenomenal growth of exports and imports and the accompanying increase in the national economy's dependence on the rest of the world. Korea had been a country virtually sealed off from the rest of the world until it embarked on export promotion in the early 1960s. As described earlier, exports have so far been Korea's engine of growth; the country has

Table 2.2 Industry shares of GDP at current prices (percentages)

Industry	1953–61	1962–66	1967–71	1972–76	1977–81	1982–86	1987–91
Agriculture, forestry, and fishing	40.4	39.6	27.8	24.7	17.7	12.9	9.4
Mining and manufacturing	14.4	18.7	22.0	27.3	30.4	31.6	30.6
Manufacturing only	12.7	16.8	20.5	26.1	29.1	30.5	30.0
Construction, electricity, gas, and water	4.0	4.5	6.6	5.8	9.4	10.4	13.8
Other services	41.2	37.2	43.6	42.2	42.5	45.1	46.2

Sources: Bank of Korea, *National Income in Korea,* 1982; *National Accounts,* 1990; *Economic Statistics Yearbook,* 1991 and 1992.

22

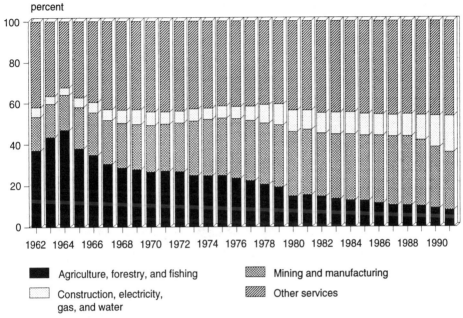

Figure 2.5 Korea: sectoral shares of industry in GNP, 1962–91

percent

1962 1964 1966 1968 1970 1972 1974 1976 1978 1980 1982 1984 1986 1988 1990

■ Agriculture, forestry, and fishing

▨ Mining and manufacturing

☐ Construction, electricity, gas, and water

▨ Other services

Sources: Bank of Korea, *National Income in Korea,* 1982; *National Accounts,* 1990; *Economic Statistics Yearbook,* 1991 and 1992.

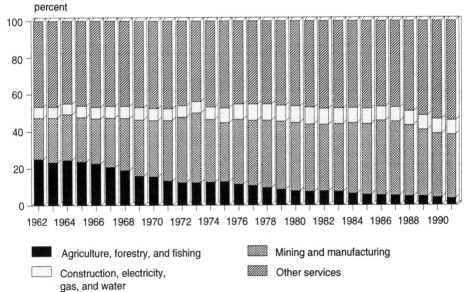

Figure 2.6 Taiwan: sectoral shares of industry in GNP, 1962–91

percent

1962 1964 1966 1968 1970 1972 1974 1976 1978 1980 1982 1984 1986 1988 1990

■ Agriculture, forestry, and fishing

▨ Mining and manufacturing

☐ Construction, electricity, gas, and water

▨ Other services

Source: Director-General of Budget, Accounting and Statistics, Executive Yuan, *National Income in Taiwan Area of the Republic of China*, 1991.

Table 2.3 Korea: trade balance, 1962–91[a]
(millions of dollars)

Year	Exports	Imports	Trade balance
1962	55	390	−335
1963	87	497	−410
1964	119	365	−246
1965	175	416	−241
1966	250	680	−430
1967	335	909	−574
1968	486	1,322	−836
1969	658	1,650	−992
1970	882	1,804	−922
1971	1,132	2,178	−1,046
1972	1,676	2,250	−575
1973	3,271	3,837	−566
1974	4,515	6,452	−1,937
1975	5,003	6,674	−1,671
1976	7,815	8,400	−585
1977	10,047	10,523	−476
1978	12,710	14,491	−1,781
1979	14,705	19,100	−4,395
1980	17,214	21,598	−4,384
1981	20,671	24,299	−3,628
1982	20,879	23,474	−2,595
1983	23,204	24,967	−1,763
1984	26,335	27,371	−1,036
1985	26,442	26,461	−19
1986	33,913	29,707	4,206
1987	46,244	38,585	7,659
1988	59,648	48,203	11,445
1989	61,409	56,812	4,597
1990	63,124	65,127	−2,003
1991	69,582	76,561	−6,979

a. All figures are valued at f.o.b. and based on balance of payments statistics.

Source: Bank of Korea, Economic Statistics Yearbook, various years.

enjoyed extremely favorable domestic and international economic environments, which have contributed to the success of the export-led growth strategy.

Exports of manufactured goods were practically nonexistent before 1962, and imports, as has been noted, were almost completely financed by US aid. Due to the vigorous emergence of light industries and strong export promotion, Korea witnessed a tremendous increase in exports since the early 1960s, as shown in table 2.3. Despite the rapid increase in exports, however, the balance of trade generally worsened in the 1960s and 1970s because of a rapid increase in imports. As will be explained in chapter 7, the Korean government vigorously promoted exports, and at the same time it fostered import-substitution industries as well by erect-

Figure 2.7 Korea, Taiwan: trade balance, 1962–91

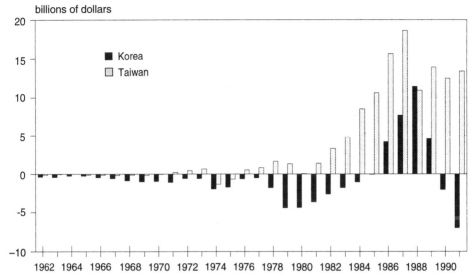

billions of dollars

Sources: Bank of Korea, *Economic Statistics Yearbook*, various years; Council for Economic Planning and Development, *Taiwan Statistical Data Book*, various years.

ing tariff barriers. Imports consisted, therefore, mostly of capital goods and the raw materials needed for export industries and import-substitution industries.

Korea's balance of trade accounts, which were deeply in the red throughout the 1960s and 1970s, finally registered a surplus in 1986 (figure 2.7). Although more detailed analysis on Korea's foreign trade will be conducted in chapter 7, it may be noted here that, ironically, the rapid growth of the trade surplus caused many difficulties during subsequent periods. One ought to review carefully the long-run impacts of the nature of the surplus: it is a testimony to the fact that a surplus is not always a blessing for a country.

To recapitulate, the Korean economy during the last three decades has achieved extremely high rate of growth of GNP and per capita income with considerable inflation, great structural transformation from an agricultural economy to an industrial one, a high rate of employment growth, and an extremely rapid increase in exports and imports. All these changes took place within the span of one generation, through a process that can be characterized as one of "condensing" the much longer industrialization path traversed by the advanced countries. Korea has been able to condense what was condensable through the physical expansion of the economy, but continued growth depends on factors that are not condensable through physical expansion alone.

3

Five-Year Development Plans: An Overview

First Five-Year Economic Development Plan (1962–66)

The Democratic Party–led government came into power after the Rhee regime was overthrown by student demonstrations in April 1960. It attempted to launch an economic development plan in early 1961, but it was preoccupied with social disorder until it was toppled by a military coup in May 1961. The military government was to last until 1979, when its leader, the late President Park Chung Hee, was assassinated.

In 1962 the government launched the first five-year economic development plan; its plan period, 1962–66, was the most important five-year period in the history of Korean development. It was during this period that the government established the basic strategies for economic development to which it adhered for the coming decades. When the military government came to power, however, it did not have a clear strategy for economic management. Through trial and error, the government came across a set of basic guiding principles for development. Let us first see the background of the plan and the nature of the process through which it was developed.

The economic situation during this period required the government to make strenuous efforts at development. As the economic aid from the United States gradually decreased, so did the rate of investment, accompanied by a fall in the rate of growth and a rise in unemployment. The economy, which had depended heavily on the aid, faced a great challenge. The people were deeply frustrated and yearned for a government initiative to vitalize the depressed economy.

On seizing power, the military government declared that economic development would be its prime objective. In the beginning, however, it did not have a clear direction for accomplishing this. Driven primarily by nationalism, the military government tried to provide the initial impetus for development by mobilizing domestic capital. In June 1962, it tried to finance an ambitious investment program funded by the Emergency Monetary Measure, which purported to mobilize domestic capital through currency reform. This policy ended in failure; hoarded money amounted to only a meager sum.

Discarding the advice of the Korean-American Joint Economic Committee, which had worked for economic stability, the government adopted an inflationary method of financing its investment programs: it increased the money supply. This policy also failed, along with several important projects, seriously eroding the foreign exchange position of the country. Among the most important projects was investment for producing Saenara passenger cars; the government gave up the project due to the lack of foreign exchange. Another project was a plant for producing television sets; it, too, was given up in 1962. An attempt to produce watches in 1962 was also unsuccessful.[1]

Realizing early that such white-elephant investments were prone to failure, the military government revised the original five-year plan in 1964, putting an end to the inflationary method of mobilizing domestic capital. The government reintroduced a financial stabilization plan, discarded those projects which exhausted foreign exchanges, and adopted more active policies for export promotion.

Targets and Performance

The first five-year plan was a hastily prepared document, based on the three-year economic development proposal drafted by the Ministry of Reconstruction in 1957. The revised version of the proposal had been promptly approved in a cabinet meeting on 15 April 1960, just a few days before the breakout of student demonstrations that led to the downfall of the Rhee government.

In view of the declining aid from the United States, the first five-year plan aimed at establishing a self-sufficient economy. As discussed earlier, this original plan was designed to achieve high economic growth based on domestic capital. As the achievement of the original target (an average annual growth rate of 7.1 percent) appeared impossible in the early phase of the plan period, due to excessive and ineffective investment plans, the government revised the original plan during the third year of the plan, adjusting the projected growth rate downward.

---

1. For more detailed accounts on these projects, see Richard Luedde-Neurath (1986, 53–58).

Table 3.1 Targets and performance of the first five-year plan (1962–66)

Indicator	Targets	Performance
Economic growth rate (percentage)	7.1	7.8
Investment as a share of GNP	22.6	17.0
Domestic saving as a share of GNP	9.2	8.8
Foreign saving as a share of GNP	13.4	8.2
Current account in 1966 (millions of dollars)	−246.6	−103.4
Exports in 1966[a] (millions of dollars)	137.5	250.4
Annual average percentage change		43.7
Imports in 1966[a] (millions of dollars)	492.3	679.9
Annual average percentage change		19.1

a. Denotes figures on balance of payments basis.

Sources: Economic Planning Board; Bank of Korea, *National Accounts,* 1990.

Table 3.1 shows the original targets and actual performance under the plan. As seen in the table, this plan was successful in terms of economic growth. While the targeted economic growth rate in the plan was 7.1 percent, the actual performance was 7.8 percent despite the fact that both investment and saving were below the target level. The share of saving in GNP was low; while the targeted saving ratio was 9.2 percent, the actual performance was only 8.8 percent.[2] The actual investment ratio was 17.0 percent, compared with the targeted ratio of 22.6 percent. This served as a policy signal to the government; saving had to be increased. In order to increase saving and thus sustain a high investment ratio, the government took two measures: one was to increase interest rates at banking institutions to increase domestic (and especially financial) saving, and the other was to encourage borrowing from abroad. Another cause of the high rate of growth during this period was an unexpected, rapid increase in exports. This was another policy signal; export-led growth would be possible. The great potential of export-led growth began to manifest itself at this stage. However, imports also exceeded the targeted figure because firms competed in making investments, which required imports of capital goods and raw materials.

Innovative Economic Policies

As mentioned earlier, the military government succeeded in formulating the fundamentals of a development strategy guided by trial and error

---

2. The saving and investment ratios for the first to fifth plans in this chapter are ratios to GNP, while those for the sixth and seventh plans are ratios to gross national disposable income.

rather than by any preconceived strategy. The government made some remarkable policy innovations in the course of implementing the first five-year plan. Among them: depreciation of the value of the Korean currency (the won) to make the exchange rate reflect the market value of the currency, a sharp increase in the interest rates at banking institutions to increase financial savings, and stimulation of the inflow of foreign capital to make up for the shortage of domestic savings.

These policies, which conform with standard economic theory, were nevertheless new to the government circle at that time—they marked a new approach to economic development. These policies brought, on the whole, successful results, and they deserve a more detailed description.

First, the reform of the exchange rate system in May 1964 included not only the revaluation of par value, but also the adoption of a unitary fluctuating exchange rate system.[3] This reform was motivated primarily by a desire to promote exports. However, this did not mean the adoption of an import liberalization policy. Instead, the government reinforced the import-quota system and adopted a special tariff system, imposing higher tariffs on consumption goods. The policies for export promotion and import restriction were adopted simultaneously.

Second, interest rates on savings accounts were raised sharply in September 1965 from about 15 percent to 30 percent, and lending rates were raised accordingly to increase savings and to induce the efficient use of loans. The increase in interest rates resulted in a high increase in savings deposits, shifting a considerable amount of funds from the unorganized into the organized financial system. The increase in interest rates was aimed not only at increasing financial savings, but also at improving the efficiency of the use of bank credits. The high interest-rate policy contributed to efficient use of bank loans and price stability, but it had an unexpected side effect: a large inflow of foreign capital. As the lending rate increased sharply at domestic banks, domestic firms tried competitively to borrow foreign capital at much lower rates. Thus, the adoption of a high interest-rate policy contributed to an increase in savings deposits, price stability, and an increase in the inflow of foreign capital, all of which made a high level of investment possible.

The raising of the exchange rate and interest rates implied that the government had abandoned two of the "three lows," policies that, as described earlier, had been maintained since the 1950s. Edging these

---

3. In this system, the official exchange rate of the Korean won against the US dollar was quoted periodically after due consideration of the market rate of the foreign exchange certificate. Foreign exchange banks were allowed to issue this certificate to residents in exchange for the designated foreign exchange or against the sale of gold. The certificate could be freely traded among residents or used for import certification (or opening of letter of credit), payment abroad with guarantee of the Bank of Korea, and purchase of foreign exchange.

rates toward market levels, the government improved the workings of the price mechanism in the financial market and foreign exchange market and provided the basis for export-led economic growth.

Third, in order to promote the inflow of foreign capital, the government asked the government-owned domestic banks to guarantee repayment of domestic firms' foreign currency borrowing in cases where the firms went bankrupt.[4] The government also guaranteed remittance of principal and profits for foreign direct investment. However, as Korean firms were not accustomed to borrowing from abroad, the actual amount of foreign capital inflow turned out to be far lower than the targeted amounts during the first five-year plan.

The policy of encouraging firms to borrow foreign capital, however, proved successful. Firms imported capital from abroad, employed labor, manufactured and sold labor-intensive products, and made handsome profits. The wage rates were low, due to the abundant supply of labor, making the labor-intensive industries established during this period cost-competitive in the international market.

The technology that entrepreneurs used was mostly simple and well-known. In addition, there was never any great uncertainty about demand for Korean products in the international market. For example, major export items such as wigs, artificial eyelashes, textiles, and plywood were standardized items in terms of prices and content. These items were mostly the goods of perfectly competitive markets, where the only decisive factor for an exporter was cost of production.

Basic Philosophy of the Plan

During the first five-year plan period, the government established a set of basic principles, which, though not stated in so many words in the plan documents, were to become guidelines for economic policies for years to come. The leading elite in the government, who determined this basic development strategy, were innovative and resilient. The principles can be summarized as follows:

- Korean economic development should be achieved through industrialization. While in the initial stage the light industries should be established to increase income and employment, the heavy and chemical industries would be established as the industrial structure is deepened.

- Economic development should be achieved under government control and leadership. The government should determine the direction of policies based upon economic development planning. The goals of

---

4. The banks were owned by the government but were operated by the staffs of the banks, who were appointed by the government.

economic development should be achieved partly through the price mechanism and partly through government investment and financing. The government may employ other means than the price mechanism for promoting priority industries.

- Although in principle firms should be owned and managed privately, the government could complement and replace private decisions in the case of major investments.

- To finance investments required for economic development, foreign capital inflow should be induced. To increase employment and repay foreign debts, the increase in exports should have top priority among economic policy measures.

- For economic development, growth should have a higher priority than redressing imbalances in income distribution and unevenness in industrial development across geographical regions because growth was expected eventually to take care of these problems. Furthermore, some inflation should be tolerated; it is natural that high growth rates should be accompanied by some inflation.

The five principles enumerated above are regarded as the basic development strategy to which the government adhered throughout the 1960s and 1970s. While these strategies do not seem novel today, they contain a few aspects that can be considered innovative in the light of the political and economic atmosphere at that time.

First, consider the direction of industrialization. Industrialization was also the ultimate goal of economic policies of the two previous governments: the Liberal Party government and the Democratic Party government. The only debates were about the means and methods of carrying out industrialization. The novelty lay in the way in which industrialization was pursued: through government-led planning that stressed growth as a primary objective.

Although it was not a new idea that the government should exercise appropriate leadership for economic development, the Korean military government envisaged a much stronger role for development than did previous governments. Korea has had a very centralized government, charged with the full responsibility of carrying out a development plan. Many developing countries, including Taiwan and India, adopted economic plans before Korea did. However, Korea's economic plan had characteristics very different from those of other countries: the government was to play a much more direct and active role than did other countries' governments, and the attainment of targets was considered essential. The strong central government was to command the ways in which development was pursued.

To carry out the development plan, the government made some important organizational innovations in government structure and operations. The Economic Planning Board (EPB) was established in 1963 by reshuffling the Ministry of Reconstruction, whose main function had been administration of US aid, and absorbing the Budget Bureau of the Ministry of Finance. The EPB later absorbed the Statistics Bureau of the Ministry of Home Affairs. The minister of the EPB, who concurrently holds the title of deputy prime minister, was to lead all economic ministers and was responsible for drafting and implementing the economic development plan. Furthermore, the military government placed the central bank—the Bank of Korea—under its control by revising the Bank of Korea Act. Commercial banks were also brought under government control by confiscating the stocks of the banks, which had previously been privately owned. The government also strengthened its control over many government organizations and quasi-public institutions.

The economic development plan during the 1960s included programs for establishing infrastructure projects and targets for the private sector. The elaborate industrial targeting policies for specific industries—the practices of designating specific industries to be established and the means to do so that dominated the economic policies in the 1970s—were not yet widely practiced. Infrastructure projects were financed through the government budget, and targets for the private sector were to be attained primarily through price mechanisms.

The government allowed private ownership and management in all industries except for important public utilities. However, the government intervened in major decisions on investment, finance, imports of foreign capital, and location of major industries, even if the firms were privately owned. Furthermore, toward the late 1960s, the government started to carry out industrial targeting practices. In effect, the Korean economic system in the 1960s and 1970s was a variant of authoritarian capitalism, in which enterprises were privately owned but management was shared between the government and the owners.

The military government promoted exports as well as the inducement of foreign capital. Maximization of exports was the top priority over all other policy objectives. As already noted earlier, the Liberal Party government during the 1950s emphasized the importance of earning foreign exchange reserves and later, the Democratic Party government during 1960–61 also set up regulations with a view to increasing exports. However, it was the military government that adopted the most thorough policy measures to promote exports. For example, the government monitored the export performance of major firms, the president presided over monthly Export Promotion Meetings, and prizes were awarded to major companies that had contributed to achieving export targets.[5]

5. It has to be emphasized, however, that import substitution and the expansion of exports proceeded simultaneously.

As discussed in chapter 1, promotion of exports is an appropriate strategy for developing countries whose pattern of resource endowments is like Korea's. In the Korean case, the basic strategies for economic development were not based on any established ideology—except for nationalism—but were instead derived through the experience of government authorities from the early 1960s. These strategies ignited the people's "will to economize," to borrow W. A. Lewis's expression, and swept away the sense of despair that had prevailed in the 1950s (Lewis 1955). These strategies were effective and brought great success, but in ensuing years, arbitrary decision making by the government became more common and increased the rigidities of the centralized bureaucratic managment.

Development Strategies Pursued Further: the Second Five-Year Plan (1967–71)

Targets and Performance

The second five-year plan period is characterized by rapid economic growth, based in part upon the political stability of the regime made possible by the easy victory of the incumbent president in the 1967 presidential election. Table 3.2 summarizes the targets and performance of the second plan. The actual annual growth rate of the economy surpassed the targeted 7.0 percent to reach 9.5 percent, and the actual rate of investment was 26.1 percent of GNP, far ahead of the planned 19.0 percent. A portion of investment was financed through domestic savings (16.1 percent). These figures alone underscore the fact that one of the main driving forces of rapid growth during the period was foreign capital inflow. The inducement of foreign capital was a way to make the fullest possible use of the abundant supply of labor.

As discussed earlier, firms heavily dependent on foreign capital in the 1960s earned considerable profits by manufacturing standardized products based upon simple technology, and this in turn caused a rapid increase in the foreign capital inflow (mainly in the form of suppliers' credits) during the second five-year period. Thus, foreign capital played a vital role in initiating Korea's industrialization, but as many firms vied for it, the amount generated in certain industrial areas became excessive. Some firms established by foreign capital became "unsound"—that is, unprofitable—one of the characteristic features of some Korean firms.

The growth of exports in this period was remarkable, with an average annual growth of about 35.2 percent in dollar terms, far in excess of any reasonable expectations. In 1971, the last year of the first plan, the actual export volume more than doubled the planned amount. However, this increase in exports was accompanied by an even greater increase in im-

Table 3.2 Targets and performance of the second five-year plan (1967–71)

Indicator	Targets	Performance
Economic growth rate (percentage)	7.0	9.5
Investment as a share of GNP	19.0	26.1
Domestic saving as a share of GNP	11.6	16.1
Foreign saving as a share of GNP	7.5	10.2
Current account in 1971 (millions of dollars)	−95.8	−847.5
Exports in 1971[a] (millions of dollars)	550.0	1,132.3
Annual average percentage change		35.2
Imports in 1971[a] (millions of dollars)	894.0	2,178.2
Annual average percentage change		26.2

a. Denotes figures on balance of payments basis.

Sources: Economic Planning Board; Bank of Korea, *National Accounts*, 1990.

ports, resulting in a widening trade deficit. This was rather inevitable, since the majority of the manufacturing firms, whether in export or import-substitution industries, were engaged in the assembly of imported, half-finished products. The rise in imports, therefore, occurred not so much in final consumption goods as in intermediate goods.

Application of Basic Development Strategy

The second five-year plan more or less followed the basic development strategy established during the first five-year plan, since both the domestic and international environments had not changed significantly. The following is a summary of the ways in which this strategy was applied.

Progress of Industrialization

Industrialization proceeded during this period at a much more rapid pace than was originally envisaged. Over the five years, the proportion of GNP attributable to primary industries declined from 34.8 to 27.2 percent, while that from mining and manufacturing industries rose from 20.5 to 22.5 percent. Employment in the manufacturing industries increased about 60 percent during this period. This period also saw a shift from light manufacturing to heavy industries, including petrochemical, mineral, and steel. While a sizable investment had already been made in basic industries such as cement, steel, and fertilizers in the first plan period, the second plan implemented a more conscious effort toward promoting the growth of technology-intensive industries. Industry-specific legislation was instrumental in this process—it included the Industrial Machinery Promotion Act (1967), Shipbuilding Industry Promotion Act (1967), Electrical Industry Promotion Act (1969), Steel Industry Promotion Act (1970), and the Petrochemical Industry Promotion Act (1970). The Free Trade Zone Act in 1970 allowed the establishment of such zones in Masan in 1970 and in Iri in 1973. Also established during this period were the petrochemical industry complex in Ulsan and the electrical export industry complex in Kumi.

The Role of Government

The legislative efforts discussed above imply that the government seriously embarked on a policy of industrial targeting. Since the 1950s, the Japanese Ministry of International Trade and Industry had practiced industrial targeting in order to develop intensively those industries with a potential for high technological progress and high income elasticities. During the second plan period, Korea adopted a similar policy. The successful creation of the Pohang Iron and Steel Company, the Seoul-Pusan Highway, and the Seoul-Inchon Highway, which were pursued despite considerable opposition, gave the government confidence in its ability to pursue investment policy, including the practice of industrial targeting.

Direct intervention by the government in the national economy was still relatively rare at the beginning of the second plan period. However, with the onset of promotion of heavy and chemical industries in the late 1960s, the scope of government intervention widened. In addition to a large number of special banks established during the period, the government saddled the commercial banks with a large share of the priority loans to investors in heavy and chemical industries.

Relationship between the Government and Firms

The rapid inflow of foreign capital in the late 1960s created a fair number of unsound firms among those that borrowed excessively from abroad. The term "unsound firms" in Korea refers to firms that continue to operate at a loss without any prospect of solvency but nonetheless survive with a continued infusion of relief loans made by the government on their behalf. Particularly when these firms were large, the government resorted to measures such as emergency "rescue" loans to avoid the massive layoffs that would accompany bankruptcy.

Specific measures for rescue included relief loans or the arrangement of other business groups to acquire the firms in trouble, providing the former with favorably termed loans in return for taking over the latter. Industrial targeting in any country necessarily involves government assumption of a sponsorship role. In the case of Korea, government intervention has been of a direct nature, and the government had to assume some responsibility for those investments with which the government had been involved directly.

Foreign Capital and Exports

We have already noted that both foreign capital inflow and exports increased remarkably during the second plan period but that firms incurring excessive debts were having trouble with their loan repayment schedules. The government responded to this situation in the early 1970s by discouraging foreign loans in favor of foreign direct investment in the form of joint ventures between foreigners and domestic firms.

Export promotion became the first priority in economic policy, with various measures to achieve this end being fully developed during this period. Specific measures for export promotion were numerous, but the most important of them were preferential credits for exporters, tax subsidies, the establishment of free trade zones, and tariff exemptions for raw material imports earmarked for exports. Most of these measures were implemented during 1963–68. Furthermore, when export industries were threatened by inflation, the government usually devalued the local currency so as to sustain the profitability of the exporters.

Equity and Balance

The export promotion policy was undoubtedly effective in increasing exports, but unfortunately it brought with it an industrial structure heavily skewed in favor of export industries, big businesses, and an unequal distribution of wealth. This trend was already visible in the latter half of the 1960s but became more conspicuous in the 1970s.

While industrial policy was unmistakably geared toward manufacturing industries, notable new developments occurred in economic policy-making during this period. The first was the price support program for domestic production of rice. In 1969, the government adopted a policy of supporting the price of rice at a higher level than that of the free market. This was in contrast to the previous policy of keeping the price of rice artificially low, which discouraged the farmers' from producing rice. The government began to offer somewhat higher prices for the rice it purchased in order to prevent the rapid relative decline of the agricultural sector. This about-face reflected the government's awareness that economic improvement in rural areas is politically and economically necessary as well as essential to sustain domestic demand for manufactured goods.

The second development began in 1970, when the government embarked on a large-scale rural modernization program called the Saemaul (New Community) movement. It was a spiritual revival program under the slogan of "industry, self-help, and cooperation," that aimed at encouraging a spirit of self-reliance among the farmers by developing new sources of agricultural income. The movement provided initiatives for the improvement of rural roads, modernization of rural housing (using the excess supply of cement in the urban areas), development of a new leadership from the ranks of successful modern farmers, and the generation of new income-earning sources. This movement initially did achieve some success in encouraging greater efforts from farmers. But, it failed to face the problems of agriculture and of the rural economy from a long-run perspective and to provide rural areas with much-needed nonagricultural sources of income.

Buildup of Heavy and Chemical Industries: the Third Five-Year Plan (1972–76)

Changes in Domestic and Foreign Economic Environments

The third plan period was marked by high growth rates in both GNP and exports, largely due to the policy of establishing heavy and chemical industries and of export promotion in the midst of rapidly changing domestic and foreign economic environments. At the same time, it became evident that the efficiency of investment was on the decline and the structural imbalance in the economy was being aggravated.

On the political front, President Park, who had been reelected for a third term, adopted in 1972 the Yushin (Revitalization) Constitution under martial law, with the intent of securing a life tenure for the presidency. The Yushin government concentrated on promotion of exports and high economic growth to legitimatize the forcible constitutional amendment and ban on political activities. The third plan started in 1972 with an official target of a $10 billion export volume and a per capita GNP of $1,000 by the year 1980, together with three main goals: "energetic development of agricultural and fishing industries, epoch-making increase in exports, and buildup of heavy and chemical industries."

The first of the three goals soon gave way to the remaining two, as the achievement of annual export goals and the growth of heavy and chemical industries assumed importance over the development of rural and coastal areas. In January 1973, President Park announced a "Heavy and Chemical Industrialization Declaration," setting top priority on the development of the following six industries: steel, petrochemicals, shipbuilding, industrial machinery, nonferrous metals, and electrical industries. Some long-term goals to be achieved by the year 1980 were 10 million tons of steel production, 5 million tons of shipping capacity, 940 thousand barrels of refined oil, and 500 thousand automobiles, all per annum. The government thereafter mobilized all economic policies at its disposal—fiscal, monetary, credit, trade, and labor policy—to promote the development of heavy and chemical industries. This all-out effort reflected the fact that the regime was betting its own destiny on the success of this program. Measures for the buildup of heavy industries were in the same vein as those proven effective in building light industries in the 1960s: to build a few large-scale industrial complexes for heavy and chemical industries and designate a number of firms to build plants with government-arranged foreign capital and domestic financing.

This basic framework put forward by the Yushin regime, however, was met with a series of adverse events, both domestic and foreign. In regard to the domestic economy, the most important were the widespread financial difficulties of firms established with foreign capital during the 1960s. As discussed earlier, a large number of firms dependent on foreign capital had become excessively leveraged since the latter half of the 1960s, and bankruptcy appeared to be inevitable for many of them. It was difficult to promote heavy and chemical industries when potential investors were heavily burdened with debts and "unsound firms." On the international scene, in the wake of the stagflation in the developed economies around 1970, the first oil crisis erupted in October 1973, dealing a devastating blow to the Korean economy.

The government responded to these troubles with a series of policy measures. First, as regards the problem of "unsound firms," in August 1972 President Park announced in a sweeping presidential decree an emergency measure purported to effectively write off existing domestic debts of the beleaguered firms. The decree and the subsequent measures implementing it gave the indebted firms a breathing spell. Second, the government decided, betting on a more favorable turn of events in the future, to go ahead with the original plan for establishing heavy and chemical industries, despite the difficult conditions magnified by international stagflation and the oil crisis. It was a great act of faith: despite the disadvantageous turn of events abroad, the basic policies of heavy and chemical industrialization and export growth were continued.[6]

Unexpected events brought fortuitous windfalls the economy badly needed. First, the agreement in 1973 by developed countries on international exchange-rates adjustment brought about an appreciation of both the Japanese yen and German mark, providing the Korean exporters with greater competitive advantage in the international market. The rapid recovery of the world economy that started in 1975 added further impetus for Korea's export growth. Second, on account of the entry en masse of Korean construction firms into Middle East countries, whose demand for construction activities increased tremendously with the steep rise in their oil revenues, the current account of Korea improved very substantially, bringing an unexpected welcome relief to the Korean economy.

Targets and Performance

Let us review the changes in macroeconomic indicators over the third plan period and their causes. The rate of foreign capital inflow and the

---

6. For an excellent comprehensive analysis on the background, process, and effects of the heavy and chemical industries in the 1970s, see Yoo Jung-ho (1990).

Table 3.3 Targets and performance of the third five-year plan (1972–76)

Indicator	Targets	Performance
Economic growth rate (percentage)	8.6	9.1
Investment as a share of GNP	27.6	27.1
Domestic saving as a share of GNP	19.5	20.8
Foreign saving as a share of GNP	5.4	6.7
Current account in 1976 (millions of dollars)	−359.0	−313.6
Exports in 1976[a] (millions of dollars)	3,510.0	7,814.6
Annual average percentage change		47.1
Imports in 1976[a] (millions of dollars)	3,993.0	8,405.1
Annual average percentage change		31.0

a. Denotes figures on balance of payments basis.

Sources: Economic Planning Board; Bank of Korea, *National Accounts,* 1990.

rate of investment growth remained high (table 3.3). Heavy investment and favorable export performance from 1973 on were responsible for the high average growth in GNP in the subsequent years. Although heavy and chemical industrialization was characterized by high capital intensiveness and great cost, it was nevertheless compensated for by an overall reduction in unemployment. The unemployment rate declined from 4.5 percent in the last year of the second plan period to 3.9 percent in that of the third plan period.

The growth of exports in dollar terms continued at a rapid pace after the appreciation of the Japanese yen and German mark in 1973 and achieved a remarkable 56.2 percent increase in 1976 due to a rapid recovery of the world economy. The average annual growth rate of exports in the dollar terms over the entire plan period was 47.2 percent. However, the increase in imports (31.0 percent) was also substantial, so that the current account deficit remained significantly above the plan target.

The remarkable growth in both real GNP and exports, achieved in the face of what appeared to be insurmountable difficulties, gave the government still greater confidence to continue the policies of heavy industrialization. However, the continuation of the high growth policy, despite the oil crisis, ingrained in the economy a great inflationary pressure. While most other countries were adopting anti-inflationary policy measures, Korea alone persisted in maintaining a growth-oriented, expansionary policy. The excessive investments in heavy and chemical industries geared toward exports, accompanied by duplication of investment and increased cost caused by excessive foreign and domestic debts, reduced efficiency in many investment projects and eventually brought about the breakdown of these policies toward the late 1970s. In April 1979, the government announced a Comprehensive Stabilization Program to redress the excesses of the heavy and chemical industry policy of the 1970s, calling for restrictive budget management, restrictive monetary policy, a scaling down of the heavy and chemical industry program, measures to increase the supply of consumption goods and stabilize their prices, measures to prevent real estate speculation, and measures to support low-income earners.[7]

Application of Basic Development Strategies

We have seen that the government adhered with remarkable consistency to the basic policy line established in the previous decade. In the following sections, several aspects of Korean economic growth during the third plan period will be reviewed by discussing the ways in which the government applied what I have called the five basic development principles for implementing the heavy and chemical industrialization program.

Industrialization Strategy

The drive for heavy and chemical industrialization that started in the latter half of the 1960s accelerated in the 1970s. This strategy was deemed necessary to increase exports and to achieve a more advanced industrial structure like that of developed countries. The government made the case that Korea needed to attain the same proportion of heavy and chemical industries in the manufacturing sector that Japan or West Germany achieved by the early 1960s.

A Heavy and Chemical Industry Planning Council was established by the president in 1973 to take charge of the planning and implementation of the heavy and chemical industry buildup. The public did not know exactly how the board operated, but it seems that the board was more concerned with engineering aspects (e.g., difficulties in technological development or locations) than economic aspects (e.g., cost of buildup, demand for products, or its impact on the national economy).

The heavy and chemical industry emphasis gradually became the sacred cow in economic policymaking. A dual structure in economic planning emerged, with the Heavy and Chemical Industry Planning Council on one side and the Economic Planning Board on the other. The Industrial Base Development Promotion Act was enacted in 1973, on the basis of which 13 heavy and chemical industry complexes were established throughout the country to establish plants in steel, petrochemical, industrial machinery, automobile, and electrical industries. In addition, the

---

7. In 1979, the government estimated that the investment in heavy and chemical industries as a proportion of total investment in 1976 and 1979 was 74 percent and 82 percent, respectively (Yoo 1990, 44). The industrial targeting policy supporting the heavy and chemical industrialization program in the 1970s was formally terminated in 1986 by enactment of the Industrial Development Act.

Local Industry Development Act was enacted to promote the growth of local industrial complexes.

The Role of the Government

The role of the government in promoting economic growth was further strengthened during the third plan period. Slogans such as "growth first" or "export first" colored all the government's actions. In order to finance investments in heavy and chemical industries, the government took control of available funds at all banking institutions, including commercial banks. According to the National Investment Fund Act, which was enacted in the wake of the Heavy and Chemical Industry Declaration in 1973, the National Investment Fund purported to supply available funds to investments in essential—that is, heavy and chemical, and export—industries. According to this law, the owners or managers of savings deposits in all banking institutions, pension funds established under the National Welfare Pension Act, postal savings deposits, or life insurance funds were required to purchase National Investment Bonds or deposit their money with the National Investment Fund, regardless of other legislation governing the use of the funds (Article 8). In other words, each and every type of savings was to be mobilized on a compulsory basis; these provisions underscore the degree of determination and the scope of government power at the time of developing heavy and chemical industries.

The influence of the government in the national economy went even further. Almost every price—even the prices of fast food items—was under government control, and the government's control on wages was quite complete. Since the labor movement was practically outlawed, the role of the unions in wage determination was unimportant. The government set guidelines for wage rates, taking into consideration their impacts on the price level and on exports. Firms were not allowed to set their own dividends to stockholders; the guideline for determining dividend rates was set by the government, which was concerned with their impacts both on interest rates and on the development of the stock market.

Relationship between the Government and Firms

During the heyday of the promotion of heavy and chemical industries, the most important decisions of the firms investing in priority industries (e.g., size of foreign loans, size and conditions of commercial loans, type and size of investment, and product prices) were relegated to the government. Under these circumstances, the government was obliged to assume the risk of investment, which under normal circumstances would have been assumed by private businesses. As a follow-up to the measures bailing out unsound firms in the late 1960s, the government announced in 1972 the Emergency Decree on Economic Stabilization and Growth, popularly known as the August Third Measure. To save businesses suffering under deteriorating financial conditions due to foreign loans and massive domestic debts, the decree froze all curb loans to businesses and converted them into either a long-term debt with very favorable terms (including three years' moratorium) or into capital investment in firms, and it lowered official interest rates on both deposits and loans. These measures greatly benefited the indebted businesses at the expense of the lenders in the curb market. Over the long term, however, such measures further encouraged the Korean firms to incur debts without being seriously concerned about default.

Behind the increase in exports and the expansion of conglomerates was the establishment of general trading companies. A general trading company was an institution, unique to Japan, that at the initial phase of its development handled trade on behalf of the government and other firms. These companies were dissolved after Japan's defeat in World War II, but they reemerged in the early 1950s in a much more flexible form and made an important contribution to the galloping increase in Japanese exports. The Yushin regime in the early 1970s thought it was appropriate to introduce a variation of the Japanese institution in Korea. The government selected a small number of large firms that met certain criteria, gave them special benefits, and made them handle export business for other exporters as well as for themselves. This enabled the firms to accumulate expert knowledge on exporting and to take advantage of economies of scale. The general trading companies were expected to expand exports and to make it easier for the government to achieve export goals. In the beginning, the government seemed to have expected these trading companies to handle about 50 percent of total exports (Cho 1987, 50) because the proportion of Japanese general trading companies' exports in total exports was at about the same level.

The special benefits granted to the general trading companies, in addition to those granted to exporters in general, included a number of administrative and financial benefits and special allowances for foreign exchange. More important to the companies, however, were the benefits of a more informal nature, including low-interest loans granted when the companies exceeded export goals, favorable positioning of the conglomerates to which each company belonged, and other benefits in investment opportunities. The proportion of the general trading company exports in total exports rose from 13.6 percent in 1975 to 41.0 percent in 1980 and further to 51.3 percent in 1985 (Cho 1987, 55).

These were the special features of Korean general trading companies during the period under study: First, they concentrated on exports (especially those for their own groups) and paid little attention to imports and other trading matters.[8] Second, these general trading companies

---

8. The proportion of imports through general trading companies in total imports was only 8.3 percent in 1983, in contrast to 55–65 percent for the case of Japan.

expanded into conglomerate groups. Each group established a large number of new companies within the group to achieve export goals and to increase the group's total export volumes. The profitability of the general trading companies is reported to have decreased over the years,[9] but net revenues to the groups after taking into account other official and unofficial benefits must have been fairly high.

Foreign Capital

Essentially, the approach the government took for building up the heavy and chemical industries was no different from the one it took during the 1960s when light industries were established—that is, to attract foreign capital. Thus, the big push for heavy and chemical industrialization was naturally accompanied by a rapid increase in external debt. One notable feature of foreign capital inducement was that foreign loans outvalued foreign direct investment. The government did emphasize in the early 1970s the desirability of drawing in foreign direct investment, but during this period, almost all important investments were made by local entrepreneurs, who relied principally on borrowing. The Korean system of industrial targeting leaned more toward foreign borrowing than foreign direct investment.

Equity and Balance

A strong policy emphasis on exports and heavy and chemical industries naturally meant that resources were preponderantly allocated into these areas. As exports and heavy and chemical industries were captured by general trading companies and their affiliated conglomerates, industrial balance and distributive equity became substantially skewed in favor of the large firms. The inflationary pressure also favored the indebted class at the expense of the small savers; the statistical data show that distribution of income and wealth became more unequal during this period than in previous periods.

The Aftermath of the Heavy and Chemical Industry Program: the Fourth Five-Year Plan (1977–81)

Targets and Performance

As the government believed it had successfully overcome the oil crisis, the goal of economic growth during the fourth plan was set at an ambi-

---

9. The annual average rate of profit was 1.4 percent in 1977, 0.4 percent in 1980, and 0.3 percent in 1983 (Cho 1987, 57).

tious average annual rate of 9.2 percent. The plan also aimed at reducing foreign capital inflow, increasing domestic savings, achieving improved current account balances, and raising the proportion of heavy and chemical industries to almost 50 percent.

During the early years of the plan period, there were tremendous investments in priority sectors: investments in exports and heavy and chemical industries were so heavy that the amount invested in these industries during the first three years of the plan period surpassed that planned for the entire period. Conversely, investment in light industries fell far short of the plan's goal; clearly the country's all-out effort lay in heavy and chemical industries.

The current account remained in deficit with the exception of 1977, when it was momentarily in surplus due to an export boom as well as the thriving construction business in the Middle East. Furthermore, the second oil crisis in 1979 dealt a much greater blow to the Korean economy than the first one; the balance of payment worsened, and foreign debts snowballed.

As table 3.4 shows, the actual share of investment in GNP during the plan period exceeded the plan target, while the actual share of saving in GNP fell short of the planned one. Thus the actual gap was as much as 5.9 percent, compared with the planned 2.0 percent. This implies that the drive for heavy and chemical industrialization was at such a large scale that it was impossible to achieve it without large-scale foreign capital inflow and that the drive was largely executed outside the normal course of economic planning.

Even if the macroeconomic indicators shown in table 3.4 appeared strong enough; under the surface of prosperity were problems that boded ill for the future. Suffice it to say that the economy would have found it difficult to continue growing without substantial adjustments. While investments in heavy and chemical industries continued, a shortage of resources to sustain it began to appear in physical, human, technological, and financial areas. A wage-price spiral began to appear, accompanied by speculation on buildings, land, and durable goods.

The rate of economic growth in 1977 and 1978 was 9.8 percent for both years, which was ahead of projected figures. But later the economic growth rate slowed to 7.2 percent in 1979, –3.7 percent in 1980, and 5.9 percent in 1981, with an average annual rate of only 5.7 percent over the entire period. In contrast, the shares of investment in GNP were as high as 27.3 percent in 1977, 31.1 percent in 1978, and 35.4 percent in 1979. The investment ratios remained high—at 31.5 percent in 1980 and 28.4 percent in 1981, presumably to complete the investment projects started before 1980. On the other hand, the high investment ratios in 1980 and 1981 resulted from the fact that even though investment decreased absolutely, it continued at a high level, while GNP growth fell or even turned negative, reflecting the recessionary effect of the second

Table 3.4 Targets and performance of the fourth five-year plan (1977–81)

Indicator	Targets						Performance					
	Average	1977	1978	1979	1980	1981	Average	1977	1978	1979	1980	1981
Economic growth rate (percentage)	9.2	10.0	9.0	9.0	9.0	9.0	5.7	9.8	9.8	7.2	-3.7	5.9
Investment as a share of GNP	26.2	27.0	26.3	25.9	25.9	26.0	30.7	27.3	31.1	35.4	31.5	28.4
Domestic saving as a share of GNP	24.2	22.0	23.0	24.0	25.1	26.1	23.5	25.1	26.4	26.6	19.9	19.6
Foreign saving as a share of GNP	2.0	5.0	3.4	1.9	0.8	-0.1	5.9	0.6	3.3	7.6	10.2	7.9
Current account (millions of dollars)	—	-634	-237	235	679	1,172	—	12.3	-1,085.2	-4,151.1	-5,320.7	-4,464.0
Exports[a] (millions of dollars)	—	9,700	11,970	14,519	17,292	20,242	—	10,046.5	12,710.6	14,704.5	17,214.0	20,670.8
Annual average percentage change	21.6						21.6	28.6	26.5	15.7	17.1	20.1
Imports[a] (millions of dollars)	—	10,133	11,925	14,043	16,345	18,872	—	10,523.1	14,491.4	19,100.0	21,598.1	24,299.1
Annual average percentage change	24.1						24.1	25.2	37.7	31.8	13.1	12.5

a. Denotes figures on balance of payments basis.

Sources: Economic Planning Board; Bank of Korea, *National Accounts*, 1990.

oil shock as well as the low efficiency of earlier investment in heavy and chemical industries.

One cannot overlook the performance of imports and exports in comparing planned and actual accomplishments. As noted above, achieving export goals was one of the overriding priorities of Korean economic policy in the 1970s, and it is reflected in the hairsbreadth accuracy with which the annual export figures corresponded to planned figures. The planning bodies believed that the success of the economic plan depended upon achievement of export goals, and thus exports were promoted by all means available. On the other hand, actual imports, which received less attention, far exceeded planned levels.

Wages and Prices

A large increase in the supply of money to support heavy and chemical industrialization necessarily produced a rapid rise in the price level during the fourth plan period. The GNP deflator rose about 20 percent every year. Many believed, however, that actual inflation exceeded official figures. Although not confirmed, the possibility did indeed exist. Almost every price was under government control, giving rise to different prices for the same goods—official prices, announced prices, and unofficial market prices—making accurate information on a uniform price very difficult. Under these circumstances, the official price data, no matter how objectively compiled, could easily be wide of the mark.

The wage level also increased dramatically during this period. Korean wages, originally under rather strict government control, suddenly began to skyrocket in 1976, triggered initially by the shortage of highly skilled labor. This induced fierce competition among large business groups for college graduates fresh from universities and colleges, whose wages increased sharply. Other wages soon followed suit. Furthermore, as the capital intensity of industries increased with investments concentrated on heavy and chemical industries, the wage level in these industries uniformly rose, and the wage increase, in turn, tended to increase investment in labor-saving techniques of production and in capital-intensive industries.

Price Stability and the Structural Adjustment of the Economy: the Fifth Five-Year Plan (1982–86)

The assassination of President Park in October 1979 and the Yushin regime's collapse were accompanied by a prolonged crisis in political, economic, and social spheres. After a slow and ultimately abortive process of democratization, a new regime emerged in 1980 with social justice as its slogan. During the fifth five-year development plan period, 1982–86, the government brought about many welcome changes, though with a few important undesirable side effects.

Growth of Income and Exports

As shown in table 3.5, the fifth plan set a goal of 7.6 percent average annual growth compared with the actual 9.8 percent. The actual ratios of investment and domestic saving to GNP were 29.2 and 31.9 percent, respectively, in the final year of the plan period; contrary to the preceding plan period, then, the saving ratio exceeded the investment ratio. This period also witnessed the narrowing of the gap between imports and exports, with the attainment in the final year of a sizable surplus in the current account. While the surplus was due to the stabilization policy during the period, the rapid appreciation of the Japanese yen that began in September 1985 provided Korean exporters with a substantial competitive advantage over their Japanese counterparts in the international market. Korea's chronic balance of payments deficit had gradually been narrowed, heralding that eventually it would completely disappear and a surplus would be achieved. But, because of the steep appreciation of the Japanese yen vis-à-vis the dollar, Korea was able to record a sizable and premature surplus in the current account as early as 1986. The surplus skyrocketed to $14.2 billion in 1988 and turned back to deficit in 1990.

Stabilization of Price Level

Another important development is that a stabilization of the price level was achieved for the first time in recent memory. The rate of change of the wholesale price index dropped from 39.0 percent in 1980 and 20.4 percent in 1981 to 4.6 percent, 0.2 percent, 0.7 percent, 0.9 percent, and –1.5 percent for the years from 1982 through 1986, respectively. The worldwide trend toward stable prices, coupled with the government's efforts to tighten fiscal and monetary policies, contributed to this achievement. The stabilization effort included freezing the purchase price of rice and other agricultural products and freezing the salaries of civil servants, resulting in a decline in the propensity to consume that contributed considerably to price stability. But on the other hand, the severe contraction of government spending resulted in a shortage of spending on infrastructure and public services, including environmental protection, education, and welfare spending for the poor.

Restructuring and Liberalization

The third noticeable development was that there was considerably less government intervention—such as direct control, extreme forms of in-

Table 3.5 Targets and performance of the fifth five-year plan (1982–86)

Indicator	Targets						Performance					
	Aver-age	1982	1983	1984	1985	1986	Aver-age	1982	1983	1984	1985	1986
Economic growth rate (percentage)	7.6	8.0	7.5	7.5	7.5	7.5	9.8	7.2	12.6	9.3	7.0	12.9
Investment as a share of GNP	31.6	31.1	31.2	31.2	31.7	32.5	30.0	29.8	29.7	30.9	30.3	29.2
Domestic saving as a share of GNP	27.4	24.2	25.7	26.9	28.3	29.6	27.2	21.8	26.2	28.0	28.3	31.9
Foreign saving as a share of GNP	4.2	6.9	5.4	4.3	3.4	2.9	2.6	7.0	3.9	3.5	2.2	−3.1
Current account (billions of dollars)[a]	—	−4.9	−4.4	−4.1	−3.8	−3.6	—	−2.6	−1.6	−1.4	−0.9	4.6
Exports[a] (billions of dollars)	—	23.5	30.5	36.5	44.0	53.0	—	20.9	23.2	26.3	26.4	33.9
Annual average percentage change							10.8	1.0	11.1	13.5	0.4	28.3
Imports[a] (billions of dollars)	—	29.3	34.2	39.7	46.8	55.5	—	23.5	25.0	27.4	26.5	29.0
Annual average percentage change							4.3	−3.4	6.4	9.6	−3.3	12.3

a. Denotes figures on balance of payments basis.

Sources: Economic Planning Board; Bank of Korea, *National Accounts*, 1990.

dustrial targeting, and an all-out export drive—as public opinion began to favor giving freer rein to the private sector. The most notable measure for promoting the "private initiative economy" was the privatization of commercial banks. The government sold its portion of bank stocks to the public between 1981 and 1983, and it abolished numerous regulations and control on the management of the banks. In connection with this, the authority for enforcing a comprehensive directive on the business operation and management of banks, given to the superintendent of banks of the Bank of Korea in accordance with the General Banking Act, was abolished, and the appointment of bank executives was allowed to take effect without the *ex post* approval of the superintendent of banks. Moreover, the Agreement of the Group of Banks, which was often criticized for its collusive character in setting deposit and loan interest rates and other commission rates, was also abolished to promote fair competition among banks. This was supposed to be a prelude to the eventual self-management of commercial banks and the opening of the domestic financial market. In reality, however, government control over the business of commercial banks continued, particularly the control on personnel and loans for unsound firms. What the government achieved was privatization, not liberalization.

One of the most important changes during the period was in the international economic scene. As the balance of payment surplus appeared, the country began to be pressed for import liberalization from the United States and other trade partners. This forced Korea to liberalize its trade policies and to readjust its economic structure.

The Sixth Five-Year Plan (1987–91)

As the 1980s progressed, it became increasingly clear that the Korean people were deeply dissatisfied. They began to demand more democratization and greater equity in both the political and economic spheres. The prevailing sentiment manifested itself in the general election of February 1985, in which the ruling Democratic Justice Party failed to get the majority vote, though it managed to hold the majority seat in the National Assembly. Alarmed by the sudden eruption of resentment, the government announced the sixth five-year development plan in September 1986. It heralded the goal of achieving an "advanced economy" with "social welfare and balanced growth." The highlights of the plan are summarized in table 3.6 (original targets) and incorporated the following six-point directives.

■ Maintain a 7.2 percent average annual economic growth rate to absorb 382,000 new entrants yearly into the work force each year and keep the rate of unemployment at 3.3 percent. Maintain an average

Table 3.6 Targets and performance of the sixth five-year plan (1987–91)

| Indicator | Targets[a] | | | | | | Performance | | | | | |
	Aver-age	1987	1988	1989	1990	1991	Aver-age	1987	1988	1989	1990	1991
Economic growth rate (percentage)	7.2	7.5	7.5	7.0	7.0	7.0	10.0	13.0	12.4	6.8	9.3	8.4
Investment as a share of GNDI	30.7	30.2	30.6	30.8	30.9	31.0	34.5	29.6	30.7	33.5	37.1	39.3
Domestic saving as a share of GNDI	32.3	31.4	32.0	32.4	32.7	33.0	36.3	36.2	38.1	35.3	36.0	36.1
Foreign saving as a share of GNDI	-1.6	-1.2	-1.4	-1.6	-1.8	-2.0	-2.3	-7.4	-8.0	-2.3	0.9	3.1
Current account (billions of dollars)	—	2.3	2.7	3.1	3.6	4.0	—	9.9	14.2	5.1	-2.2	-8.7
Exports[b] (billions of dollars)	—	35.6	39.8	44.2	49.1	54.4	—	46.2	59.6	61.4	63.1	69.6
Annual average percentage change							16.3	36.4	29.0	3.0	2.8	10.2
Imports[b] (billions of dollars)	—	32.6	36.3	40.3	44.7	49.6	—	38.6	48.2	56.8	65.1	76.6
Annual average percentage change							21.0	29.9	24.9	17.9	14.6	17.6

GNDI = gross national disposable income.

a. Original targets set in 1986.
b. Denotes figures on balance of payments basis.

Sources: Economic Planning Board; Bank of Korea, *National Accounts*, 1990.

annual rate of investment at 30.7 percent of GNP and of domestic savings at 32.3 percent with negative foreign savings.

■ Maintain sound fiscal policy and effective monetary management and achieve price stabilization through wage and exchange rate stabilization. The increase in the wholesale and consumer price indices should be arrested at 3.0 percent and 5.0 percent, respectively.

■ Avoid volume-oriented export goals in favor of goals for increasing foreign exchange earnings, and liberalize imports at the same time, with the annual current account surplus maintained at a level of $5.0 billion. Pay back $19.2 billion of foreign debt in net terms, and reduce net foreign debt outstanding to $13.5 billion in 1991.

■ Improve industrial structure through developing resource-saving and skilled, labor-intensive industries such as industrial machinery, electrical equipment, and automobiles. Promote import substitution of parts and components necessary for heavy and chemical industries, encourage the growth of small and medium enterprises, expand research and development investment, and achieve a balance between demand and supply of energy resources.

■ Increase investment in less-developed regions and decentralize and transfer essential government functions in such areas as education, medicine, banking, information, and technology to local authorities, thereby reducing the gaps in income and growth in rural and urban areas. Achieve income growth in rural areas by establishing more than 150 agricultural-industrial areas, and improve the standard of living in rural and fishing villages.

■ Provide a basic social welfare system: improve labor-management relations, gradually introduce social welfare measures, improve the quality of education, and establish a national pension system. Promote development of a market economy and reassess the role of the government in the economy.

Revision of the Plan and Demand for Democratization

The contents of the sixth plan looked reasonable enough, especially if one accepted the optimistic assumption the government adopted as it began planning in 1986—that the conditions prevailing in 1986 would be maintained during the entire plan period. The basic perspective upon which this plan was based was essentially similar to that of the past five economic development plans: that the basic structure of the national economy was sound and only certain quantitative and minor adjustments were needed to solve problems that might arise. If this perception had indeed been valid, then the planned figures for the macroeconomic indicators should not have been unreasonable. But it was clear that the economy needed more adjustment than what the plan envisaged, and the plan, in order to serve the government as well as the people, had to be revised to solve the numerous problems Korean society encountered during the plan period.

President Chun Doo Hwan's government was in February 1988 replaced by President Roh Tae Woo's government after a spell of perhaps the most turbulent eruption of popular cries for more democratization, more human rights, greater equity in income distribution, and social justice. President Roh, who was elected in December 1987 with 36 percent of the popular vote, announced that he was unswervingly for democracy and greater equity and that he was an "ordinary man," in an effort to earn confidence and support of the people. During the first two years of President Roh's term, the nation was to witness ceaseless political turmoil in and outside the National Assembly, which was dominated by the three opposing parties; social disorder; and erosion of social discipline with the demise of the authoritarian regime.

In response to the irrepressible demands of the people, the government in October 1988 revised the sixth plan, the main tenets of which were to establish self-regulation, fairness, and balance in the economy. The revised plan was to undertake reforms with respect to land tenure, financial transactions, concentration of economic power in conglomerates, and labor-management relations. It further promised to undertake social welfare measures for the poor and needy in urban and rural areas and to introduce a public health-insurance program and an extensive pension system. The macroeconomic targets of the plan were revised upward, reflecting economic performance that by far surpassed the original targets.

Targets and Performance

As shown in table 3.6, the performance of the sixth plan was characterized by a quite high growth rate and dramatic changes in the current account. The actual average annual rate of growth was 10.0 percent, much higher than the original target rate of 7.2 percent. The ratios of investment and domestic saving to GNP also exceeded the original targets. The current account showed a reverse J-curve trend during the period, and the surplus, which was $4.6 billion in 1986, was doubled in the next year and recorded a peak of $14.2 billion in 1988. It went down sharply, however, and returned to a deficit in 1990; the deficit snowballed to $8.7 billion in 1991.

The achievements during 1987–88 are mainly due to a high rate of increase in exports and investments. The so-called three lows—low oil prices, a weak US dollar, and low international interest rates—made possible a rapid expansion of exports and reduced the burden of imports and interest payments on foreign debts. From 1989, however, the price competitiveness of Korean exports weakened due to wage hikes beginning in the second half of 1987 and to the appreciation of the Korean won. The pressures to open the domestic market and the appreciation of the Korean won were strengthened as the current account surplus expanded during 1986–88. As a result, the rate of increase in exports shrank while that of imports went up, and the growth rate went down to 6.8 percent in 1989. To cope with the assumed recession, the government implemented several strong measures to boost domestic demand: expanding bank credit for equipment investment and encouraging construction of residential buildings. In 1990 and 1991, growth regained its momentum, but the balance of payments deteriorated sharply, and price stability was threatened along with the rapid expansion of domestic demand while export was in the doldrums due to weakening competitiveness.

Enhancing Equity and Balanced Growth

During the sixth plan period, demands were made for a fair distribution of the economic pie and for political democratization, which had been restrained since the early 1960s. The year 1988 was marked by ceaseless labor disputes and the rapid increase in real wages. Not only labor but almost all sectors of the economy demanded that their shares be increased. The business community, which enjoyed huge profits with the increase in sales, engaged in land other real estate speculation, triggering a skyrocketing increase in real estate prices between 1988 and 1990.

The prospects for the future after the Olympic Games in September 1988 were bleak, and toward the end of the year a new perspective for economic management was called for. The author was called upon to serve as deputy prime minister and minister of the Economic Planning Board in December. In the face of the ceaseless eruption of labor disputes and the constant cries of business for more assistance, the government found it enormously difficult to pursue what it perceived to be the right policy direction: an austerity program as a part of macroeconomic management and microeconomic reforms to stem the intensive speculation in land, to establish a fair trade system, and to institute fair financial transactions.

The government, with popular support, did institute three laws aimed at restricting land speculation and encouraging the more efficient use of land: the Act Limiting the Maximum Size of Housing Landholdings, the Act to Recoup Development-Induced Profits and the Act on Windfall Capital Gains Land Tax. It also launched a new policy for agriculture and established a basic scheme for social security, including a minimum wage scheme and a national pension system in 1988, and a nationwide public health program in 1989.

These policy measures emphasized establishing stability, fairness, and balance in the economy. However, the business community, which had enjoyed protection and assistance from the government for a long time, suffered as a result and therefore objected to these policies. Thus, when the economy showed a relatively low growth rate in 1989, the new economic policy team, installed by the cabinet reshuffle in March 1990, was directed to place lower priority on the above-mentioned policies. It initiated measures for regaining high growth rates, and the pace of reforms to enhance equity and fairness slowed relatively.

Liberalization and Market Opening

With the 1985 Plaza Agreement, the pace of liberalization and market-opening quickened throughout the world economy. As a country with a trade volume that placed it 12th among all nations, Korea could not afford to stand aloof from this trend. Taking this new responsibility into consideration and in response to the calls from its trading partners, Korea stepped up measures of liberalization and market opening. The import liberalization ratio for manufactured goods increased to 99.9 percent during the sixth plan period so that it now almost matches those of advanced countries. The ratio for the import of agricultural products also went up to 84.7 percent. Foreign exchange regulations have largely been revoked, and the government accepted the obligations of Article VIII of the International Monetary Fund Agreement in 1988. In March 1990, a new exchange rate system, called Market Average Exchange Rate System, was introduced as a major step toward a free float. In this system, the government and the Bank of Korea are no longer directly involved in setting foreign exchange rates. The daily basic won-dollar exchange rate is determined by the weighted average of the interbank won-dollar exchange rates applied in spot transactions on the previous business day.[10]

One thing to be noted concerning the sixth plan period is that Korea then formally initiated trade with the communist nations, including the former Soviet Union, China, and Eastern European countries. The Korean peninsula has been divided into two political systems, a capitalist regime in the south and a communist regime in the north, since 1945. The Cold War continued until the late 1980s, and there was no formal

---

10. When this new exchange rate system was initiated, the daily fluctuating band of the interbank won-dollar exchange rates was set at 0.4 percent of the prevailing basic won-dollar exchange rate, but it was widened to 0.6 percent effective from 1 September 1991. The band was further widened to 0.8 percent as of 1 July 1992.

trade between South Korea and communist countries, including North Korea. Encouraged by the end of the Cold War and the successful Seoul Olympic Games, Korea strengthened its diplomacy toward communist countries. As a result, Korea opened its market to them and became one of their trade partners.

The Seventh Five-Year Plan (1992–97)

Major Targets

In the early 1990s, the disorders that had erupted in the process of democratization calmed, but the people's desire for balanced development and for social welfare remains unsatisfied and continues to grow. With the termination of the Cold War, national reunification became an important issue and one that was perceived as reaching resolution in the near term.

The structural problems that are the legacy of "condensed growth" remain. In addition, the volume and structure of the economy has grown too big and too complicated to be dealt with by simple solutions of macroeconomic management. The external environment is also worsening, and the pressures for market opening and technological protectionism are strengthening.

To cope with those domestic and external challenges and to achieve sustained growth, it is perceived to be important to pursue qualitative improvement centering on the "software" of the economy rather than the quantitative or volume-oriented expansion of the past 30 years. It is also deemed important to harmonize macroeconomic stabilization with microeconomic reforms. Thus, although the seventh plan set its macroeconomic targets—such as a 7.5 percent average annual economic growth rate, balance in the current account, and improvement of the industrial structure (table 3.7)—it also emphasized major qualitative tasks to be solved.

The seventh five-year plan set as its principal goal "pursuing an advanced economy and society and heading toward national reunification." For this, the following three major strategies were adopted: strengthening competitiveness of industry, enhancing equity and balanced development, and pursuing internationalization and liberalization, as well as providing the basis for national reunification. Under these three strategies, 10 major tasks were selected.

To strengthen competitiveness of industry:

■ Reorganize the educational and human resources development system so that they supply human resources such as technical manpower to meet the demands of an industrialized society.

Table 3.7 Targets of the seventh five-year plan (1992-96)

	Targets					
Indicator	Average	1992	1993	1994	1995	1996
Economic growth rate (percentage)	7.5	7.0	7.0	7.5	8.0	8.0
Investment as a share of GNDI	36.4	38.2	37.1	36.3	35.4	34.8
Domestic saving as a share of GNDI	35.5	34.7	34.8	35.2	36.1	36.6
Foreign saving as a share of GNDI	-0.6	-2.7	-1.6	-0.4	0.5	1.4
Current account (billions of dollars)	—	-8.0	-5.0	-1.5	2.0	6.5
Exports[a] (billions of dollars)	—	78.5	89.4	101.8	116.0	131.6
Imports[a] (billions of dollars)	—	85.5	93.7	103.3	114.5	126.1

GNDI = gross national disposable income.
a. Denotes figures on balance of payments basis.
Source: Economic Planning Board.

■ Promote technological development and innovation, and keep pace with the information age.

■ Furnish and expand infrastructure and promote the efficiency of the transportation system.

■ Raise the efficiency of business management and the industrial structure by dispersing the ownership of conglomerates and establishing a professional management system. Also, strengthen the competitiveness of small and medium enterprises.

To enhance equity and balanced development:

■ Restructure the regional and coastal society to cope with further agricultural market opening and to raise income levels. Also enhance balanced development among regions.

■ Alleviate the housing problem, improve the scheme for curbing real estate speculation, and pursue measures for environmental protection.

■ Improve the social security system, such as expanding the coverage of the national pension scheme to include farmers and fishermen, and promote culture and the arts.

To pursue internationalization and liberalization and to provide the basis for national reunification:

- Liberalize the financial system, including deregulation of interest rates, foreign exchange, and foreign investment in the capital market. Also reduce government intervention in private economic activities.

- Expand service and agricultural market opening, and strengthen competitiveness of these sectors. Reorganize the areas of the economic system that do not meet international trade norms to cope with the worldwide liberalization movement (e.g., the Uruguay Round), and promote overseas investment of domestic firms.

- Provide the basis for national reunification through economic cooperation with North Korea.

Recent Developments

As shown before, during 1990–91 the Korean economy regained momentum, but inflationary pressures mounted, and the current account deficit widened sharply. To cope with these problems, measures to suppress domestic demand were initiated in the second half of 1991. They included the restraint of overheated construction activities, curbs on intensive speculation in real estate, and a relatively tight control over the money supply. Thanks to such measures, the Korean economy returned to stability with a comparatively low inflation rate and a reduced current account deficit in 1992. Consumer price inflation dropped remarkably to 4.5 percent from 9.3 percent a year earlier, and the current account deficit declined to $4.5 billion, about half that of 1991. In the first half of 1993, consumer price inflation remained at around 4 to 5 percent, and the current account also exhibited a narrow deficit.

The Korean economy paid the price for its stabilization with a slowdown of GNP growth. The growth rate slipped to 4.7 percent in 1992 and 3.8 percent in the first half of 1993, from around 9 percent in 1991. Fortunately, however, recent movements of the major economic indicators show that the Korean economy appears to have passed through the trough of the business cycle and to be on a mild recovery track. Exports are exhibiting a moderate increase due to the surge in exports of heavy industrial and chemical products, and several investment-related leading indicators have improved somewhat. Such developments are helped by the strong Japanese yen, the relatively low interest rates since the second half of 1992, and possibly by the policy actions of the new government.

In February 1993, President Kim Young Sam's government took office and was lauded as the first civilian government since May 1961. The government made "Construction of a New Korea" its watchwords and placed policy emphasis over the short run on revitalizing the national economy through the 100-day New Economy Plan in order to prevent its growth potential from dwindling away. For the long term, the government directed policies toward restructuring the economy and launched the Five-Year Plan for a New Economy. In essence, this differs little from the seventh plan with respect to its targets and major policy tasks. Be that as it may, the verdict on the achievements of the plan must be left to the future.

4

Industrial Organization

Entrepreneurship and Industrial Structure

During the last several decades, Korea has witnessed a spurt of businessmen with entrepreneurial qualities such as drive and innovative spirit. Korea owes much to these business leaders; through their efforts the country has made remarkable strides in economic development. They certainly contributed much to transforming the country from an impoverished agricultural society to what it is today.

Despite their achievement, or rather because of it, the popular image of business in Korea is less favorable than what is deserved. One might ascribe this to the antibusiness propaganda of the radicals, but this may be a prejudiced opinion. The unfavorable image, formed during the condensed growth period, is likely to be corrected as entrepreneurs adjust to a more normal growth process.

The condensed nature of growth of Korean business parallels the condensed economic growth of the economy as a whole; one mirrors the other. Many of the most important Korean conglomerates today are by-products of an industrial policy that sparked condensed growth. They were well-suited to achieving this growth. But just as the Korean economy as a whole needs to adjust to more normal growth, so do the Korean conglomerates. This chapter will examine these entrepreneurs' behavior and the industrial structure of the Korean economy. It will then suggest the basic direction policies to transform the entrepreneurial operation should take.

Business-Government Relations

Korea's burst of entrepreneurship has impressed many observers, and a few large Korean conglomerates have become household names throughout the world. This is all the more surprising when one takes into account the conspicuous lack of such entrepreneurship before 1945 and a social atmosphere that had appeared quite inhospitable to industrial and commercial activities. The Yi dynasty of Korea (1392–1910) certainly did not witness the growth of commerce and industry comparable to that of, say, Tokugawa Japan (1603–1868). In addition, during the colonial days, the Japanese authority effectively shut the Koreans out of important industrial activities by enacting the Kaisha-Rei (Decree on Corporations) in 1911.

What has made the emergence of vigorous entrepreneurship possible? One factor undoubtedly is the innate drive and shrewdness of Korean business leaders. Another factor is the government's guardianship of them, and particularly the leaders of big business. Since its establishment in 1948, the Korean government has consistently embraced the free enterprise system and established the goal of industrialization on market principles as the first priority of its economic policy.[1] The government has adopted all available measures to implement its goal, although the industrialization effort, particularly at the initial stage of development, encountered a great many constraints.[2] The ideology and the basic goal of the government has made the relationship between government and business exceedingly close.

As described in chapter 2, the government of Syngman Rhee sold formerly Japanese-owned enterprises at favorable prices to potential Korean businessmen, who were subsequently given preferential treatment to promote their firms' development into import-substitution industries. These enterprises mostly produced and sold daily necessities that had been in short supply in a protected market, and most of them made easy profits. By the end of the 1950s, the military government in 1961 uncovered enterprises gathering what it regarded as "illicit fortunes," which it confiscated after the military coup. Soon afterward the government turned to these same businessmen to enlist their support and to stimulate their business activities. Some of these fortunes were subsequently dissipated in the course of socioeconomic vicissitudes, but others survived and were successful.

Government's Entrepreneurial Functions and Conglomerates

The "growth-first" policy that accelerated the condensed growth of the 1960s and 1970s, implemented by an all-out effort of the government,

---

1. The ideological underpinnings of the Korean government since its establishment was discussed in chapter 1.

2. One may recall difficulties such as inflation, a low rate of saving, the shortage of capital, and a low level of technology, particularly in the 1950s.

further cemented government-business relations. With the constitutional amendment in 1972, the power elite of the government sought to target heavy and chemical industries and exports. Since the short-term goals of achieving growth targets were easy to achieve through aid to big businesses, the government mobilized all available policy measures to support them. Industrial targeting policy in the early 1970s and the introduction of a system of general trading companies in 1975 gave great stimulus to growth and expansion, and a group of "vertically integrated," family-owned conglomerates merged in less than a decade.[3] From then on, the government-business relationship took on the image of "Korea Inc."

In many cases, the government simply designated an individual to invest in a particular project, allocating to him designated amounts of bank loans and imported foreign capital. This practice implied that it is ultimately the government's role to assume the risk of investment; when the investment fails, the government often has come to the rescue of the private investor. In fact, the government did assume such responsibility during the late 1960s and 1970s by giving relief loans to unsound firms or by liquidating them so they could be taken over by other large firms at preferential terms.

This system made it possible for firms investing in priority industries to shift risk to, or at least to share risk with, the government. Entrepreneurs thus assumed much less risk in making investments than when they invested under normal circumstances, and this made them less concerned about risk than they otherwise would have been. Few would maintain that a true entrepreneurial spirit was lacking among Korea's business leaders, but it certainly was bolstered by unstinting government support.

Whatever it may have achieved in the short run, government assumption of business functions, if continued for a prolonged period, must necessarily be inimical to the development and efflorescence of entrepreneurship because the government's decisions are easily swayed by noneconomic considerations and are bound to stifle it. Even when the enterprise does succeed, this success only partly results from the innovation that marks the genuine entrepreneur. The system does not reward genuine innovators; rather, it supports partly those who are effective in public relations.[4] Furthermore, it erodes people's sense of fairness and their trust in government policy.

---

3. When the government established these "upstream" industries through its support of private business, the policy invariably ended up with "vertically integrated," family-owned conglomerates. This is one of the reasons why some governments, such as that of Taiwan, established public corporations to which investments in these upstream industries were entrusted.

4. The concluding chapter of this book further underscores the significance of this point.

The government's practice gave rise to conventional wisdom that it was the job of government (and of the banks) to support businesses and to prevent business failure. It nurtured a psychology among the businessmen of dependence on the government, encouraged them to pursue easy gains originating from dubious sources, and impelled them to expand as fast as practicable. They leaned on the support of authorities in times of difficulties, and such support rendered them impatient at a slower and sounder pace of business.

The industrial targeting policy of the 1970s is now gone, and the government-business relationship has accordingly changed. With the demise of this industrial policy, the government has relinquished its practice of making business decisions. Much of the relationship still survives, but it can no longer be characterized as "Korea Inc." The common purpose and the clear and visible system of command and communication between them that characterized the earlier system have since become very much blurred.

Government and the Small and Medium Enterprises

It is not fair to say that only the conglomerates were favored; the government also tried to assist small and medium enterprises (SMEs).[5] As mentioned earlier, one of the first things that the government of President Park Chung Hee did in the early 1960s was to establish the Industrial Bank of Korea, a specialized bank for financial support of the SMEs, and the Korea Federation of Small Business, a private body for protecting SMEs' interest. The government also established a government-supported fund to make loans to SMEs and instructed the commercial banks and other lending institutions to lend a certain proportion of bank loans to SMEs. Thanks partly to government support, a good number of successful SMEs emerged during the 1970s and 1980s, sustaining a spurt of exports during the last several decades.

One may recall, however, that the basic thrust of economic policy, particularly during the 1970s, was to achieve growth and export targets through the support of large businesses. The SMEs were thus relegated to a disadvantageous position. To be sure, the government, through its five-year economic plans, never failed to mention the strengthening of SMEs as an important economic policy goal, but this goal has never been fully implemented. It was naturally not possible to realize both goals; one had to give way to the other. The goal of assisting SMEs has

---

5. According to the Small and Medium Industry Basic Act, an SME is an enterprise with less than 300 full-time employees in mining, manufacturing, and transportation industries, less than 200 in the construction industry, and less than 20 in trade and service industries. A manufacturing enterprise with less than five employees, however, although technically a small enterprise, is usually categorized separately as a "petty" firm.

been thwarted as consistently as the policy of assisting large businesses has been strengthened. The more large enterprises were favored, the more the SMEs were disadvantaged because disproportionate amounts of the factors of production, including high-quality human resources, low-cost financial resources, and physical capital were directed toward conglomerates. Few good resources were left for the SMEs.

As the conglomerates diverted productive resources away from the SMEs, the prices of remaining resources tended to be pushed up. For example, as the conglomerates pushed up wage rates in their capital-intensive industries, the wage rates in the SMEs' labor-intensive industries also tended to increase. One might think that the increase of wage rates in the capital-intensive sector would release labor from that sector to the labor-intensive sector and thereby reduce wage rates in the latter sector. This inference is true from a static point of view, but the dynamic wage behavior of Korea belies this expectation. The increase of wage rates in the capital-intensive sector tended to pull up wage rates in the labor-intensive sector due to what appears to be a "communication effect" that was developing in Korean industrial relations. The labor unions, which in Korea are primarily firm-based, eyed the gains made by other firms and demanded that their employers pay comparable wages to them with little regard to their productivity. Thus, the rise in the wage rates in one sector of the economy tended to be communicated to other sectors of the economy.[6] As a result, the labor-intensive SMEs suffered from a higher cost of production than would otherwise be the case. Indeed, when a small economy such as that of Korea builds up superconglomerates and devotes more than the normal amount of resources to them, it will naturally leave less for SMEs. The opportunity cost of the conglomerates was retarded growth of the SMEs from both the static and, in the Korean context, dynamic viewpoints.

Degree of Industrial and Economic Concentration

The establishment and growth of heavy and chemical industries in Korea during the 1970s and to a lesser extent during the 1980s is first and foremost the story of the conglomerate expansion. Any telling of it devoid of conglomerates is a tale with the protagonists missing. Likewise, future development cannot be assessed without taking into consideration their predominant role. Conglomerates make the major investments in Korea today, and these firms will almost certainly grow faster than the rest of the economy.

The vigor and speed with which the Korean economy had until the

---

6. For the behavior of wage levels and the relationship between wage levels and industrial policy, see the next chapter.

end of the 1980s been growing suggests that the accompanying system of the resource use was sufficiently efficient. Recently, however, the economy has started showing signs that its efficiency and competitive advantage are being lost, and Korea began debating whether its economy would be able to maintain similar efficiency in the future.

Industrial efficiency is rooted importantly in industrial organization, which can be viewed from macroeconomic and microeconomic perspectives. Macroeconomic aspects include the degree of industrial concentration or competitiveness of Korean industry taken as a whole. Microeconomic aspects relate to the internal structure of individual firms. Both are very important determinants of the efficiency of the economy as well as that of individual firms.

Macroeconomic Aspects of Industrial Organization

Macroeconomic aspects of industrial organization can be discussed from two vantages. One has to do with the degree of competitiveness (or the degree of concentration) in a specific industry; this can be measured by the market share of a dominant firm or firms in a specific industry. This coincides with the notion of industrial concentration in the traditional sense—for example, monopoly or oligopoly in the steel industry. The other has to do with a measure of the extent of the dominance of a conglomerate (or group of conglomerates) in a particular sector of the economy such as the manufacturing sector. This notion is not prevalent in the economic literature because concentration in this sense is not a conspicuous feature of industrial organization in advanced countries. It is, however, very relevant in developing countries, including Korea, where a few firms dominate the industrial sector.

To begin with, let us consider the problem of industrial concentration in Korean manufacturing in the traditional sense of the term. The Fair Trade Commission, a part of the Economic Planning Board,[7] defines the "monopolistic or oligopolistic firm" as "a firm that has more than 50 percent of market share of a particular commodity or one of the three or fewer firms that collectively have more than 75 percent of the market share of a commodity in an industry whose value of total domestic supply exceeds 30 billion won." In accordance with this definition, the commission reports the number of monopolistic and oligopolistic firms and commodities each year. Table 4.1 shows the increase in the number of market-dominating commodities and firms from 1982 to 1991. It shows

---

7. The Fair Trade Commission, created by the Monopoly Regulation and Fair Trade Act enacted in 1980, belonged to the Economic Planning Board until January 1990, when the law was amended for the second time, making the commission more independent of the board. However, the work of the commission is closely related to that of the EPB.

Table 4.1 Number of market-dominating commodities and firms, 1982–91

Year	Commodity	Firm
1982	43	87
1983	59	107
1984	71	136
1985	85	151
1986	100	181
1987	106	161
1988	122	177
1989	131	178
1990	135	180
1991	136	183

Source: Economic Planning Board.

that the number of the market-dominating commodities increased three-fold and the number of firms twofold during the 1982–91 period. This partly reflects the fact that the Korean domestic market for any commodity is so small that it is very susceptible to oligopoly. Furthermore, as more new goods and services are produced, the number of the market-dominating firms naturally increases. To the extent that industrial concentration is a natural outcome of genuine competition and not the result of other powerful forces, a mere increase in the number of market-dominating firms should be of little concern.

When one looks at the World Bank study on monopolies in the Korean economy (table 4.2), using slightly different definitions, one can see that economic concentration was indeed high in Korea—higher than in Japan or Taiwan—and that it increased during the 1970s, with approximately 80 percent of commodities produced in Korea and over 60 percent of commodity sales deemed noncompetitive. According to this study, there was some progress between 1982 and 1985 in reducing industrial concentration. Other recent data on this problem are not available, but in view of the tendency of conglomerates to grow faster than the rest of the economy, there is little reason to believe that industrial concentration is declining.

Let us now turn to the economywide dominance of the conglomerates and their significance to the Korean economy. First, conglomerates are ubiquitous. No aspect of Korean life, noneconomic or economic, the poor or the wealthy, are entirely free from their imprint.

The preponderance of the conglomerates notwithstanding, reliable studies in Korea on any aspect concerning them are few.[8] Available

8. The only fairly comprehensive study on economic concentration in Korea, widely cited by commentators on this problem is Lee and Lee (1985).

Table 4.2 Commodities and sales from noncompetitive[a] Korean manufacturers, 1970–85 (percentages)

	1970	1974	1977	1982	1985
Commodities	81.5	82.8	83.7	82.1	77.7
Sales	61.1	67.9	61.2	68.6	62.2

a. Top three firms produce more than 60 percent.

Source: World Bank, *Korea—Managing Industrial Transition*, vol. II, 1987, p. 30.

information is unreliable as well as fragmentary. Virtually the only economic data on this matter are summarized in table 4.3, which show conglomerates' shares in total sales and employment in the manufacturing sector between 1977 and 1989.

A few notes of caution are in order.[9] First, in both the cases of the top 10 and top 30 conglomerates, their respective shares of shipments in the economy as a whole increased through the first half of the 1980s and then declined. This implies that concentration of economic power in Korea has diminished as a whole since the mid-1980s due to continuing government policy measures to help SMEs. Second, the share of employment has been on the decline throughout the 1980s, and the ratio of shipments to employment increased during the first half of the 1980s while it declined during the second half. This shows that the labor-saving activities of the conglomerates as a whole were more vigorous than those of the SMEs in the first half of the 1980s, but not during the second half. One last observation is that the top 10 conglomerates are overwhelmingly large—their combined shipments exceeded three times that of the next top 20, and these shipments are growing faster than those of the rest of the top 30.

Microeconomic Aspects of Industrial Organization

The most notable feature of the conglomerates is individual ownership. The owners retain a tight control of all the firms belonging to their "group"; some firms in the group have gone public, but many are still closely held. Even for the "open" firms, the owners hold tight reins on

---

9. With due regard to the analyses that yield these figures, one would nevertheless have substantial reservations about the accuracy of the information upon which the analyses must have been conducted. The conglomerates are extremely complex phenomena, and any report on their performance would contain a sufficient amount of irregularities to render the analyses performed on them less than fully accurate. As a measure of the preponderance of conglomerates in the economy, the figures in the table are at best misleading, in the sense that the importance of the conglomerates exceeds by far whatever impression is conveyed by the figures.

Table 4.3 Conglomerates' shares in manufacturing shipments and employment, 1977–89 (percentages)

	1977	1981	1985	1987	1989
Shipments					
Top 10	21.2	28.4	30.2	27.9	27.0
Top 30	32.0	39.7	40.2	36.8	35.2
Employment					
Top 10	12.5	12.1	11.8	11.6	11.8
Top 30	20.5	19.8	17.6	17.6	16.6
Ratio of shipments to employment					
Top 10	1.70	2.35	2.58	2.41	2.29
Top 30	1.56	2.01	2.28	2.01	2.12
Ratio of top 10 to next top 20					
Shipments	1.96	2.51	3.02	3.13	3.29
Employment	1.56	1.57	2.03	1.93	2.46

Source: Economic Planning Board.

the firms belonging to the group. Legally, the firms in a conglomerate are independent of the rest of the firms so that the presidents of the member firms, who might be the owner's family members or professional managers employed by the owner, can make decisions affecting their firms, but in reality the owner retains final decision-making authority.[10] The conglomerate owner maintains the secretariat and/or the office of planning and coordination through which policies governing the entire conglomerate are formulated and implemented. The internal organization of the biggest conglomerates in Korea are very similar to one another.

Another important organizational characteristic is the fact that the Korean conglomerates encompass many firms operating in different industries. The major Korean conglomerates have expanded their domain by starting firms in services as well as manufacturing industries. Their sphere of manufacturing operations ranges from food processing to automobiles, electronics, and aviation. Their service industries include retail trade, hotels, finance and securities, real estate, newspapers, universities, and research institutes. The largest conglomerates, during their formative days, did originate in specialized fields and still retain them. As they pushed into new territories, specializations have become blurred, and the groups have become even more similar.

---

10. The closest prototype of the largest Korean conglomerates may be the Japanese *Zaibatsu* in the prewar days. The Japanese *Zaibatsu* firms were dissolved by the US occupation authority, but they have been revived and restructured into what is called *Keiretsu*.

Table 4.4 Small and medium enterprises'ᵃ shares in manufacturing, 1960–91 (percentages except where noted)

	1960	1970	1980	1990	1991
Number of SMEs	15,063	25,037	31,466	67,679	71,105
SMEs as share of total firms	99.1	97.0	96.6	98.3	98.5
Employees	78.1	48.2	49.6	61.7	63.5
Value added	66.3	28.0	35.1	44.3	45.8
Exports	n.a.	n.a.	n.a.	42.1	39.9

n.a. = not available.

a. Defined as a firm with 5–200 employees for the years 1960 and 1970 and as a firm with 5–300 employees for the years 1980 through 1991.

Source: Economic Planning Board.

Small and Medium Enterprises

Before the 1960s, Korean SMEs were engaged mainly in processing agricultural, forestry, and fishery products and traditional handicraft industries to meet the demands of the agricultural society. Examples of the processing industries were breweries, rice milling, lumbering, paper, and earthenware, and some examples of the handicraft industries were textiles and briquets. The number of SMEs with 5 to 200 employees significantly increased during 1960–70 (table 4.4). At the same time, the larger firms recorded a more impressive increase—from 141 in 1960 to 779 in 1970. During this period, the import-substitution and export industries expanded greatly with the inflow of foreign capital, and firms in these industries were generally large. Since these firms held large shares of the employment and value added, the SMEs' shares in these categories declined substantially despite the increase in the number of enterprises. The share of SMEs in the number of employees declined precipitously from 78 percent in 1960 to 48 percent in 1970, and the share in value added also declined, from 66 to 28 percent during the same period.

The 1970s marked a period in which large enterprises grew very quickly as the government supported heavy and chemical industries. SMEs increased in number at a much lower annual rate in the 1970s than in the 1960s and 1980s. The annual rate of increase was 5.2 percent in the 1960s, slowed to 2.3 percent in the 1970s, and surged to 8.0 percent in the 1980s. From 1970, the SMEs' shares in both number of employees and value added have increased, but the relationship between employees and value added shows that SMEs have experienced relatively weak labor productivity improvement within the entire manufacturing sector.

**Table 4.5 Korea, Japan, Taiwan: comparison of SMEs'
shares in manufacturing, 1990 (percentages)**

	Korea	Japan	Taiwan
Shares of SMEs in total firms	98.3	99.1	98.7[a]
Employment	61.7	72.4	70.6
Value added	44.3	55.5	50.0

SME = small and medium enterprise.

a. Figure is for 1987.

Sources: Economic Planning Board, the Ministry of Trade and Industry.

Furthermore, the Korean SMEs are relatively weak compared with those of Taiwan and Japan, even though the countries have similar historical and economic backgrounds (table 4.5). In particular, Japan greatly exceeds Korea in terms of the SMEs' shares in both number of employees and value added.

Behavioral Characteristics of Korean Entrepreneurs

As noted above, Korean industrial structure is marked by the dominance of conglomerates and the relative weakness of SMEs. Though the quality of the entrepreneurship in both types of enterprises is generally excellent, their patterns of behavior are naturally dissimilar. This is more or less expected because the pattern of business behavior has to reflect the environment in which an enterprise operates.

The organizational structure of the Korean conglomerates, for example, reflects the pattern of growth during the condensed-growth days. The most outstanding characteristic of the conglomerates' entrepreneurial behavior is their predilection for expanding in size and territory. Many Korean entrepreneurs succeeded during the last three decades by simply plunging themselves into new industries with or without adequate preparation in terms of technology, capital, and markets. This mode of behavior persists among them today.

Not only are they willing to enter new industries, they have also shown readiness to invest abroad. At times, these overseas investments were made with or without sufficient information about the market and host-country economic conditions, as exemplified by their great interest in the East European countries.

The urge to expand has sprung partly from the conglomerates' desire to internalize the production of components and parts used for producing final output. Instead of having an out-of-group SME supply components, the conglomerates have had incentives to establish their own subsidiaries, crowding out existing SMEs operating in the same field. Such vertical integration permits them to economize on transactions costs and improve the quality of parts.[11]

A keen sense of competition among the conglomerates has also impelled expansion. They perceive increasing market share as more important than the rate of profit. Two or more groups often have made large-scale investments simultaneously in the same industrial fields in order not to fall behind rivals, to the great woe of smaller, independent companies already operating successfully in these industries. The coordination of investment among the conglomerates themselves as well as with others was not the distinguishing characteristic of their behavior.

The conglomerates tend to expect the government to do whatever is needed to facilitate this expansion and to come to their rescue when necessary. Nonetheless, until recently they were subject to a variety of regulatory restrictions, and they are naturally loath to have government impede their expansion. For example, they urge the government to lower interest rates in order to reduce their debt service burden and the cost of new investments. It is difficult to generalize the patterns of business behavior of SMEs because they are so diverse in terms of industry type and size. They may also feel the urge to expand, but in the absence of government assistance, their ability to do so is limited. They have faced a perennial want of high-quality labor and bank loans. To them, finance availability has been more important than the level of interest rates. There are many innovators among them, who earn trust and respect from their employees as well as from the public. Though many have been doing well as suppliers of components and parts, they also want to produce and sell finished products.

Efficiency of the Conglomerates and the Economy

From the individual conglomerate's point of view, such enterprises are very efficient. Their efficiency springs from many sources. First, they have sufficient command of financial resources to invest in research and development. They are able to learn from imported technology, and in many cases they have succeeded in assimilating and improving imported technology. The technological advances made by the Korean conglomerates in machinery, electronics, shipbuilding, and automobiles have been quite remarkable. In many cases the conglomerates reaped initial success

---

11. If the parts and components produced by SMEs in Korea tend to be low in quality, so that the large-scale enterprises have an incentive to make those parts and components themselves, it is a testimony to the weakness of the Korean SMEs, and not the inherent weakness of the SMEs as such.

from large-scale investments in new technology-intensive industries without adequate prior knowledge or experience.[12]

The groups have monopsonistic access to the best human and other resources available in the country, including those who have been trained abroad; the salaries they offer can compete easily with foreign multinational corporations. They have easy access to bank loans and other financial resources. They have excellent public relations channels and can influence public agencies. Their overall economic power can generate so much "rent" that few would expect the individual firms under their umbrellas to fail.

In general, the economic power of conglomerates, along with the rents originating from it, will increase commensurate with the number of enterprises they add to their groups. These additions, however, dilute their focus and specialization and lure them to encroach upon SMEs. Thus, even though the "economic power" of a conglomerate grows as it adds firms in new areas, an individual firm belonging to the conglomerate, mutually unrelated, may not be as efficient and strong as the group.

The economic efficiency of conglomerates becomes doubtful when considered from the viewpoint of the economy as a whole. Expansion is the primary source of conglomerates' strength, but it is the primary source of weakness of the economy as a whole. To the extent that the strength of the conglomerates is rooted in rents rather than profit, the individual efficiency of a conglomerate does not necessarily ensure efficiency for Korea. When a conglomerate crowds out an SME and performs better than the SME, it does not necessarily mean that the former is more efficient than the latter, when the "efficiency" of the former rests upon quota rents. The size of the rents the conglomerates collect represents a deadweight efficiency loss for the economy.

Knowledgeable people have lately debated the need for Korean businesses to ramp up their technological capability in order to improve their competitive position in international markets. They argue that Korean enterprises are not making enough effort here and that government as well as businesses should increase research and development spending. True enough, but money alone does not buy technology, which should be broadly interpreted to include a variety of innovations in all aspects of business operation. What is important is not increased capability in a selected set of high-technology industries, but a cluster of innovations in commercially productive technologies, in conventional as well as high-technology areas. The organization and mode of the enterprise is not

---

12. However, trade data show that between the late 1970s and the mid-1980s, Taiwan's market share in OECD markets with respect to both the heavy and chemical industry and light industry groups exceeded that of Korea by increasingly greater margins even though Taiwan has no conglomerates (Yu 1990, 93–102).

irrelevant to technological improvement with commercial application. An enterprise geared to expansion is not necessarily bound to produce innovations. Korean businesses wanting to upgrade technological capability need to reevaluate their structure and organization with respect to ownership, management, channels of command, and exchange of information.

The preceding discussion centers on the question of efficiency rather than equity. There are those who believe conglomerates are undesirable from an equity and social justice perspective, even if they are efficient.[13] From the point of view of economic development and development policy, equity should be looked upon as the socially acceptable degree of "fairness" in the systems of capital accumulation, resource use, and provision of opportunities. It is important to provide reasonably equal opportunities for all economic actors so as to motivate them to do their best.[14] Equity in the sense of equality of opportunity is the *sine qua non* of development. Viewed from this standpoint, excessive expansion of conglomerates, to the extent that they have encroached upon SMEs, will be detrimental on both efficiency and equity grounds to the development of the economy as a whole.

Past Policies for Achieving a Balanced Industrial Structure

The government has been aware of the industrial structure's tendency toward polarization and of its long-run political and economic cost. Since the first half of the 1970s, it has adopted policy measures to establish a balanced industrial structure. One of the earliest of these was the Presidential Emergency Decree of May 1974, which restricted the supply of bank loans to conglomerates and induced them to raise investment funds in the capital market. The decree was aimed at modernizing the structure of ownership of the closely held, family-run corporations and at developing the capital market. The major firms belonging to conglomerates were induced to decrease their debt-equity ratios by going public, increasing paid-in capital, selling subsidiaries, issuing corporate bonds, and merging or restructuring. To make these measures effective, the government terminated low-interest financing for any recalcitrant enterprises. In 1974, the government adopted the Prime Bank System, under

---

13. Efficiency of conglomerate groups should not be confused with efficiency of an individual firm belonging to the group. The former can be "efficient" even though the latter is not: the strength of a conglomerate as a whole is much greater than the sum of the strengths of member firms. The strength of the former springs from the size of the group, with or without efficient member firms.

14. The problem of equity should be viewed from a broader angle than that of simple redistribution of a given amount of income.

which the largest lending bank was designated the prime bank responsible for monitoring the business performance of the borrowers and their loans from all banking institutions and for advising them.

In 1975, the government enacted the Price Stabilization and Fair Trade Act to "maintain price stability and establish fair and free competitive order." The law enabled the government to set maximum prices on important goods, including public utilities and monopoly products, and prohibited unfair trade practices and unjust restraints on competition.

In December 1980, the government enacted the Monopoly Regulation and Fair Trade Act, which prohibited business collusion. This law was amended in December 1986 to ban interlocking directorates, establishment of holding companies, and the practice of reciprocal investment by a group of firms in the stocks of other firms. The purpose of this law was to restrain monopoly or oligopoly and to foster competition. Moreover, it was intended to prohibit excessive economic concentration and the abuse of market-dominating power. The Fair Trade Commission was created to deliberate upon and resolve matters of importance regarding this law.

The law, however, had many loopholes and has not proved very effective in restraining monopolies or checking the conglomerates' power. There are, for example, many provisions that allow business combinations and restraints of competition if they are deemed necessary for the rational restructuring of the industry concerned or for the strengthening of international competitiveness. Also, the Fair Trade Commission, a five-member body, remains insufficiently organized to function effectively as an overseer.

Most importantly, the weakness of government policies in stemming the consolidation of the conglomerates' economic power is the consequence of government policies since the 1970s to maximize export growth and GNP through promotion of conglomerates. This basic policy is incompatible with principles such as prohibiting concentration of wealth, promoting social justice, and fostering equity.

In the past, the government alienated the SMEs by pursuing policies that favored conglomerates. In the 1960s, the main concern of Korean industrial policy lay in promoting exports, and government policy on SMEs was primarily designed as a means to increase exports. The share of the SMEs in total exports in the beginning of the 1970s was about 40 percent. Considering that the share of the SMEs in total value added was 28 percent in 1970, it is apparent that until the beginning of the 1970s the SMEs specialized more in exports than did large enterprises.

Since the early 1970s, when the heavy and chemical industries began to be vigorously promoted, the SMEs' role in producing and providing components for large enterprises began to be recognized. The government began in 1975 to advocate the *Kye-Yul-Hwa* policy to streamline the process of production and prevent mismatch between the mass production capability of the large enterprises and the ability of the small and medium enterprises to supply them with parts on demand. A law to promote the alignment of enterprises was enacted in 1975.

Government policies on SMEs after the adoption of the alignment policy in the 1970s had two principal goals. One was to increase financing for the SMEs, and the other was to determine and designate the suitable fields of business for SMEs. The former policy was implemented by administrative guidelines that instructed the banks to increase the share of bank loans to SMEs. This policy sparked an increase in bank loans for the SMEs, but there still remained considerable difficulties due to SMEs' lack of security and to the complicated administrative procedure. The contents of the latter policy of securing specific markets for the SMEs were as follows: designation of fields of industries as exclusive realms for the SMEs and barring the entry of the large enterprises into these fields, designation of specific portions of the production process as exclusive fields for the SMEs, and protection of the SMEs from being unfairly hurt by the large enterprises in subcontracting.

With the help of these policies, the number of the SMEs has greatly increased since the latter half of the 1970s, as shown in table 4.4. However, the policy of alignment has not been fully successful. The large enterprises tend to oppose it, asserting that the policy causes inefficiency, and the SMEs tend to prefer producing finished goods to producing parts for large enterprises.

Since the early 1980s, the correction of imbalances in industrial structure has become the focus of economic policy. In 1982, the Small and Medium Industry Promotion Act was enacted in order to establish the Small and Medium Industry Promotion Fund and to build the industrial complex for SME promotion. The main objectives of this law were to expedite modernization of the SMEs, to encourage joint effort among them, and to furnish managing and technical skills for them. In 1986, the Small and Medium Industry Startup Promotion Act was enacted to help entrepreneurs start SMEs through tax incentives and financial support. In 1986, the Industrial Development Act signified a change in the direction of the policies from supporting specific industries to encouraging the "rationalization" of the entire industrial structure.

Despite all these policies, SMEs in Korea are generally still weak, especially in the manufacturing sector. They continue to prefer finished-goods production, and large firms continue to create their own small subsidiaries. The weakness of the SMEs—the source of innovation in most modern industries—is one of the most vulnerable features of the Korean economy.

Structural Adjustment Policy for the Future

The industrial policy of the last several decades facilitated both condensed growth and structural imbalance, marked with strong conglomerates and weak SMEs. The structural imbalances have been accompanied by, and are concomitant with, other seemingly unrelated problems of the Korean economy, such as the underdevelopment of the financial sector, built-in inflation, inadequate development of human capital, slow improvement in productivity, and discord in industrial relations.

The Korean economy is undergoing a transition; factors that accounted for past growth are changing rapidly. Unless the structural imbalances discussed above are redressed, it will be difficult to generate new factors for growth, and economic performance will deteriorate. The government and the business community need to understand the nature of the transition and do their share in bringing it about.

Actually, the government does not have to devise many new measures to bring about structural adjustment. Legal and administrative frameworks, though inadequate, have already been provided: the Monopoly Regulation and Fair Trade Act, regulations on bank lending, and various measures for assisting the SMEs. A tighter and more consistent application of the existing frameworks would be necessary to check the further growth of conglomerates, to encourage appropriate entrepreneurial traits, and to foster the SMEs. In the past these policies failed not primarily because legal and administrative provisions were inadequate, but mainly because the government was not prepared to pay the short-run price for structural adjustment. This in turn reflects inadequate understanding of the nature of the structural imbalance and of a lack of political will.

To be sure, existing frameworks cannot quite cope with the problems of structural readjustment. For instance, the government has since 1986 formally abandoned industrial targeting by enacting the Industry Development Act, in itself the right policy. It has divested itself of the authority to coordinate industrial activities for restructuring. This appeared to be the right policy, and the government ought to have stuck to it. Since then, however, the government has been exercising informal means of control on conglomerates' investments. For example, the government has been imposing on commercial banks an informal loan management regulation, under which the banks are required to restrict the number of loans to large conglomerates. This regulation is designed to check the excessive growth of the conglomerates. Recently, the government established informal guidance to induce the conglomerates to specialize. Each of the 10 top conglomerates was told to choose three industries and each of the next 20 conglomerates two industries in which to specialize, and then the government is to grant bank loans without limit to finance investment in these industries. While the government's intentions are understandable, one may doubt if this rule can serve the purpose. Not only is it contrary to the policy of financial liberalization, it may result in inefficient investments. Indeed, one may doubt if the rule can in fact be enforced. The conglomerates should be left to themselves; they should be allowed to specialize in more than, or less than, two or three industries. Furthermore, the financial resources of the commercial banks in Korea have become so limited that even when all five big city banks are combined, the amount of loans that they can collectively make may fall far short of what is needed for a few large investment projects. Consequently, it is not realistic to promise bank loans without limit. The best way is to let the commercial banks themselves decide how much, when, and to whom they should make loans.

Policies should be devised or refined to encourage the kind of entrepreneurship that is suited to achieving intensive growth, now that the process of condensed growth is coming to an end; to strengthen policy measures to encourage SMEs; to discourage sources of unearned income in order to make normal long-term entrepreneurial activities relatively more attractive; to eliminate the source of built-in inflation so as to ensure that entrepreneurs can have a long time horizon in which to conduct business; to take an impartial and neutral stance with respect to technological development; and to overhaul the system of regulations and controls so as to increase industrial efficiency and social equity. Let us elaborate upon these points.

Encouraging Entrepreneurs

The best way to encourage genuine entrepreneurship in Korea is to let the notion of "creative destruction" guide development. The country must let enterprises go bankrupt. Korean economic policy has been based upon the idea that the government should do its best to prevent firms from failing. Korean businesses, especially large ones, likewise expect the government to take appropriate action to rescue them. In other words, Korean development has proceeded on the notion of development without cost. As long as this is a criterion for economic policy, true entrepreneurship will not emerge.

Entrepreneurial enterprises come in many varieties: some are particularly suited for expansion; others are conducive to technological innovations; still others may be noted for promoting harmony with labor. So far in Korea, the policy thrust has primarily focused on expansionary ability. The entrepreneurial trait that the country now needs most is excellence in specialized areas. Korean entrepreneurs have demonstrated a drive to expand, but not the tenacity, quality consciousness, and professionalism upon which an advanced industrial economy can be built. In particular, government policy should be aimed at inducing Korean business to base expansion less on existing technology, organization, and government assistance and more on their own technological and organizational innovations. The Korean business community, aside from the SMEs, should be encouraged to depend less on government support and more on their own efforts at creating and improving their competitive abilities. The government policy will be effective only to the extent that the business community takes its own initiatives to foster its own growth potential. Both government and business should dispel the prevailing notion that business should not be allowed to go bankrupt.[15]

The source of innovation is specialization. In the modern industrial environment, innovations result only from long-term commitment of resources on clearly focused goals. In the same vein, the overhaul of organizations should be done so as to encourage the emergence of professional managers and the development of individuals with specialized knowledge.[16]

Strengthening SMEs

For the industrial structure of a country to be efficient, there must be a balance in the relative size of large enterprises and SMEs and a proper division of labor between them. They are essentially complementary, in that the large enterprises assemble parts made by SMEs into modern capital-intensive or technology-intensive goods. Thus, the large enterprises are relatively efficient in exploiting economies of scale—the assembly line has to be large—while the SMEs are relatively efficient in exploiting economies of small scale and/or economies of diversification. Even when the SMEs are the producers of finished goods, the large enterprises and SMEs are still complementary; the SMEs are suited to producing many different goods in small quantities, whereas the large enterprises are suited for mass production of relatively standardized items. In order for an economy as a whole to be efficient, it has to be efficient in both fields, and industrial organization should be such that there is a fair balance between the large enterprises and SMEs. The SMEs are the lifeblood of an economy; this is where needed innovation has to be induced. This policy will guarantee that effective competition prevails in the economy and that a reasonable degree of equality of opportunity can be secured. This is in fact the core of the policy for structural adjust-

---

15. For the last several years, Korea has witnessed the heirs of leading conglomerates' owners inheriting the reins. Most of these young men have been trained in fine schools in and out of the country. As expected, they have shown drive and willingness to innovate, and it is hoped that they will provide their businesses with new entrepreneurship to cope with the increasingly competitive environment in the future.

16. From a long-run point of view, it seems strongly desirable for Korea to have more professional managers manage businesses and more technology-oriented personnel attain executive positions. So far, the educational and professional background of the business leaders has been predominantly that of business or of economics, which was suitable in the days of condensed growth but increasingly is unsuited to achieving innovations in technology and conducting more vigorous on-the-job training for the workers—indispensable if Korea is to cultivate competitive abilities.

ment. The Korean government has been forming policies to assist SMEs, but few of them have been effective.

Most of these measures taken recently are aimed at alleviating SMEs' financial difficulties. These measures invariably prescribe in minute detail the ways in which commercial banks and the Bank of Korea are to lend: how much they are to lend, to whom, and on what terms.

These policy loans to SMEs were not successful because what SMEs need most badly are real resources, such as high-quality workers, skills, technology, and managerial capability. As long as these are not available, more policy loans will be of little avail. In order for SMEs to obtain these real resources, resources have to be released from other sectors, such as conglomerates or the public sector. But, since the government also promotes non-SME sectors, the resources SMEs need are not released from other sectors. There is in fact little mobility of resources between the SME sector and other sectors. Under such circumstances, the increase in bank loans on favorable terms will merely aggravate the indebtedness of the SMEs. Indeed, this is precisely what has happened on many occasions.

Thus, the policy on SMEs cannot succeed as long as it is isolated from other related policies. SMEs can flourish only when economic policy has been freed from the mercantilist notion that the government must foster and protect SMEs and that the government should prevent business failures.

Discouraging Emphasis on Windfall Gains

It is very important that the sources of unearned income, such as windfall gains of landowners due to increased land prices, should be discouraged as much as possible. Such windfalls do exist in any economy; to some extent it is desirable that they exist because they help achieve equilibrium in the economy. But excessive windfall gains trap the economy in a whirlpool of speculation and dissipate entrepreneurial talent. The entrepreneurial abilities of the Korean business community have been sapped by such activities; so has the propensity of workers to work hard.

Reducing Built-In Inflation

As will be discussed in chapter 6, the Korean economy has a built-in inflationary structure, which has to be eliminated to discourage entrepreneurs from engaging in short-term gains and to encourage them to pursue long-term excellence. Furthermore, built-in inflation has retarded the development of financial institutions, and there has been a perennial shortage of bank loans for SMEs. Under these circumstances, business always opts for high rates of short-term profit and shuns steps toward long-term competitive advantage.

Targeting Technologies

As argued earlier, a current policy of industrial targeting like the one of the 1970s is unnecessary and even harmful.[17] Technological targeting will be no less unnecessary or harmful. The government cannot pinpoint the technologies that the economy needs any more than it can pinpoint industries' needs. The experience with technological targeting in developing countries shows that it almost always ended in disaster.[18] The government should be neutral in this regard; it should be the market that induces the development of technology.

Regulation to Ensure Social Equity

The argument against government targeting technologies does not imply that the government should abandon all industry and technology policies and adopt a strictly laissez-faire approach. The government should maintain its policy on industrial development from a broader point of view; it should maintain systems and institutions that are fair to all and provide the economy with fair and equal opportunity. It should restore industrial balance and encourage innovations across industries. This leads us to the problems of the proper level of government regulations. Korea has elected so many cumbersome regulations and controls that stand in the way of industrial efficiency. It is very difficult for new entrepreneurs to start; regulations, rules, and controls that mainly benefit bureaucrats pile up businesses' overhead costs and should thus be abolished. Some new regulations and controls are needed. As new industries are developed, fresh conflicts of interest emerge, and the importance of environmental control looms ever larger. Despite the almost universal call for deregulation, laissez-faire should find no berth in Korea. The country certainly cannot give license for disorder, lawlessness, and unscrupulous pursuit of self-interest. Korea—or any country, for that matter—cannot deregulate as much as is needed so long as the freedom accorded to enterprises is misused for pursuing only private gains that shows disregard of social responsibility.

The industrial policy aimed at structural readjustments does involve a cost—in the form of a short-run reduction of the growth rate and some loss of privileges on the part of those who fared well during the old

---

17. It is widely understood that the policy of industrial targeting in Japan in the 1960s brought prosperity to Japan. But it is by no means clear that it was industrial policy in the sense of industrial targeting that made it so successful. Some industries did succeed, but many others failed despite policy emphasis (Okimoto 1989).

18. A notable example might be Brazil, which tried to foster domestic technology by discouraging imports of foreign technology. The policy did not succeed, but of course there were those who benefited from this policy.

days. But eventually these policies will benefit all. For those accustomed to the rapid growth of the past and for the businesses that took government support for granted, the reduced growth rate that might attend structural adjustment might appear as a permanent slide toward crisis. They should not be carried away by a crisis of confidence.

It is important to design economic policy with a view toward helping the conglomerates help themselves by restructuring their organizations and their operations; the interests of the conglomerates and that of the economy as a whole should be made to merge in the long run. Let the government help the conglomerates adjust to emerging conditions, and furthermore, let conglomerates help the government restructure its policy framework.

5

Labor

The primary source of Korea's condensed growth lies in labor; so far the country has made effective use of it. Those familiar with Korean development would readily admit that while government's and entrepreneurs' roles in achieving high economic growth were significant, the key factor has been the abundance of good laborers. Governments collapsed and there were many sociopolitical crises, but the economy has been able to sustain robust growth thanks to the "unlimited" supply of productive laborers. The government has been able to carry out its development policy unconstrained by a shortage of labor, and firms have been able to carry out their plans, taking low wages for granted.

However, things are changing. The labor problems rising on the winds of democracy since August 1987 and the extensive changes that have been taking place in labor-management relations suggest that the single most important factor of growth in the past is now being eroded. For the last several years, wage rates have risen tremendously, with the increase in labor productivity lagging behind. Furthermore, as substantial labor forces have shifted to either construction or service sectors with better working environments, many manufacturing firms are experiencing shortages of labor, despite higher wages. These developments will force the economy to make extensive adjustments. Although labor disputes have cooled down in recent years, the basic factors underlying the severe disputes during 1987–89 still exist. This chapter will investigate basic causes of labor-related problems and suggest solutions.

Productivity of Labor

Good studies on labor-related problems are scarce, and reliable time series data on these are not readily available. Data certainly can be, and have been, collected and used, but unguarded use of them may lead to different conclusions because different data sets may not be directly comparable and may rest on different operational definitions of the same terms. Under these circumstances, it is difficult to be very precise on employment, labor productivity, and wages, and the discussion in this chapter is limited to broad accounts of these variables.

The Korean labor situation at the initial stage of industrial development in the early 1960s was one W. A. Lewis (1955) would characterize as possessing an unlimited supply of labor. The industrial sector was very small; the labor employed by firms with more than five employees amounted to only 235,000, or about 15.6 percent of the total labor force, and disguised unemployment was widespread in the rural-agricultural sector. In 1960, when the student revolution broke out, the fully employed labor force was only 57 percent of the potential labor force while the "completely unemployed" labor force was about 2.9 percent. The remainder, or about 40 percent of the total, can be considered as a measure of the extent of disguised unemployment. The underemployed labor in the rural sector was willing to be employed at the subsistence wage rate offered by then-upstart firms using relatively simple technologies in labor-intensive industries. The process of "condensed growth" began, accompanied by a great increase in employment. The abundant supply of labor, whose productivity during the period under study increased more rapidly than real wages, was the most important source of condensed growth. The rapid increase in labor productivity enabled the economy to absorb the growing proportion of employable labor into productive activities. The increase in employment throughout the period under study was phenomenal; between 1963 and 1991, the labor force employed in the manufacturing sector increased by as much as 833 percent.

It is difficult to measure the increase in labor productivity—one has to have man-hour and output data, which are often unavailable. However, a reliable statistical analysis on this question with respect to manufacturing industries shows that the increase in labor productivity during the past two decades has been extremely rapid (table 5.1). The rate of increase of labor productivity in the manufacturing sector has been marked by many ups and downs, but it did register two-digit average annual increases for 12 out of 21 years.

It is true that the increase of labor productivity in industries other than manufacturing was slower, but data show that it was almost uniformly high throughout all industries. The high labor productivity increase would naturally be due, among other factors, to vigorous invest-

Table 5.1 Labor productivities in manufacturing, mining, and utilities, 1971–91 (percentages)

Year	Physical productivity[a] increase rate			Marginal physical productivity[b]		
	Manu-facturing	Mining	Electricity	Manu-facturing	Mining	Electricity
1971	4.7	8.1	11.1	0.53	0.82	1.05
1972	12.7	4.0	12.5	0.53	3.71	-3.29
1973	8.4	8.7	20.7	0.37	2.07	2.83
1974	7.0	1.5	3.8	0.49	0.62	0.70
1975	7.5	0.9	3.5	0.83	0.90	0.69
1976	7.0	0.5	9.1	0.48	0.58	1.30
1977	10.9	4.2	17.2	0.82	1.61	-5.00
1978	12.0	1.9	15.6	0.91	0.44	5.00
1979	15.8	7.4	1.0	-1.83	0.00	0.88
1980	10.6	3.7	-0.9	0.09	0.22	0.65
1981	18.2	0.2	7.4	-1.60	0.70	10.20
1982	7.8	3.7	3.8	-3.70	3.00	1.96
1983	13.6	4.3	6.5	8.36	-0.15	1.88
1984	10.5	5.4	1.1	3.39	1.97	1.08
1985	7.1	5.0	4.6	-1.18	1.34	2.32
1986	18.0	1.1	0.7	8.84	1.04	0.94
1987	14.5	4.0	6.7	5.44	-2.17	1.99
1988	-1.9	4.7	1.9	1.07	0.08	1.23
1989	9.8	15.6	19.8	-0.65	0.50	-1.50
1990	15.7	13.1	44.4	-2.17	0.60	-0.85
1991	16.3	8.1	28.6	-2.21	0.29	-1.23

a. The index of output at constant prices as a ratio of the index of regular employees (1985 = 100).
b. Changes in the index of output at constant prices as a ratio of changes in the index of regular employees.

Source: Korea Productivity Center, *Quarterly Productivity Review*, various issues.

ments, which made the workers better equipped; improvement in the quality of labor in terms of skills, knowledge, and attitude toward industrial work; and the lengthening of working days and hours. It would appear that all these factors were present during the period under study.

As already seen in chapters 1 and 2, Korean businessmen made vigorous investments throughout the period. During the 1960s, the business community vied for investment opportunities in all branches of light industries. Since the investment was "extensive" in nature, the capital/output ratio remained at a fairly low level, and the expected rate of profit remained high. Thus, the firms had great incentives to invest by importing capital and technology from abroad.

With the launching of heavy and chemical industries in 1972, Korea witnessed many duplicate investments. A number of bottlenecks appeared in the economy: shortages of skilled labor, technological know-how, and managerial capability; shortages of financial resources; and lack of demand for output. These phenomena presaged an eventual decline of the marginal efficiency of investment, as borne out by developments in the early 1980s, but the high investment rate in the 1970s did sustain the marginal physical productivity of labor, which remained largely positive in the 1970s, as shown in table 5.1.

The part of the improvement in labor productivity that was due to improvement in the quality of workers in terms of knowledge, skill, and willingness to work is believed to be quite considerable. Thanks to the expansion of education in all grades during the 1950s, the workers in general were highly literate and versed in the simple knowledge their work required. There was very high morale among the newly employed workers, who were relieved from the sense of hopelessness their previously dim prospects had imposed upon them. Employment in the modern sector and the lure of urban life were enough to enkindle the "will to economize" of potential workers. They were eager to learn new skills and to earn more by working long hours. The real wage rates certainly were low by international standards, but they did increase considerably over time, and the workers had incentives to work harder and longer.

Wage Rates

When there is a great reservoir of labor in the rural sector—where the wage rate is more or less constant at the subsistence level—one would expect that wage rates in the industrial sector would not significantly depart from rural wage rates. The behavior of wage rates in Korea from the early 1960s, however, does not seem to bear this out. From the beginning of the 1960s, wages began to move significantly upward from the subsistence level, even though the rural labor pool was far from exhausted. Table 5.2 shows the rate of increase of nominal wage rates in the manufacturing industries during the 1960s. Since the increase in nominal wage rates surpassed that of consumer prices, real wage rates started increasing almost from the beginning of the 1960s. The real wage rate increased almost uninterruptedly throughout the entire period, and furthermore, it registered high two-digit consecutive increases during 1967–69, 1976–78, and 1988–90.

As discussed in chapter 3, the initial stage of export and import substitution in a wide variety of consumption goods was nearly completed toward the end of the 1960s, when the increase of nominal manufacturing wages by far outpaced the increase in price level, reflecting shortages of labor that appeared for certain types of work. Although the total labor force was so large as to be characterized as "unlimited" in supply, the supply of particular types showed bottlenecks, so that the increase in demand for a given kind of labor easily pulled up the wage rates in that area. Another factor that pressed Korean wage rates upward was the stratification of the Korean labor market with respect to education,

Table 5.2   Wage increase rates, 1966–92 (percentages)

Year	Nominal wage increase rate		Real wage increase rate[a]	
	Manufacturing	Nonagricultural	Manufacturing	Nonagricultural
1966	15.6	n.a.	3.3	n.a.
1967	22.6	n.a.	11.0	n.a.
1968	26.5	n.a.	14.2	n.a.
1969	34.2	n.a.	20.0	n.a.
1970	26.9	n.a.	9.1	n.a.
1971	16.2	15.4	2.6	1.9
1972	13.9	17.5	1.9	5.2
1973	18.0	11.5	14.3	7.9
1974	35.3	31.9	8.5	5.8
1975	27.0	29.5	1.5	3.7
1976	34.7	35.5	16.8	17.4
1977	33.8	32.1	21.7	19.8
1978	34.3	35.0	17.3	18.1
1979	28.6	28.3	8.8	8.6
1980	22.7	23.4	−4.6	−4.2
1981	20.1	20.7	−1.2	−0.6
1982	14.7	15.8	7.1	8.1
1983	12.2	11.0	8.6	7.4
1984	8.1	8.7	5.7	6.2
1985	9.9	9.2	7.3	6.7
1986	9.2	8.2	6.2	5.3
1987	11.6	10.1	8.3	6.9
1988	19.6	15.5	11.7	7.8
1989	25.1	21.1	18.3	14.5
1990	20.2	18.8	10.7	9.4
1991	16.9	17.5	6.9	7.5
1992	15.7	15.2	8.9	8.4

n.a. = not available.

a. Real wages are calculated by deflating nominal wages by the consumer price index.

Source: Ministry of Labor, *Report of Monthly Labor Survey,* various issues.

geographical origin, and gender. Because certain work can be performed only by workers with qualifications such as a college degree or residence in a certain area, the Korean labor market was more imperfect than would otherwise have been the case. As bottlenecks appeared, not only did wage rates rise in sectors where specific labor was in short supply, it eventually pulled up all other wages. The rapid increase in wage rates during 1967–69 seems to reflect these bottlenecks.

The problem of labor shortages became all the more apparent in 1974, immediately after the government started its strenuous effort to develop heavy and chemical industries. The nominal wage rate in the manufacturing sector increased about 34 percent in the year, and during the remainder of the 1970s the annual rate of increase of nominal wage rates was 30 to 35 percent.

The steep rise in nominal wage rates during this period was accompanied by a rise in the price level. But the nominal wage increase far outstripped the price increase, so that the real wage rate increased nearly 20 percent during 1976–78. The increase in the wage rate subsided from 1979 into the early 1980s while inflation accelerated, so that the increase in the real wage rate was negative in 1980 and 1981.

It might appear that the 1974–79 period marked a turning point for the Korean economy; the period of excess supply of labor was over, and labor shortages set in. While this observation originates from wage statistics, one has to bear in mind that the great increase in wage rates during the 1970s was caused not by a general shortage of labor but by bottlenecks in particular types, which were forcibly induced by the targeting of heavy and chemical industries. The great spurt of investment in heavy and chemical industries was accompanied by the competitive bidding up of wages by firms participating in priority industries. These firms, in order to get increasingly scarce high-quality labor, vied to attract new college graduates, often many months before their graduation—a practice that effectively diverted the best graduates from the rest of the job market. These firms, furthermore, often engaged in fierce "scouting," as the word is popularly used in Korea, for better-qualified personnel from other firms. The standard of wages and salaries in Korea is usually set by those for new college graduates; when this wage level is set, contracts are made for other types of employees, whose wages maintain a certain set proportion in relation to the wages for new college graduates. When the latter goes up, all other wages follow suit. The great wage increase of 1975–79 reflected the keen competition of large businesses at that time. The shortage of high-quality labor has since become a perennial problem, but during the second half of the 1970s, it was more apparent than real—artificially pronounced rather than justified by underlying real forces. As the frenzy of heavy and chemical industries subsided, so did the artificially inflated demand for high-quality labor, and the rate of increase of wages returned within normal parameters.

The democratization movement that has been sweeping the country since 1987 triggered an intensive demand for higher wages and better working conditions. As will be described in the next section, a spell of labor disputes ensued. In most cases, employers were forced to grant at least part of labor's demands. The annual average of wage rate increases was approximately 22 percent during 1988–90, but in many manufacturing industries the increase rates were much greater.

To Korean workers, the special favor government gave firms during the 1960s and 1970s appeared as a glaring injustice. They perceived their employers' capital accumulation as of their own making, and consequently that they deserved a greater share. Furthermore, they noted that frequently when their employers were in financial trouble, the government bailed them out. Impelled by a sense of deprivation, the workers demanded higher wages, even when their employers were not making a profit. Because of the intensity of the demands, employers often granted at least some of them.

Particularly noticeable was that wages increased much more steeply for large conglomerates than for small and medium enterprises. Wage hikes are usually contagious: when the wage rates rise in one industry, they trigger demand for higher wages in other industries—first for the same types of labor and then for other types.[1] The large conglomerates are usually more responsive to labor's demand for higher wages because, for them, the proportion of wages in their total costs is relatively small, and it is therefore less costly to grant the demands than to engage in prolonged labor disputes. But these wage increases burden small and medium enterprises, which are generally labor-intensive, subjecting them to intense pressure to increase wages and making it difficult to attract good labor.

Fortunately, however, labor disputes largely subsided after the fourth quarter of 1989; the real wage rate increase for 1990 dropped to around 11 percent—much less than the 18 percent in 1989. There were many indications in 1990 that the worst of the labor disputes were over and that labor as a whole would be much more willing to abide by the laws and regulations governing labor disputes. Industrial relations in Korea have shown considerable improvement since 1990 due to the efforts of workers, businesses, and government. In 1991, nominal wages increased by 17 percent, but real wages grew at a stable 6.5 percent. In 1992, nominal wages rose by 15 percent, showing a moderate slowdown, though real wages continued to increase at the high rate of 8.4 percent.

Labor Share in National Income

Over the last several years labor has clearly demonstrated that their grievances were quite considerable. Were their demands, particularly for higher wages, justified? One yardstick might be the proportion in the work force of low-wage earners whose monthly wage is, for example, less than 150,000 won in 1990 constant prices. If this proportion is large, the demand for higher wages might be considered legitimate from a social policy point of view. Another important yardstick might be labor-share trends in national income. If national income were distributed unfavorably, so that the workers' share in it is reduced over time, labor disputes would be expected. Wage differentials by occupation, industry, size of firm, and region would be yet another factor related to labor disputes. If

---

1. This process is either prompted by inflation, as in the case of a demand-pull variety, or is accompanied by an inflation characterized by a cost-push price rise.

the same labor fetches different wages, there would be legitimate grounds for complaint on the part of those who are discriminated against. Wage differentials can be, and often are, caused by institutional and traditional factors as well as by the laws of supply and demand. However, if wages are determined arbitrarily and without economic justification, labor disputes are likely. Let us consider the three aspects men-tioned above, using some recent studies by labor economists on wages.

First of all, let us see the proportion in the total labor force of low-wage earners.[2] According to a survey of the Ministry of Labor, workers earning below 100,000 won per month—considered to be the absolute poverty line—amounted in 1986 to a low 1.5 percent of the total work force; women constituted 84 percent of these low-wage earners (Ministry of Labor 1986, 22). However, judging from earlier related studies on wages, the proportion of wage earners excluded from the Ministry of Labor survey could be as high as 49.3 percent (Fun-Koo Park and Se-Il Park 1984), a large number of whom were earning less than those with the lowest pay in the survey. Furthermore, the wage corresponding to the absolute poverty level should be increased to 160,000 won, or about $200.[3] In 1986, the proportion of workers earning less than 160,000 won per month was 17 percent of the total work force. Although most workers whose earnings fall below absolute poverty were young, single, and not married heads of households, special attention has to be paid to improving the welfare of those lowest paid-wage earners.

Second, the issue of whether Korean workers have been adequately compensated for their contribution to production ought to be investigated from a macroeconomic perspective. Although a reasonable wage level or the share of wages in national income cannot be determined completely objectively, a "fair" level can be construed by reviewing existing statistics and research results. Most studies based on published data seem to conclude that wages are largely at a satisfactory level and that government labor policy during the period under study cannot be characterized as a low-wage policy. These studies note that real wages have

---

2. Wage rates rose significantly, following massive labor disputes. Specifically, manufacturing wages rose by 22.9 percent during the fourth quarter of 1987 as compared to the same quarter of 1986, and by 19.6 percent during 1988 as compared with 1987. Thus, to help understand the labor situation and the causes for labor disputes in subsequent years, the statistics for years before 1987 have been presented.

3. The Minimum Wage Act was introduced in January 1988. During the first year, a two-tier system was adopted: 111,000 won for lower-wage industries and 117,000 won for higher-wage industries. In 1989, a uniform minimum wage of 144,000 won was applied to all industries. Actual wages received by employees whose basic wages are at the minimum wage level are about 55 percent larger than minimum wage because of overtime pay, allowances, and bonuses. In this regard, the actual monthly pay of those who receive the minimum wage amounts to approximately $335.

Table 5.3 Labor income shares in GNP and growth rate, 1971–92
(percentages)

Year	Compensation of employees as a share of GNP	Real wage increase rate (w)	GNP growth rate (g)	Employment increase rate (emp)	w / (g−emp)
1971	34.7	1.9	8.6	3.3	0.2
1972	34.5	5.2	5.1	5.0	0.5
1973	34.6	7.9	13.2	5.5	0.4
1974	33.1	5.8	8.1	4.0	0.5
1975	33.5	3.7	6.4	2.1	0.4
1976	34.4	17.4	13.1	6.1	0.9
1977	36.0	19.8	9.8	3.0	1.5
1978	37.9	18.1	9.8	4.3	1.3
1979	39.5	8.6	7.2	1.3	1.0
1980	41.2	−4.2	−3.7	0.3	1.2
1981	40.8	−0.6	5.9	2.5	−0.1
1982	41.2	8.1	7.2	2.5	0.8
1983	41.8	7.4	12.6	0.9	0.5
1984	41.6	6.2	9.3	−0.5	0.7
1985	41.4	6.7	7.0	3.7	0.6
1986	40.4	5.3	12.9	3.6	0.3
1987	41.1	6.9	13.0	5.5	0.4
1988	42.1	7.8	12.4	3.2	0.5
1989	44.5	14.5	6.8	3.8	1.4
1990	46.4	9.4	9.3	3.0	0.8
1991	47.6	7.5	8.4	3.0	0.7
1992	47.8	8.4	4.7	1.9	1.3

Sources: Bank of Korea, *National Accounts,* 1990; *Economic Statistics Yearbook,* 1991 and 1992.

increased steadily throughout the period, and even during the early 1980s (1982–86), the annual average growth in real wages was about 6 percent, a very high level by international standards.

As illustrated in table 5.2, real wage rates in the manufacturing industries increased sharply from 1967 to 1969 and from 1976 to 1978, though they also recorded increases during other periods. During 1981–86, in particular, real wages increased at an annual average of 6.1 percent, so it may be concluded that wage increases in Korea have been sustained at a substantial level. This seems to contradict the conventional view that the success of export-led economic development policies in Korea has been based on low wages, and that wage policy has focused on keeping real wages low. Be that as it may, the real wage rates increased most substantially in 1988 and 1989, reflecting the outburst of labor disputes during the democratization movement.

Table 5.3 demonstrates similar results. The second column shows the ratio of compensation of employees to GNP. In 1971, this labor share was only 34.7 percent, but it increased to 42.1 percent by 1988. This share is certainly lower than that in advanced countries, but it has been steadily increasing for several decades. There are indications that Korean workers were not quite adequately paid until about 1987, when the democratic movement set in. The wage level has since risen so considerably that Korea is no longer a low-wage country.

The labor share in GNP alone is not a good measure of the welfare of labor relative to the rest of the population because the labor share in GNP reflects increases in employment. In order for the welfare of labor to keep abreast of that of the rest of the population, the rate of increase of real wages (w) should at least be equal to the rate of increase of GNP (g) minus the rate of increase of employment (emp). That is, a ratio of $w/(g–emp)$ greater than or less than one can be interpreted as an improvement or deterioration in workers' welfare, respectively.

As is illustrated in the last column of table 5.3, this ratio has fluctuated widely. However, the average ratio during the period of 1971–91 is certainly more than one, which can be interpreted as an indication of improvement in workers' welfare. The sum of w and emp exceeded g in the 1970s, except for 1971 and 1975. This tendency also continued from 1989–92.

Working Hours

The above analysis shows real wages of Korean workers rising considerably throughout the 1970s and 1980s and the labor share of GNP being maintained at a satisfactory level. However, the unusually long working hours of Korean workers are relevant. Taking the number of working hours per week into consideration, there emerges a somewhat different picture of low wages not revealed in the above statistics.

As shown in table 5.4, the work week in manufacturing industries in Korea was 13 hours longer than that of Japan and 6 hours longer than that of Taiwan in 1986. Korea has the ignominious distinction of having the longest working hours of all the Asian newly industrializing economies and in most other developing countries. Moreover, the figures in the table in fact are believed to be lower than actual working hours. Indeed, workers in Korea, including public officials, do not have a clear concept of "regular working hours," although the situation is fast changing with democratization. One peculiar feature to be noted in table 5.4 is that, although per capita income has increased steadily over time, working hours in Korea remained at about the same level until 1986. In Japan and Taiwan, working hours have tended to decline with rising income, as expected from a theoretical perspective.

According to the "Survey Report of the Wage Situation by Occupation" by the Ministry of Labor (1986), average monthly working hours in all industries amounted to 227.2—that is, about 52.4 hours per week,[4]

---

4. Total working hours per week = total working hours per month times 12/52.

Table 5.4 Korea, Japan, Taiwan: average working hours per week, 1970–91

Year	Korea	Japan	Taiwan
1970	52.5	43.3	n.a.
1971	51.9	42.6	n.a.
1972	51.6	42.3	n.a.
1973	51.2	42.0	52.2
1974	49.9	40.0	49.9
1975	50.5	38.8	50.8
1976	52.5	40.2	51.3
1977	52.9	40.3	51.3
1978	52.9	40.6	50.9
1979	52.0	41.1	50.6
1980	53.1	41.2	51.0
1981	53.7	41.0	48.5
1982	53.7	40.9	48.4
1983	54.4	41.1	48.4
1984	54.3	41.7	48.9
1985	53.8	41.5	47.4
1986	54.5	41.1	48.2
1987	54.0	41.3	48.3
1988	52.6	41.8	47.7
1989	50.7	41.4	47.0
1990	49.8	40.8	46.6
1991	49.3	n.a.	n.a.

n.a. = not available.

Source: International Labor Organization, *Yearbook of Labor Statistics,* various years.

and in manufacturing industries the average working hours per month were 236.2, or 54.5 hours per week. The real wages and the labor share in GNP recorded in table 5.3 partly reflects such long working hours, and one might question the assumption that the welfare of the Korean labor force had been improving steadily and noticeably. It would appear that wages, which account for total remuneration, have been increasing satisfactorily, but this to a significant extent reflects long working hours during the 1960s and 1970s.

Finally, the so-called unreasonable wage structure needs to be examined since it may be a source of workers' grievances and, thus, labor disputes. In Korea, production and service work traditionally have been paid less than clerical and managerial work. Also, middle and high school graduates have been paid considerably less than college graduates. Table 5.5 shows the trend of wage differentials by types of work: production, service, clerical, and professional.

Wages for professional workers may be high due to the high productivity of the group. However, the wide wage differentials between production and clerical types of work do not necessarily reflect differences

Table 5.5 Wage differentials by types of work, 1971–91
(average monthly wage in thousands of won)

Year	Professional, technical, and related workers	Administrative and managerial workers	Clerical workers	Sales workers	Service workers	Production workers
1971	40	61	34	20	16	18
1972	44	68	33	24	17	18
1973	51	83	41	32	21	21
1974	60	99	54	35	26	29
1975	83	147	65	39	33	33
1976	119	196	89	47	43	43
1977	135	225	102	70	52	53
1978	179	291	122	87	69	72
1979	233	403	163	106	95	100
1980	266	438	177	109	115	118
1981	303	493	213	137	139	144
1982	363	534	240	193	161	164
1983	394	590	258	224	176	182
1984	423	632	279	242	193	200
1985	448	680	297	269	202	212
1986	479	701	319	281	216	233
1987	545	752	344	292	239	260
1988	575	840	397	337	293	314
1989	630	921	452	367	319	371
1990	695	1,035	519	413	370	430
1991	777	1,362	602	454	433	511

Source: Ministry of Labor, Yearbook of Labor Statistics, various years.

in their respective productivity. These differentials may be a serious source of production workers' discontent.

Although detailed study is needed, I suspect that the real differentials are not likely to be as large as those shown in table 5.5. The reason, as mentioned earlier, is that the notion of overtime work cannot be readily applied to clerical and managerial workers. Their working hours may actually be longer than those of production workers. Usually, there is a visible correspondence between labor input and output in "production" work, so working hours can be calculated objectively, and the distinction between labor input and output becomes clear. In clerical and managerial occupations, there is usually no distinction between regular and overtime work. Thus, observed overtime working hours are much longer in production work than in clerical and managerial work. However, there are many cases in which clerical and managerial workers do overtime informally. The relatively high wages of the clerical and managerial workers are thus likely to reflect unobserved, longer working hours relative to those of production workers. In addition, given the Korean system of promotion, future executives of companies are usually drawn from the pool of managerial workers, while it is unusual for production workers to be promoted to such a rank. Thus, production workers tend to be relegat-

Table 5.6 Wage differentials by education levels, 1971–91
(average monthly wage in thousands of won)

Year	Middle school and less	High school	Junior college	College or university
1971	18	27	n.a.	47
1972	19	28	n.a.	51
1973	21	33	n.a.	61
1974	29	41	58	81
1975	35	56	76	120
1976	47	73	106	168
1977	54	89	131	205
1978	73	117	174	270
1979	104	158	233	364
1980	124	181	265	413
1981	151	219	313	492
1982	174	249	326	552
1983	194	267	373	605
1984	214	287	378	651
1985	226	303	393	687
1986	251	324	417	718
1987	279	348	442	779
1988	340	414	501	839
1989	405	487	580	930
1990	477	569	668	1,056
1991	568	671	788	1,203

n.a. = not available.

Source: Ministry of Labor, *Yearbook of Labor Statistics,* various years.

ed to inferior positions, creating a sort of class consciousness and invoking feelings of deprivation among the equality-conscious Korean workers.

There are some other factors in the wage differentials between production workers and clerical and managerial workers. As already explained, some able and promising production workers have had opportunities to be transferred or promoted to higher positions involving clerical or managerial duties as they accumulate experience in a wide range of production work. Therefore, clerical and managerial workers are usually older and more experienced than production workers. Moreover, different levels of educational achievement are required for the different types of jobs: in a country such as Korea (that is, having a labor-intensive industrial structure) much production work could be accomplished by workers with a basic level of education, but some clerical and managerial duties required higher education. Thus, the wage differentials between production workers and clerical and managerial workers in part reflect differences in educational levels.

Table 5.6 also shows wage differentials by education level. It indicates that college graduates are paid much higher wages than middle and high school graduates. Because college graduates are in general more productive than non–college graduates, it is natural that the former should earn more than the latter. But there is a tendency for college graduates to be paid a larger share than less-educated workers regardless of productivity; the college diploma has become a social status symbol. Thus, the wage differential originates partly from this social status system in Korea. Wage determination depends as much on who one is as on what one does. While the future participants in a firm's decision making are drawn from the pool of college graduates, the middle and high school graduates are usually not expected to reach such positions. The distinction between officers and enlisted men in the military is an apt analogy to describe the difference between college graduates and non–college graduates in Korea. However, the wage differentials by education level have been continuously narrowed during the past two decades.

So far, wage trends, upon which workers' complaints are centered, have been examined from several viewpoints. The conclusions, which have to be verified by further study, can be summarized as follows.

- Statistics do not indicate a large number of workers earning extremely low wages, but in actuality there are a significantly large number of such workers.

- The share of labor in national income has shown considerable improvement over the years, and the workers' welfare, as far as it can be measured by steady rises in real wages, has also improved. This indicates that the living standard of the workers has improved as much as that of the rest of the population. However, considering that Korean workers have been working unusually long hours to maintain a relatively satisfactory labor share of GNP, one can say that the real wage level for Korean workers has remained relatively low.

- Wage differentials between production and nonproduction workers have remained large enough to be a focus of production workers' grievances. However, in practice, nonproduction workers are not necessarily more favorably treated than production workers; the higher wages of nonproduction workers seem to reflect their longer, albeit invisible, working hours, ages, or experiences, and higher education levels.

- Wage differentials between college graduates and middle and high school graduates partly reflect differences in social standing rather than of productivity. This has bolstered the frustration of non–college graduate employees.

These conclusions seem to suggest that as far as the rate of increase of real wages and the share of the total wage bill in national income are concerned, Korean workers would not have good reasons to harbor grievances. However, their complaints do seem to be legitimate when one takes into consideration the long working hours and the high rate of industrial casualties, a feature not discussed in this chapter. Furthermore, the structure of wages also is a source of grievance for industrial workers, along with social environments inhospitable to workers.

Characteristics of Labor Disputes of 1987–89

The term "labor dispute" is neither an academic nor a legal one; it is difficult to define it strictly. For the present purpose, a labor dispute is defined as a state of friction that exists between workers and employers when the workers attempt to improve working conditions or to secure the recognition of their rights through sabotage, sit-in demonstrations, or other means.

The labor disputes that swept the country during 1987–89 were surprising to both Koreans and foreign observers. The country had never experienced such disputes: many people were baffled, and most of the employers were frightened. Certainly, government and the business community should analyze the nature and causes of those disputes carefully so as to avoid them in the future.

The main features of these disputes can be summarized as follows. First of all, most of the disputes proceeded from and were settled through labor laws and regulations.[5] In many cases, workers harassed their employers using various means, destroying facilities in their work places and blocking streets. For most disputes, sit-ins preceded negotiations. That is, action was taken before demands were presented. This situation spread nationwide very quickly. These actions underscored the fact that money, rather than attachment or devotion to their companies, was the workers' chief incentive. Furthermore, the workers had clearly come to believe that the existing laws and social order hindered advancement of their legitimate causes and that their demands could not be conveyed effectively to their employers through legal procedures. Workers' behavior was thus the characteristic result of the unleashing of pent-up grievances long suppressed by discipline and regimentation.

Second, the progress of a dispute often ran counter to social convention and often defied logic. The disputes occurred and progressed in a fitful and precarious fashion, and agreements were reached "dramatically," as foreign newspapers so often characterized them. On many instances, considering the scope of workers' demands, settlements on disputes might have appeared impossible to outsiders. However, in

---

5. During the initial phase of the disputes, not only workers but also employers adopted extra-legal means to advance their causes. Fortunately, this is no longer the case.

virtually all cases, both parties demonstrated unusual brinkmanship, coming to agreements at the last minute. This phenomenon underscores the lack of institutionalization of labor-management relations. The origin, the progress, and the settlement of the disputes mystified outsiders. Accordingly, workers' demands and the settlement of disputes were bound to be viewed as "dramatic." Workers called for large increases in wages even when they fully understood that their firms were making no profits. Employers, for their part, accepted workers' demands, despite the losses they incurred and the dim outlook on profits. On some occasions, the negotiations between labor and management were not based upon facts regarding labor productivity or profits and losses of the companies concerned, and the disputes invariably were charged with emotion, usually magnified by the lack of trust between the two parties.

It is noteworthy that despite the agonizing process of the disputes, dialogue between the two parties finally brought settlements. This was the lesson learned—there is no substitute for peaceful, sincere, and voluntary dialogue; it implies that the perfunctory meetings held each quarter, as prescribed by the Labor-Management Council Act, will little avail.

The fact that many disputes were settled outside legally prescribed methods underscores the fact that the legal system pertaining to labor-management relations is not adequate in dealing with present industrial relations. More specifically, none of the labor-related laws—the Trade Union Act, the Labor Dispute Adjustment Act, the Labor Relations Commission Act, and the Labor-Management Council Act—have been very effective in bringing about harmonious labor-management relations.

In many labor disputes, there were instances of conflicts between "management-supported" labor unions and the so-called democratic labor unions. The former represents the officially recognized labor unions while the latter refers to those unlawful ones, according to the current union law. In cases in which workers did not endorse the representatives appointed by the officially recognized unions, or where the employers declined to negotiate with representatives of the "democratic" unions, disputes arose over leader representation.

Disagreements over representation often gave rise to the question of legitimacy of the agreement reached between the two parties. Sometimes, groups of workers denounced the hard-won agreement on the grounds that it was reached between "illegitimate" labor representatives. Other times, employers canceled agreements unilaterally on the grounds that the workers were not properly represented.

Situations like this are attributable to the provisions of the law concerned, which specifies the principle of a single labor union per firm, whereas actually, multiple labor unions operate within the firm. The situation is also attributable to the loopholes in the laws and regulations pertaining to the actual formation of labor unions; according to the present law, the formation of a union cannot be officially acknowledged if the official in charge refuses or delays receipt of the letter of notice of union formation.

From a broader point of view, however, the confusion on union representation originates from the lack of transparency and consistency in labor and industrial policies in the 1970s, which limited the activities of the union despite the fact that they were guaranteed by laws and regulations. In short, labor-management relations in Korea have been driven by the dynamics of the relative power of the two parties, and the outcomes of the disputes are determined outside the prescribed rules and institutionalized procedures.

In sum, the above characteristics of labor disputes in Korea in recent years seem to suggest that the relationship between labor and management and the behavior of the economic agents are the products of condensed growth. Industrial relations are not yet fully institutionalized. The "industrial culture" in Korea is still relatively immature; both workers and management are still inexperienced in negotiation. Fortunately, labor disputes since 1990 have largely subsided, and there appear to be a few signs that more mature industrial relations are being established.

Recent Developments of Labor Problems

Table 5.7 shows the remarkable decrease in the number of labor disputes, especially those focused on wage negotiations, which dropped to 167 cases in 1990 from 2,629 cases in 1987. Despite this dramatic decreases, real wage rates rose to a fairly high level—10.7 percent in 1990—indicating that a satisfactory level of wage increases can now be attained through peaceful negotiations.

Another sign of improvement was the recovery of strong growth in labor productivity. Labor productivity in the manufacturing sector increased by 15.7 percent in 1990 and 16.3 percent in 1991. These figures contrast with the 1.9 percent productivity decrease in 1988 and the 9.8 percent productivity increase in 1989.

These desirable changes were also aided by the relatively poor performance of the Korean economy since 1990. Even though GNP growth was high in 1990–91, this was mainly attributable to a construction boom and the expansion of consumer expenditure. The manufacturing sector has lost its competitive edge in the world export market because of its heavy wage-cost burden, which caused the reemergence of the trade deficit in 1990. In this environment, severe and unauthorized labor disputes were censured by public opinion, and this enabled the government to enact tough policy measures to stabilize wages. In 1992 the government implemented a strong stabilization policy, inducing firms to limit overall nominal wage increases to less than 5 percent. It appeared that this 5 percent guideline was-well observed by workers and

Table 5.7 Labor disputes by causes, 1975–92

Year	Total disputes	Delayed wage payment	Demands for wage increases	Closed or reduced operations	Fire	Illegal labor	Improving working conditions	Other
1975	133	32	42	7	10	19	4	19
1976	110	37	31	8	3	8	4	19
1977	96	30	36	4	4	6	2	14
1978	102	29	45	3	1	2	–	22
1979	105	36	31	5	6	3	–	24
1980	407	287	38	11	5	–	14	52
1981	186	69	38	11	9	4	32	23
1982	88	26	7	4	2	–	21	28
1983	98	35	8	9	6	–	19	21
1984	113	39	29	2	5	7	14	17
1985	265	61	84	12	22	12	41	27
1986	276	48	75	11	34	16	48	44
1987	3,749	45	2,629	11	51	65	566	382
1988	1,873	59	946	20	110	59	136	543
1989	1,616	59	742	30	81	10	21	673
1990	322	10	167	6	18	–	2	119
1991	234	5	132	–	7	–	2	88
1992	235	27	134	–	4	–	–	70

Source: Korea Labor Institute, *KLI Labor Statistics,* various years.

nesses; the firms reported that they were observing it. But there apparently were several instances in which nominal wages increased 15 percent in 1992, compared with 17 percent the previous year. This is evidence that the wage guidelines hardly worked and that they exacerbated problems in wage bargaining between workers and firms.

These changes notwithstanding, the shift of labor from the manufacturing sector to services continued, as workers sought a better working environment. The proportion of employees in manufacturing dropped from 27.6 percent in 1989 to 26.7 percent in 1990. In 1991 the proportion fell further, to 26.6 percent. This reflects the prevalence of the "3D" syndrome in the Korean economy: there is a strong tendency on the part of workers to avoid "difficult," "dangerous," and "dirty" jobs. But the more serious effect of this trend is that it is detracting from the quality of labor in the manufacturing sector. This is a fundamental cause of the declining competitiveness of Korean products in the world export market. Recently, the government has allowed employees in some manufacturing firms to be exempt from military service in order to overcome the disincentives that are causing the labor shortages in manufacturing.

Labor Policy

Generally speaking, the policy on labor in Korea has been subordinate to overall development policy; the function of the former is to support the latter. Since the development policy has been focused on maximizing the growth of income and exports, the labor policy has been focused on maximizing the supply of labor for the manufacturing industries. Since it has been assumed that there is an unlimited supply of labor, particularly in the rural sector, where disguised unemployment is widespread, the focus of the government's policy has been the demand for labor. The demand for labor is a function of wage rates, and therefore, to maximize employment, the labor policy has been directed toward maintaining low wage rates. On the whole, the assumption of an unlimited supply of labor at that time was valid, and the government did succeed in achieving the "growth-first" objective.

We have already seen in the preceding section that the government on some occasions adopted a "high wage" policy—the most notable example being the policy adopted during the second half of the 1970s, when the government encouraged or at least acquiesced in a big increase in wages. This was partly to placate the workers and to court their political support and partly to support the heavy and chemical industries by inducing workers to do more work. But on the whole, the basic thrust of the policy has been to maintain wage rates low enough to maximize employment while at the same time maintaining the cost competitiveness of the export industries.

We have also seen above that the quality of Korean labor has generally been good enough to sustain the initial phase of extensive growth. Needless to say, the quality of the labor force has improved considerably over time, commensurate with industrial expansion, and therefore the government has made little effort to improve the quality of the labor force. Neither has the government made much effort to improve the welfare of the workers as regards protection of their health, safety, and working environment.

Recently, the government has established workers' vocational training centers throughout the country; they are purported to provide information on job opportunities as well as training. The long-run programs for improving the productivity of labor, including education, have long been negligible. The government has simply concentrated its energy on economic growth, and contrary to the impression it has often sought to give, it has paid hardly any attention to education.[6]

Securing the maximum supply of labor, coupled with maintaining industrial peace, has been the policy on labor unions. It will not be

---

6. As noted in chapter 2, one of the main achievements of the government during the 1950s was to eradicate illiteracy through expansion of educational institutions. This factor can account for the good quality of the workers during the initial phase of economic development. The educational facilities did continue to expand during the subsequent decades, but this was the result of the natural course of events, and the policy emphasis on education was negligible compared with that for economic growth.

necessary here to give a detailed account of the tortuous development of this aspect; it will suffice to describe the gist of it as background for exploring possible future policies.

The first Constitution of the Republic of Korea, enacted in 1948, guaranteed the workers' basic rights, such as the ones enjoyed in advanced countries. In March 1953, four labor-related laws were enacted: the Labor Standards Act, the Trade Union Act, the Labor Dispute Adjustment Act, and the Labor Relations Commission Act. However, these laws only imitated advanced countries' legislation—hardly suitable to the Korean situation. These laws had been enacted even before a working class existed.

At that time, the Korean economy was barely sustained by economic aid from the United States, and industrial development was just beginning. Labor movements to improve the welfare of workers could not be effective under conditions of an unlimited labor supply. The Federation of Korean Trade Unions served essentially as a supporting organization of the Liberal Party government, and the labor movement was strongly tinted with political colors.

The military government, which came to power in 1961, set economic growth as the basic goal of its economic policies, imposing limits on the activities of the labor unions by revising in 1963 the Labor Standards Act, the Trade Union Act, and the Labor Dispute Adjustment Act. During the 1960s, on the whole no serious labor problems occurred. This was primarily due to overabundance of labor as well as enthusiasm for the prospects of economic development. More specifically, manufacturing industry employment constituted less than 10 percent of total employment while agricultural employment exceeded one-half of it. Workers were satisfied with whatever job opportunities became available to them, with little regard to wage rates.

With the enactment of the Special Measures for Safeguarding National Security Act in December 1971, labor movements came to be regarded as a threat to national security, and collective union action was practically outlawed. According to this law and its enforcement ordinance, labor actions were subject to prior approval by the government, and once they occurred, the government was to intervene automatically. Whatever agreement was reached between the government and the unions was to be observed.

As a prelude to the forthcoming *Yushin* (Revitalization) system, the law aimed at bringing under government control all forces that could prove to be potential opposition to the authoritarian regime. Thus, the authoritarian government drastically limited the scope of union activities. At the same time, however, it was astute enough to encourage the workers to work harder by allowing unions to expand and to work for higher wages and other economic benefits. For this purpose, the Labor Standards Act was revised to "protect" the workers. The government

Table 5.8 Labor union membership and the unionization rate, 1970–92

Year	Labor union membership (in thousands)	Unionization rate[a] (percentages)
1970	473	20.0
1971	497	19.7
1972	515	20.4
1973	548	20.4
1974	656	22.1
1975	750	23.0
1976	846	23.3
1977	955	24.3
1978	1,055	24.0
1979	1,088	23.6
1980	948	20.1
1981	967	19.6
1982	984	19.1
1983	1,010	18.1
1984	1,011	16.8
1985	1,004	15.7
1986	1,036	15.5
1987	1,267	17.3
1988	1,707	22.0
1989	1,932	23.4
1990	1,887	21.7
1991	1,803	19.8
1992	1,735	18.5

a. The ratio of labor union membership to regular employees in the nonagricultural sectors.

Source: Korea Labor Institute, *KLI Labor Statistics,* various years.

also enacted the Vocational Training Act, which required firms of a specific size to provide vocational training. The government also adopted measures to help workers financially by treating their savings deposits preferentially.

Judging that the *Saemaul* (New Community) movement had succeeded in gaining public favor in rural areas, the government decided to extend it to urban and industrial areas in the early 1970s; the workers were induced to follow government policy directives through the "factory *saemaul* movement" in an effort to bolster the morale of the workers in the emerging heavy and chemical industries. The government program, however, began to face numerous difficulties, and it was impelled to inspire laborers to work by tacitly pursuing a high-wage policy. This change in wage policy is partly responsible for the great increase in real wage rates during 1974–79.

As shown in table 5.8, both labor union membership and the unionization rate increased steadily throughout the 1970s, and in 1978 the number of union members exceeded 1 million. The expansion of labor unions during the 1970s was mainly due to the fact that the government allowed workers to organize. Despite the sharp rise in union membership, the number of labor disputes barely increased during this period, as seen in table 5.7.[7]

Toward the late 1970s, groups of workers belonging to religious bodies began to organize informal labor movements. As a consequence, the Korean labor movement began to assume a dual structure, consisting of formal (or official) unions and the informal (or underground) ones, with the latter becoming more pronounced in the early 1980s. Faced with the challenges posed by these developments, the government amended laws related to labor activities with a view toward making collective action more difficult by erecting obstacles such as mandatory reporting of the occurrence of disputes, the establishment of a cooling-off period, and prohibition of "third parties" to take part in disputes. At the same time, the Labor-Management Council Act required each firm to establish a labor-management council, stipulating that the representatives of labor and management meet regularly to discuss issues of mutual interest. The existing industrial unions were reorganized into company unions for the purpose of reducing the outbreak of labor disputes.

The new laws, however, were unable to contain informal union activities. To cope with this situation, the government again revised labor-related laws in December 1986, liberalizing labor union activities. The prohibition of outsider intervention was somewhat watered down so that industrial labor unions were allowed to take part in the activities of company labor unions. The range of permissible activities of labor unions was also broadened, and the procedures of collective bargaining were liberalized. The unfair labor practices on the part of the employers were made punishable, and the cooling-off period was shortened. In 1987, after taking into account various aspects of the labor disputes that occurred after commencement of democratization, the government further liberalized labor-related laws.

In the 1980s, union membership did not substantially increase: the unionization rate has sharply declined from 20 percent in 1980 to 15.5 percent in 1986—very low by international standards. This was not an indication, however, that workers' discontent had abated. The decline in the unionization rate reflected workers' frustration with formal labor unions. However, the low unionization rate was reversed dramatically in 1987 with the onset of the democratization movement. Laborers began to organize into "democratic" unions, and the unionization rate rose to 23.4 percent in 1989. After 1990, the unionization rate decreased again, recording 19.8 percent in 1991.

---

7. The table shows, however, only the number of "legal" labor disputes. Those labor disputes deemed illegal and settled behind the scenes through government mediation are not shown in the table.

Policy Implications

Korean labor policy during the 1960s and 1970s was geared toward mobilizing the unlimited rural supply of labor in the industrial sector. The major policy thrusts were to keep wage rates low—though the government temporarily resorted to a high-wage policy—and to prevent labor disputes.

Since the supply of labor was abundant and its quality was generally good, the government felt little constraint regarding labor. During the latter half of the 1970s, the shortage of high-quality labor began to be felt, but few measures were taken toward long-term human development. Eventually, a shortage of high-quality labor became apparent in almost all industries. Wage rates rose steeply with the onset of democratization in 1987, while shortages even of ordinary laborers began to appear in most manufacturing industries. The government has heard recommendations from various quarters that cheap labor be imported from abroad; the manufacturing industries have begun to invest in Southeast Asian countries so they can take advantage of the region's cheap labor.

The labor market has felt the impact of Korean economic transition most keenly. A labor-surplus country has turned into a labor-shortage country; a low-wage country has turned into a high-wage country. Comparative advantage is shifting too quickly from labor-intensive to technology-intensive industries. Under these circumstances, future labor policy should be based on new and longer-run perspectives. From the short-run point of view, labor policy should aim at increasing the supply of labor by holding down the unduly rapid rise in wage rates and establishing industrial relations in such a way as to settle labor disputes through dialogue. From the long-run point of view, labor policy should develop human resources to improve the productivity of labor in all industries and establish a sound industrial culture that can promote harmony and cooperation in labor relations. These points are elaborated in the next sections.

Labor Shortages

It is imperative that the economy alleviate labor shortages in manufacturing, and in small and medium-sized enterprises in particular. Labor shortages occur in all successful economies, but this phenomenon appeared far too soon in the case of Korea. For an economy with as many as 43 million people, whose average per capita income is only $6,500, the fact that it is acutely feeling the shortage of ordinary as well as high-quality labor cannot be a normal state of affairs; it is a sign that the country is losing comparative advantage in labor-intensive industries before it can establish advantage in technology-intensive sectors.

The increase in the real wage rates must be arrested and kept within limits set by the overall increase in labor productivity. Wages rates must be determined by negotiation between labor and management, not by the government. The government has to create a favorable environment for achieving this end. The most important policy is to maintain price stability so laborers will not be pressed to demand higher wages. A "growth promotion policy" in Korea today will exacerbate the price-wage spiral; it should be replaced by a set of policies designed to foster long-run growth.

The rise in wage rates in Korea is closely tied to problems in the industrial structure, characterized by big conglomerates on the one hand and very weak small and medium enterprises on the other. The former tends to be more responsive to labor's demands for higher wages, and by doing so, pulls up the general wage level. This imbalance will continue to be the source of wage increases. Government policy should therefore prevent owners of the conglomerates from raising their wage rates.

The government should support education programs for the workers to persuade them that increases in nominal wages would be accompanied by a price rise, which would defeat the very purpose of the increase. Fortunately, Korean workers have already shown they understand this logic, and government efforts along this line could reinforce the point.

Labor Relations

During the last two decades, the government tended to regard the labor movement as a threat and a danger. Collective action was regarded as a threat to national security to be suppressed without the benefit of dialogue. Labor laws explicitly enumerated rights with regard to association, collective action, and collective bargaining, but these rights existed on paper rather than in reality. This was a constant source of frustration for workers and led them ultimately to abandon rules and moderation in their actions. To foster the law-abiding spirit among the workers and the business community, labor laws should be made as realistic as possible and strictly and impartially enforced.

During the authoritarian days, primarily the authoritarian hard-line policy preserved industrial peace. Beneath the tranquil surface, however, the sources of strife lurked. In a democratic age, the government need not regard labor disputes as a potential threat to national security; in fact they are means to settle conflicts of interest that are bound to arise in an industrial society. The government policy should help establish channels of dialogue between labor and management.

Human Resources Development

Labor policy in the future should be conceived as part of a long-run development policy. This long-run development will rest upon human resources and upon the institutions in which economic activities take place.

During the 1960s and 1970s, the government was too preoccupied with short-run economic performance to be mindful of the long-run importance of developing human resources. Education, science, health, and the like suffered from benign neglect, for which the country is now paying the price in terms of weaker long-term growth potential. Korean education has expanded enormously in terms of numbers educated, but one may doubt whether it has stimulated creativity and instilled morality and civil discipline in the minds of the students. The system and content of education need to be reevaluated, and necessary reforms should be introduced.

There is general agreement among Koreans today that the scientific and technological level of the country should be elevated and that the government should take initiatives achieve this end. Everybody agrees on the need; the problem is how to go about it. The most popular diagnosis seems to be that research and development spending should be increased—to as much as 5 percent of GNP by the end of the century. Basic science and high-technology development in particular should be supported through greater fiscal spending.

Many are urging the government to launch a massive spending program for developing a score of high-technology areas selected by the government. Admitting that the government—and, indeed, the general public—should make greater efforts, there seem to be pitfalls in the popular approach, which should be critically examined. One pitfall is the notion that money can buy science and technology. If money alone were sufficient, why should any country lag behind? Money, of course, is a factor—a very important one—but there are many other factors even more basic: institutions, organizations, the quality of and incentives for researchers, and so forth.

What the country needs is a spurt of innovations—in the Schumpeterian sense—in all industries and firms, and not in just the so-called high-tech areas. There is much room for innovation in low- or medium-technology areas, which are extremely important in the Korean economic context. Economic development depends importantly upon these low-profile innovations. Indeed, they are the determinants of long-run high-tech development. The responsibility for innovation in all industrial areas rests on industrial and social institutions. Except for some rare instances, it should not be the responsibility of the government to aid a particular industrial technology, be it in a high-tech or not-so-high-tech area. The government ought to remember the outcome of the heavy and chemical industrialization program in the late 1970s and avoid similar direct involvement in technological development efforts.

Industrial Culture

Industrial culture in Korea is still immature and premodern. Corporations, the size of which are large enough to sway the entire economy, are still closely held by the owners (and their successors)—a feature not found in developed countries. In addition, the workers have not yet cultivated the kind of ethos an industrial country needs. During rapid growth, hundreds of thousands of workers flocked *en masse* from rural areas to new industrial complexes, where they became alienated from the sedate village environment and had to adapt to an inhospitable environment in which they were atoms in a crowd. A mass society has thus developed with unprecedented speed and scale, creating a fertile ground for labor agitation and disputes. It is very remarkable that Korean workers have been able to adjust as well as they have.

The growth-first policy has nurtured a notion that economic performance is more important than the institutions through which it is achieved. This inverted sense of values, derived from the extreme emphasis on achieving given targets, may have had a positive effect on past growth by maximizing the labor supply in the short run. However, this policy failed to establish institutions that are the bases of long-term growth— civil discipline, respect for enterprises, respect for laws and regulations, fair opportunities, and the like.

6

Financial System

In the late 1970s, when the Korean government actively promoted heavy and chemical industries, certain academics and businessmen argued that the Korean financial sector was lagging behind the fast-developing real sector. The implication was that an adequate development of the financial sector, matching that of the real sector, was needed for continued economic development. This contention remains a current topic of policy discussions.

What does development of the financial sector entail? There are many criteria by which this can be evaluated. Financial business is defined essentially as the process by which financiers mobilize savings from surplus units and transfer them to deficit units. According to this definition, development of the financial industry can be gauged by how efficiently financiers mobilize savings and allocate them for investment. In a capitalist economy, financial development usually surpasses development of the real sector so that accumulation of financial assets tends to exceed the increase of real output. Financial economists commonly use the financial interrelation ratio—defined as the ratio of total financial assets in an economy to its GNP—to measure financial industry development. The larger this ratio, the more developed an economy's financial industry is considered to be.

Another criterion is the degree of financial market integration. For instance, if organized and unorganized financial markets are not integrated, or if within the organized financial system, access to loans and interest rates are quite different depending upon the types and uses of the funds, the financial market is likely not well-integrated. Segmentation of the financial market can serve as evidence of inefficient allocation of financial resources and poor financial sector development. Whatever criterion is used, the Korean financial sector appears to be lagging behind the real sector. The financial interrelation ratio is low compared with that of countries at a similar development stage, to say nothing of advanced countries. As may be seen in table 6.1, the ratios of money supply (M2) to GNP in Korea and in Taiwan in 1992 were 41.9 percent and 167.0 percent, respectively. In Korea, individuals have far less access to the banking system than do those in advanced countries, and the variety of the financial instruments available to them is limited. In addition, the Korean financial system exhibits dualism, as evidenced by the lack of integration of the organized and unorganized financial markets. The structure of interest rates is also complex, reflecting severe segmentation within the organized financial sector. All these phenomena attest to the validity of the contention that the financial sector is still very much underdeveloped, and unless this sector is made to keep abreast of the real sector, it will seriously impede the growth of the economy.

The view that the relatively underdeveloped financial sector in Korea has impeded the growth of the real sector might be considered valid if the development processes of the financial and real sectors were truly independent of each other. But these processes cannot be "dichotomized," since they have developed as an integrated whole under the same development policy. The financial sector serves the real sector, as is evidenced by the history of Korean financial institutions and financial reforms since the 1960s.

Whenever the government set up an economic development plan, it usually created new financial institutions and implemented new practices to facilitate the financing of development plan goals. As will be explained in detail later, several specialized banks were established during the early 1960s to implement the first five-year economic development plan. When the second five-year economic development plan began in 1967, regional banks were established, and foreign banks were allowed to open branches in Korea. In 1972, when the third five-year economic development plan was launched, the Presidential Decree for Economic Stabilization and Growth was enforced. During this period, a National Investment Fund was created and new nonbank financial institutions were established: investment and finance companies, merchant banking corporations, mutual savings and finance companies, and the credit unions. In the early 1980s, when the fifth five-year plan was initiated, ownership of commercial banks was transferred to private hands. In addition, foreign joint banks and more nonbank financial institutions were established.

Thus, the financial sector has never developed independently of the real sector; the former developed concomitantly with, and was subordi-

Table 6.1 Korea, Taiwan, Japan: money supply (M2) as a proportion of GNP, 1965-92 (percentages)

Country	1965	1970	1975	1980	1985	1990	1992
Korea	12.1	32.2	31.1	34.1	39.2	40.1	41.9
Taiwan	33.3	40.9	55.9	64.0	104.7	144.0	167.0
Japan	75.4	72.2	82.3	85.2	96.8	116.0	109.5

Sources: Bank of Korea, *Monthly Bulletin*; Central Bank of China, *Financial Statistics Monthly*, Taiwan District; Bank of Japan, *Economic Statistics Annual.*

nate to, the latter. The financial sector has been a tool for carrying out the targets of industrial policy. Therefore, financial development in Korea during the 1960s and 1970s cannot be discussed without reference to the development of the real sector. Just as labor-related problems should be dealt with in the context of development policy, so should the issues concerning financial development be treated in relation to industrial policy.

Industrial Policy and the Banking System

Policy Reforms on Banks and Interest Rates in the 1960s

The Bank of Korea Act and the General Banking Act were enacted just before the outbreak of the Korean War in June 1950. The Bank of Korea Act stipulated that the central bank be independent of the government and that it have the authority to carry out its financial policy. The General Banking Act formalized existing financial institutions in order to carry out commercial banking.

In the 1950s, however, neither the central bank nor the commercial banks fully performed their proper roles. At that time, the Bank of Korea's policies were not based on the notion that financial policy should be carried out through the adjustment of the money supply or of interest rates. Moreover, since commercial banks had been owned by the government until government-owned stocks were sold in the late 1950s, they exercised very little autonomy.

Considering the severe inflation of the 1950s, the loan and deposit interest rates at commercial banks were low. Though there was an interest-rate ceiling of 20 percent within the organized financial institutions, this rate was in practice imposed only on overdue bank loans, and most bank loan rates remained at around 15 percent. Such low nominal interest rates implied enormously negative real interest rates, which became a source of subsidy to borrowers. Bank managers in the 1950s appear not to have recognized the function of interest rates in adjusting demand and supply of funds. Judging from the fact that bank interest rates were almost always fixed, even during the worst bouts of inflation, it appears that bank managers were unable to escape the conventional thinking, inherited from the Japanese colonial period, that interest rates should be kept as low as possible.

After the military coup of 1961, the new government perceived, quite accurately, that the country was in dire need of economic development and that economic development could legitimize the coup. We have already seen the process through which the government came to establish basic development strategies. It assumed responsibility for carrying out the development plan and began to invest in a series of projects in major industries. To carry out these investments, the government brought the banking system under tight control.

The military government lost no time in revising the Bank of Korea Act, subordinating the central bank to the Ministry of Finance, and thereby depriving the central bank of its autonomous decision-making power. In addition, a considerable portion of the equity capital in commercial banks was transferred to the government as a result of the government's confiscation of "illicit fortunes." At the same time, voting rights of any one private shareholder of a commercial bank were restricted to no more than 10 percent of total votes. Consequently, commercial banks were, in effect, confiscated by the government. The government controlled the appointment of major bank managers and determined the budget of the banks.

In addition, the government took two steps to strengthen financial support for its favored investment projects. One was the establishment of several specialized banks, each with its own designated financial purpose. The other was the adoption of a high interest-rate policy. These two moves will now be examined briefly.

Specialized Banks

The existing commercial banks and two specialized banks (the Korea Development Bank and the Korea Agriculture Bank, established in 1954 and 1956, respectively) were not adequately supplying the financial resources required to carry out the ambitious development policies of the 1960s. The government thus created several specialized banks: the Industrial Bank of Korea (1961), the National Agricultural Cooperative Federation (1961), and the Citizens National Bank (1962). Each of these was established under its own special law and was operated outside the control of the central bank. At the same time, in accordance with traditional theory, commercial banks were to be engaged in supplying relatively short-term working capital under the control of the central bank as well as of the government.[1]

---

1. A banking institution, however, was allowed to engage in investment banking and long-term financing business as well under the General Banking Act.

Table 6.2 Interest rates of banking institutions, 1961–92
(percentages)

	1961	1965	1970	1975	1980	1985	1990	1992
Time deposits	15.0	26.4	22.8	15.0	19.5	10.0	10.0	10.0
General loans	17.52	26.0	24.0	15.5	20.0	10.0–11.5	10.0–12.5	10.0–12.5
Increase rate of CPI	8.1	13.6	16.3	24.9	28.8	2.4	8.6	6.2

CPI = consumer price index.
Source: Bank of Korea, *Monthly Bulletin.*

The highlights of the second five-year plan period (1967–71) were augmented exports promotion and the accelerated growth of major industries. To support these policies, the Korea Exchange Bank and branches of foreign banks were established in 1967. In addition, the Korea Housing Bank was established to finance housing funds for low-income households, and regional banks were created successively in the various provinces. During this plan period, the government sought to promote exports and investment in heavy and chemical industries including machinery, electronics, automobiles, and shipbuilding. These industries were singled out as preferred sectors and were therefore allowed easy access to financial resources with favorable loan conditions and interest rates from both commercial and specialized banks. For example, loans made to preferred sectors were eligible for rediscount by the Bank of Korea.

High Interest Rates

Until the financial reform in 1965, interest rates had been maintained at a low level, as explained earlier. In the early 1960s, however, the Korean government realized that development policy would not be effective unless the distorted price mechanism was corrected. It accordingly devalued the Korean won in 1964 and increased the interest rate ceiling in 1965. As is indicated in table 6.2, the bank deposit rate on time deposits with a maturity of one year rose from 15 percent to 26.4 percent (30.0 percent on time deposits for more than 18 months), and the bank loan rate was raised from 17.52 percent to 26.0 percent.

The negative interest-rate margin, in which bank deposit rates are higher than bank loan rates, was adopted to increase bank deposits by inducing the inflow of private funds from the curb market. These savings were then to be channeled to investment projects targeted by the government. Some observers hold that the sharp rise in interest rates in 1965 can be regarded as a financial liberalization measure (e.g., McKinnon 1983). This view is, however, only partially correct. The rise in interest

Table 6.3 Korea, Taiwan, Japan: savings deposits as a ratio to GNP, 1961–92 (percentages)

Country	1961	1965	1970	1975	1980	1985	1990	1992
Korea	1.8	3.8	20.7	19.2	23.3	25.9	30.6	30.8
Taiwan	12.9	18.9	26.8	36.8	43.5	86.3	116.8	141.4
Japan	28.7	32.0	30.7	33.4	37.3	43.7	68.6	61.5

Sources: Bank of Korea, *Monthly Bulletin*; Central Bank of China, *Financial Statistics Monthly*, Taiwan District; Bank of Japan, *Economic Statistics Annual*.

rates promoted financial liberalization in the sense that official interest rates moved closer toward market rates. On the other hand, it moved against financial liberalization in the sense that the government strengthened control over the banking system and its allocation of funds. Whatever the effect, the purpose of the high interest-rate policy was not to promote autonomous operation of banks but rather to attract private funds circulating in the curb loan market to the banking system and to allocate them for the uses designated by the government (Chung 1987).

Savings deposits increased approximately seven times, and bank loans increased by almost as much, until the government returned to a low interest-rate policy in 1972. Before the financial reform of 1965, the proportion of time and savings deposits to GNP, as is shown in table 6.3, was only about 2 to 3 percent, a result of the prevailing negative real interest rate. In the early 1970s, this proportion exceeded 20 percent, largely due to positive real interest rates. The enormous growth of financial savings suggests that a great portion of the private funds in the curb market were absorbed into the organized financial market.

At this point, a comparison between Korea and Taiwan on financial development and interest rate policy is in order. The Taiwanese government adopted a high interest-rate policy during its early economic development period in the 1950s. In Taiwan, real interest rates have almost always been maintained at a positive level.[2] As a result, the ratios of time and savings deposits and money supply (M2) to GNP were much higher than those of Korea. The Taiwanese high interest-rate policy facilitated not only strong domestic financial institutions but also financial deepening. However, despite this policy, there still exists a fairly large curb loan market outside the organized financial market in Taiwan due mainly to the continuous interest-rate gap between the two markets as well as the concentration of funds flowing to large firms from organized financial institutions.

Korea's high interest-rate policy brought with it an unexpected side

---

2. Two exceptional cases are 1974 and 1980–81, which were highly inflationary periods caused by oil shocks.

effect: the inflow of foreign capital. The Korean government actively encouraged this inflow to finance development of heavy and chemical industries and infrastructure projects. Of course, domestic bank loans increased, too, to finance the rapidly growing investment demand in this period. Because of the interest rate gap, however, (with much lower interest rates—at about 10 percent—for foreign borrowings than those for domestic bank loans), firms preferred investment programs for which plenty of foreign capital was available, and they competitively imported foreign capital for investment. As explained in chapter 3, the rapid inflow of foreign capital created unsound firms from among those that borrowed excessively from abroad. Nevertheless, the high interest-rate policy in the end succeeded in increasing domestic savings deposits and, to a lesser extent, in supplying domestic funds for financing investment projects.

In addition to encouraging the inflow of foreign capital, the high interest-rate policy and the subsequent negative-margin system imposed considerable losses upon domestic banks, and gradually made it more difficult for them to operate. Perceiving the situation, the government reduced bank ·deposit rates and, to a lesser extent, bank loan rates several times beginning in the late 1960s until it finally returned to the low interest-rate system in 1972.

Despecialization of Banks and a Return to Low Interest Rates in the 1970s

Strengthening of Control on All Banks

With the growth of heavy and chemical industries in the early 1970s, investments became not only diverse in kind but also large in scale. To cope with this change, the government strengthened its control over the banking system, returned to a low interest-rate policy, established new nonbank financial institutions to absorb funds from the curb market, and at the same time, fostered the domestic capital market to strengthen direct financing. The first two measures will be examined in what follows, and the last two will be discussed separately later.

As explained earlier, government control over the banking system during the 1960s was characterized by the specialization of each bank. That is, in the 1960s, a sharp distinction was made between long- and short-term loans, and between commercial and specialized banks.

In the 1970s, the government began to strengthen its direct control over the banking system to direct the supply of bank loans to desired investment projects such as heavy and chemical industries. As direct control became more pervasive, the grounds for operating specialized banks were gradually undermined, and the line between commercial and specialized banks became blurred. Thus, the existing order within the financial system was disrupted, and the banking activities of the commercial banks became similar to those of specialized banks. Since the 1960s, for example, commercial banks began to deal in long-term loans in the guise of short-term loans with rollover; this practice became prevalent in the 1970s. Moreover, it became a general rule that specialized banks, with the exception of the Korea Development Bank, could accept deposits, which in consequence made their banking activities similar to those of commercial banks. Commercial and specialized banks converged, and both were held responsible for financing government-targeted investment projects.

The Return to Low Interest-Rate Policy and Its Effects

The high interest-rate policy, along with the consequent negative interest-rate margin system, began to weaken gradually in 1968 (table 6.2). As the second five-year plan got under way, the leverage ratio of many corporations became dangerously high due to excessive foreign capital imports and overborrowing. Moreover, with the heavy interest burden on these loans, the firms looked insecure. It became clear that many of these firms were unequal to the task of developing heavy and chemical industries since these capital-intensive industries required a long gestation period. Accordingly, with the birth of the *Yushin* (revitalization) regime in 1972, the high interest-rate policy gave way to a low interest-rate policy, which once again produced negative real interest rates. In short, the return to a low interest-rate policy in 1972 was intended to alleviate the heavy interest burden of faltering businesses and to expedite investments in heavy and chemical industries.

Low interest rates and the firm The promotion of heavy and chemical industries was based upon technical considerations rather than upon economic rationality, and the plan was based upon physical rather than economic terms. The government authority in charge of the program designated firms that were to invest in priority projects. In the belief that investments made with government support would be fail-safe, many firms, including those unacquainted with heavy and chemical industries, participated in these projects with enthusiasm. They were given a variety of investment incentives, one of which was low interest rates. Firms considered it a great privilege to secure low-interest bank loans because once one such a loan was obtained, it became easier to receive follow-on loans. As subsidies in the form of bank loans continued, an increasing number of firms began to subsist on low-interest bank loans; for them, government support became as important as the economic rationality of investment projects. As the size of government-supported projects became larger, so did the incentives for the firms to participate.

Industrial policy in the 1970s, which spawned the symbiotic relation-

Table 6.4 Interest rates on major policy loans as of the end of 1978

Types of policy loans	Interest rates
Exports	9.0
Export preparation of agricultural and marine production	9.0
Agricultural development	9.0
Fishery	9.0
Deep-sea fishing	9.0
Short-term agricultural production	10.0
Tourism promotion	11.5
Construction of fishing boats	11.5
Raw material imports	15.0
Machine industry promotion	15.0
Small and medium enterprises	15.0
Overseas construction	15.0
National Investment Funds	16.0
Defense industries	16.0
Equipment of export industry	16.0
General loans[a]	19.0

a. Loans on other bills with maturity of up to one year.

Source: Bank of Korea, *Monthly Bulletin.*

ship between government and business, encouraged firms to make large investments in targeted areas. The larger the investments, the easier it became to take advantage of low interest-rate loans and to transfer risk to the government. Gradually, investments of large firms spilled over to industries other than the targeted ones, as firms sought to diversify and secure profits. In addition, expansion of the firms was contingent upon the volume of exports because the amount of loans for which they could qualify depended upon it. Thus, the industrial targeting policy of the 1970s, together with the policy of maximizing exports, was bound to encourage expansion of large firms.

As indicated in table 6.4, the interest rates for "policy loans" varied significantly with the purposes of such loans. Policy loans were those bank loans made on favorable terms to investors in targeted industries or to achieve a particular goal of economic policy. Among the diverse categories of policy loans provided in the 1970s, emphasis was placed on those for the following purposes: export financing, the machinery industry, shipbuilding, tourism promotion, payment of delayed wages, buildup of an industrial complex, overseas construction, and the rationalization of industry.

The proportion of policy loans to total bank loans is not well-known. First of all, the "policy loan" concept is unclear; depending upon the use of the data, the magnitude of the proportion of policy loans to total loans can vary widely. In the late 1970s, it seems most bank loans could be classified as policy loans, in the sense that there was little room for autonomous lending. According to one fairly comprehensive study, the proportion of policy loans in total domestic credit was 47.5 percent in 1970; it increased to 53.1 percent in 1975, further to 59.1 percent in 1978, and dropped to 51.1 percent in 1980 (Yoo 1990, 42). According to one informal estimate (Chung 1982), however, this proportion was still as high as 66 percent in 1981. In addition, the proportion of new policy loans to new bank loans ranged from 60 to 80 percent throughout the early 1980s, even though the figure fluctuated substantially each year; in 1985 this proportion was 74.1 percent (Kim 1986). Although the above figures may not exactly indicate the proportion of policy loans, whose precise amount is unknown, as mentioned earlier, the proportion is undoubtedly large.

Policy loans and the banking system   Bank managers were deprived of autonomy in decision making on bank operations as well as on determination of interest rates. From the bankers' point of view, there was little incentive to review the economic rationality of proposed investment projects or to provide advice and other assistance to loan recipients. Banks had only to follow government direction in making loans, and thus they initiated little project screening, resulting in the loss of a powerful bulwark against unworthy investment. Ideally, banks should not be only passive financial intermediaries; they should be managed by "innovators," who give counsel and guidance to real investors on their investment plans. The function of bank appraisal of loan requests is important not only from the standpoint of the banks in securing a sound portfolio of assets, but also from the standpoint of the economy as a whole in screening out unworthy investments. With the banking system deprived of this function, the overall soundness of real investments in the economy, as well as banking operations, had to deteriorate. Unhealthy credits gave rise to unsound enterprises, which could only be sustained by more bank loans. Reliable data on unsound firms and the nonperforming assets of banks are not available. What is known is that there are firms that survive on extended bank lending and that the banks need relief financing from the central bank.

Upon returning to a low interest-rate policy in 1972, the rate of saving slowed. Throughout the 1970s, average real interest rates on bank loans and deposits fluctuated around zero percent (refer to appendix), and average real loan rates for policy loans (for example, export lending rates) were substantially negative. As a result, the growth of the financial sector began to stagnate, and their operations became abnormal. The curb market thrived again on a large scale, despite the Presidential Emergence Decree of 1972, which attempted to check its growth. As shown in table 6.1, the proportion of M2 to GNP, which increased sharply from 12.1 percent in 1965 to 32.2 percent in 1970, remained at around 33 percent throughout the 1970s. One should note that, in the case of Taiwan, the proportion of M2 to GNP reached 33.3 percent in 1965 and increased to 40.9 percent and 64.0 percent in 1970 and 1980, respectively. In 1992, the ratio of M2 to GNP in Taiwan reached 167.0 percent. This is a clear indication of financial deepening in Taiwan. One notes that a similar financial deepening has been taking place in Japan, where the ratio of M2 to GNP in 1992 was 109.5 percent, as shown in table 6.1.

The Presidential Decree of August 1972 and the National Investment Fund

Government control over finance was strengthened significantly by the Presidential Decree for Economic Stability and Growth on 3 August 1972 and by the foundation of the National Investment Fund in 1974. Some explanation of these measures has already been made in chapter 3. At this point, their significance will be examined from a financial standpoint.

Since the second half of the 1960s, Korean businesses had not only earned low profits but had chronically weak financial structures due to extensive importing of foreign capital, overborrowing from banks, and excessive use of curb market loans. The presidential decree proclaimed in August 1972 was largely intended to save the heavily leveraged firms. First, it decreed that all reported loan agreements made in the unorganized curb market should be converted to new ones at monthly rates of not more than 1.35 percent, which allowed the borrowers to repay their loans over a period longer than originally agreed. Second, some short-term bank loans were to be converted to long-term, low-interest loans. However, the decree implied tighter government control over the entire financial sector; in fact, it was evidence of the extent of the extralegal limitation imposed on private property rights.

Another such specimen was the National Investment Fund, which was established in 1974 "to mobilize and allocate funds for investment, aiming at boosting major industries such as heavy and chemical industries and promoting exports on the basis of nationwide savings and participation" (Article 14 of the National Investment Fund Act). Financial resources the fund was to use were secured by deposits at the fund made by all available sources of loan funds such as the Citizens Welfare Pension, the Post Office Annuity, and savings deposits at banks and other financial institutions. These funds were then distributed to the banking system, especially to specialized banks and the Korea Development Bank, to make loans for equipment investment in major strategic industries or for export promotion.

Financial Liberalization, 1980s and 1990s

In the early 1980s, the government sought to "liberalize" the economy and to encourage private initiatives in economic decision making. During 1981–82, nationwide commercial banks became "denationalized" as government ownership of those banks was transferred to private hands through the sale of equity shares. Although a fairly large proportion of bank stocks were once again in the possession of conglomerates, large shareholders' control over a bank was discouraged by limitation of the size of a single shareholder's stake to a maximum of 8 percent of the equity capital. However, even after the transfer of ownership, the banking system continued to be operated under government control. The appointments of banks' executives and senior officers was conducted by the government as before. Accordingly, denationalization only meant privatization, in the sense of change of ownership, rather than liberalization of banking operations.

Along with denationalization, entry barriers for banks and nonbanks were lowered, and a number of new banks were established in response to this opportunity. Also, the presence of foreign banks in Korea has been greatly augmented, providing foreign banks with a level playing field by lifting restrictions on their operations while reducing privileges given to them but not to domestic banks.

Furthermore, it has become increasingly necessary to liberalize interest rates and reinforce the market mechanism, thereby improving the efficiency of the financial markets. And interest rate deregulation needs to be pursued to cope effectively with the global trend toward financial liberalization.

In earlier attempts at interest rate deregulation, from the early 1980s, financial institutions were allowed to deal in a variety of new financial instruments with higher interest rates than existing instruments. For example, investment and finance companies were allowed in 1981 to deal in commercial paper (CP) at market interest rates[3] and cash management accounts (CMAs) in 1985. As a result, the flow of funds was concentrated in the higher interest-bearing financial instruments of nonbank financial institutions, though certificates of deposit (CDs) were introduced, as they were for banks in 1984. This was one of the reasons for the deepening weakness of banking institutions.

In the latter half of the 1980s, favorable macroeconomic fundamentals in the form of price stability, a high rate of growth, and a current account surplus gave the Korean economy another chance to proceed further along the road toward financial liberalization.

A wide-ranging deregulation of interest rates of banks and nonbanks was attempted in December 1988. Most bank and nonbank lending rates and some long-term deposit rates were deregulated, except for interest rates on some policy loans and short-term deposits. In parallel with this, the issuing rates on marketable financial instruments such as CP, financial debentures, and corporate bonds were completely

---

3. Interest rates on commercial paper were regulated soon after its introduction.

deregulated. However, a few months after the deregulation, Korea's macroeconomic fundamentals showed some instability. In particular, the current account surplus was reduced considerably, prices started moving up, and market interest rates rose steeply. The result was that the government again intervened in the market, and bank lending rates and most rates in the primary securities markets were regulated again. In August 1991, the government again announced a gradual interest rate deregulation plan, details of which are shown in table 6.5. Under the plan, interest rates will be deregulated incrementally, taking account of movements in the real economy and the readiness of economic entities. All lending rates and deposit rates excluding those on demand deposits are scheduled to be deregulated by 1996. Lending rates are to be deregulated relatively faster than deposit rates, and among deposit rates, deregulation will progress from those on long-term and large-denomination deposits to those on short-term and small-amount deposits in order to prevent rapid shifts of funds among financial markets and to encourage long-term deposits. The first step of the four-stage interest rate deregulation plan went into effect November 1991. After the first-stage measures, whose scope was somewhat narrow, market interest rates moved downward, reflecting the downturn of the overall economy.

Though financial conditions for further deregulation were favorable, the second-stage deregulation, previously scheduled for 1992–93, was delayed. Moving in the opposite direction, the government lowered the rediscount rate of the Bank of Korea twice in 1993 to counter the slowdown of economic growth.

The government recently revised the timetable for interest rate deregulation in accordance with the "Five-Year Plan for a New Economy" announced in June 1993. Under the new plan, the second phase of interest rate deregulation is to be implemented by the end of 1993.

Nonbank Financial Institutions and the Securities Market

During the 1970s, a dilemma developed in the Korean financial sector. While the government felt a strong necessity to control the banking system in order to execute industrial policy, the ability of banks to mobilize funds supporting those policies became progressively weakened as the banks were brought under tighter government control, in particular with respect to their interest rates. To cope with this dilemma, the government tried to supplement the traditional banking system by establishing and developing nonbank financial institutions and by fostering the capital market (securities market) to expand direct financing.

Table 6.5 Interest rate deregulation plans

Previous plan (August 1991)	Revised plan (June 1993)

Phase I: November 1991
  Loans
    Bank overdraft loans
    Real commercial bill discounts
      excluding those rediscounted by
      Bank of Korea;
    Investment and finance companies'
      commercial paper and trade bill
      discounts
  Deposits
    Certificates of deposit
    Investment and finance companies'
      sale of large-denomination
      commercial paper and trade bills,
      banks' sale of large-denomination
      commercial bills
    Large RPs
    Some long-term deposits
  Bonds
    Corporate bonds with maturities
      of over two years
	Implemented

Phase II: 1992–93
  Loans
    All loans of banks and NBFIs
      excluding loans financed by
      government and BOK rediscounts
  Deposits
    Long-term deposits with maturities
      of over two years
      Time and installment savings
      of banks, etc.
  Bonds
    Corporate bonds with maturities
      of less than two years
 	
    Bank debentures with maturities
      of over two years
	Phase I: by the end of 1993
	  Loans
	    All loans of banks and NBFIs
	      excluding loans financed by
	      government and BOK rediscounts
	  Deposits
	    Long-term deposits with maturities
	      of over two years
	
	  Bonds
	    Corporate bonds with maturities
	      of less than two years and bank
	      debentures
	    Monetary Stabilization Bonds and
	      all government and public bonds

Phase III: 1994–96
  Loans
    Loans financed by government
      and BOK rediscounts
  Deposits
    Short-term deposits with maturities
      of less than two years, excluding
      demand deposits
    Introduction of financial products
      linked to market rates, such as
      MMCs, at banks
  Bonds
    Bank debentures with maturities
      of less than two years
    Monetary Stabilization Bonds with
      maturities of less than two years
	Phase II: 1994–95
	  Loans
	    Loans financed by BOK rediscount
	      such as discount bills
	  Deposits
	    Further deregulation of short-term
	      marketable products
	      Phasing out of regulation on
	      issues and maturities
	
	  Bonds
	    Brought forward to Phase I

Table 6.5 Interest rate deregulation plans (continued)

Previous plan (August 1991)	Revised plan (June 1993)
	Phase II: 1996
	Loans
	Loans from banking funds on which the interest rate gap is made up by government funds (special equipment loans)
	Deposits
	Deposits excluding demand deposits
	Introduction of financial products linked to market rates such as MMCs, MMFs
Phase IV: 1997–	Phase III: during 1997
Deposits	Deposits
Remaining short-term deposits and demand deposits	Set up gradual deregulation plan of demand deposits
	Review abolition of restrictions on short-term marketable instruments
Bonds	Bonds
All government and public bonds	Brought forward to Phase I

NBFI = nonbank financial intermediaries; BOK = Bank of Korea; MMC = money market certificates; MMF = money market funds.

Nonbank Financial Institutions

By the time the August 1972 decree was proclaimed, the government had decided to encourage the growth of nonbank financial institutions, mainly to induce funds from the unorganized money market into organized financial institutions. In August 1972, the following new nonbank financial institutions were created, each under its special acts: the mutual savings and finance companies, investment and finance companies, and the credit unions. These nonbank financial institutions were expected to play a particularly important role in supplying short-term working capital to businesses.[4] In particular, the investment and finance companies specialized in raising funds by issuing their own bills or selling intermediate bills (including both secured and unsecured bills and commercial paper[5]) issued by those firms that met the qualifications set by the government.

---

4. While the mutual savings and finance companies and the credit unions specialized in financial services to households and small businesses, the investment and finance companies' principal operations consisted mainly of short-term financing for relatively large firms.

5. There was, in practice, little difference between CP and unsecured bills except their interest rates.

The short-term financing companies[6] were allowed to pay higher interest on their bills than the banks to help increase the supply of loan funds at these companies. This expectation was borne out by the bullish market of such bills and of commercial paper, which attracted a great volume of loan funds at the short-term financing companies. The demand for short-term loans was also heavy because the banks had been unable to meet the demand for operating funds. Short-term financing companies were able to make handsome profits.

In addition, the management of these companies was relatively free from government intervention compared with the banking institutions, which contributed significantly to their more rapid growth. For example, the value of corporate bills intermediated and discounted by the investment and finance companies equaled only 4.9 billion won at the end of 1972, but it showed a substantial increase every year, reaching 1.9 trillion won in 1980. In the early 1980s, 12 new investment and finance companies and 38 mutual savings and finance companies were established as entry barriers were lowered during financial liberalization.

Moreover, new financial instruments offering rates close to market rates, such as CMAs and CP, were introduced for short-term financing companies, whose businesses rapidly expanded with this impetus until the latter half of the 1980s.

However, the expansion of short-term financing companies has been cut short by the restructuring of the financial industry in 1991, which included conversion of eight investment and finance companies into banks and securities companies and the reorganization of the remaining businesses into intermediaries in the money market. The ratio of outstanding value of corporate bills intermediated and discounted by the investment and finance companies to the total assets of nationwide commercial banks therefore decreased from 34.7 percent in 1989 to 21.0 percent in 1992.

A detailed explanation of short-term financing and its history is beyond the scope of this chapter, but let us look at the most important characteristics of the operation of short-term financing companies during this period.

First of all, these companies were created to supplement banks in financing the investment and operations of corporations. For example, they were expected to attract funds more easily than the banks, not only by accepting and dealing in bills issued by qualified corporations, but by issuing their own bills with higher interest rates than those of banks. Although appropriate protection measures were not provided for investors who purchased commercial paper issued by the corporations and

---

6. Short-term financing companies include the investment and finance companies and the merchant banking corporations.

individual investors lacked information on the issuing companies, large volumes of unsecured bills continued to be issued and sold. This reflects the ingrained popular misunderstanding that the financial institutions, including the short-term financing companies, operate under the protection of the government, which will come to their rescue when needed. Despite the inadequate efforts of the government to protect investors, the companies did achieve great success.

Second, the functions of short-term financing companies in Korea have been substantially different from similar institutions in advanced countries. In advanced countries, these companies are usually dealers of commercial paper in large quantities and serve as intermediaries between institutional investors and the demanders of short-term money; they do not sell their own bills and do not deal with individual savings. In contrast with this, short-term financing companies in Korea have functioned much like banks; they attract funds out of people's small savings and lend funds to individual companies. This peculiar feature of the short-term financing companies in Korea originates from the government's intention; the primary purpose of these companies was to supplement the shortcomings of the banks—that is, they were supposed to attract funds circulating in the curb market by offering interest rates higher than banks and lending to those who would otherwise have borrowed from the curb market. As such, the short-term financing companies had a strong resemblance to intermediaries in the curb market.

Third, while the short-term financing companies have received favors through government policies designed to foster them, they also have been relatively free from government control and interference. However, they were not allowed complete freedom in setting the rates of interest that they offered on their bills. This limitation was presumably thought to be necessary because, if they were given complete freedom with respect to interest rates, individuals' savings would have shifted to these companies and away from deposit banks, which would have depleted the banks' supply of loanable funds. That is to say, the tight control imposed on deposit banks made it imperative to limit the freedom of operation of other financial institutions. The tradition of conservatism on the part of the financial authority usually tends toward opting for regulation and control rather than liberalization.

Table 6.6 summarizes the changes in market shares of banking institutions in Korea and Taiwan from 1970 to 1992 to show the effects of the expansion of nonbank financial institutions.

In the case of Korea, banking institutions accounted for 81.6 percent and 78.2 percent of the deposit market and loan market, respectively, in 1970. But the figures decreased gradually to 36.2 percent and 44.5 percent, respectively, by 1992. In the 1980s, the steep decline in the market share of banking institutions accelerated, especially in deposit taking, owing to the interest gap between the two competitors. It is noteworthy

Table 6.6 Korea, Taiwan: banking institutions' and NBFIs' shares of deposit and loan markets, 1970–92 (percentages)

	Korea				Taiwan			
	Banks		Others		Banks		Others	
Year	Deposits	Loans	Deposits	Loans	Deposits	Loans	Deposits	Loans
1970	81.6	78.2	18.4	21.8	86.8	97.5	13.2	2.5
1971	80.9	78.5	19.1	21.5	85.5	96.8	14.5	3.2
1972	81.7	77.4	18.3	22.6	83.6	95.1	16.4	4.9
1973	78.6	73.9	21.4	26.1	80.7	92.1	19.3	7.9
1974	77.3	75.5	22.7	24.5	80.5	93.5	19.5	6.5
1975	78.5	74.6	21.5	25.4	80.4	94.5	19.6	5.5
1976	76.1	74.4	23.9	25.6	79.8	94.7	20.2	5.3
1977	75.3	68.9	24.7	31.1	81.0	94.2	19.0	5.8
1978	74.5	67.8	25.5	32.2	76.5	92.9	23.5	7.1
1979	72.2	66.5	27.8	33.5	76.4	93.9	23.6	6.1
1980	69.1	63.8	30.9	36.2	76.1	94.5	23.9	5.5
1981	67.2	63.0	32.8	37.0	74.5	94.6	25.5	5.4
1982	64.3	62.2	35.7	37.8	73.0	94.7	27.0	5.3
1983	59.1	61.0	40.9	39.0	72.3	94.9	27.7	5.1
1984	56.3	57.9	43.7	42.1	71.1	94.8	28.9	5.2
1985	52.7	58.2	47.3	41.8	71.5	94.9	28.5	5.1
1986	49.4	56.3	50.6	43.7	70.4	95.5	29.6	4.5
1987	46.2	53.5	53.8	46.5	70.8	95.0	29.2	5.0
1988	44.3	51.5	55.7	48.5	73.1	95.1	26.9	4.9
1989	40.9	52.7	59.1	47.3	75.1	94.7	24.9	5.3
1990	40.5	49.7	59.5	50.3	73.2	93.2	26.8	6.8
1991	39.3	48.3	60.7	51.7	72.4	92.9	27.6	7.1
1992	36.2	44.5	63.8	55.5	73.7	94.4	26.3	5.6

NBFI = nonbank financial institution.

Sources: Bank of Korea, *Monthly Bulletin*; Central Bank of China, *Financial Statistics Monthly.*

that, in a country where the only financial institutions with which people are familiar are deposit banks, their importance as financial intermediaries should have fallen so dramatically.

The Korean experience is in clear contrast to the Japanese and the Taiwanese experiences. In those countries, the banking sector played a crucial role in supporting the stable growth of the real sector during development. In Japan (Suzuki 1985, 29–31), the share of bank loans in the total amount of loans made ranged from 60 to 70 percent during 1956–73, or from 75 to 90 percent, if loans made by the government-supported post office deposits are included. And in Taiwan, the share of bank loans remained above 90 percent during 1970–92, while the share of other financial institutions has been less than 10 percent. The situation is not much different in the case of deposits. In 1992, the share of deposit banks recorded 73.7 percent and that of other financial institutions was 26.3 percent, compared with 86.8 percent and 13.2 percent, respectively, in

1970. The curb market still remains larger in Taiwan than in Korea, reflecting some differences between the two economies, and this points up the limited role of nonbank financial institutions in Taiwan.

Securities Market

Recognizing the limitations of commercial banks regarding finance for the ambitious heavy and chemical industries in the early 1970s, the government tried, in addition to creation of short-term financing companies and other nonbanking financial institutions, to foster the capital market, from which firms could raise investment funds. A law was enacted in 1972 to induce firms that received bank loans over a specific amount to go public and issue stocks. Various stimuli such as tax incentives were provided.

From 1975 to 1978, the stock market experienced a great boom, led by the bullish buying of stocks of construction companies, as many of them enjoyed a major construction boom in the Middle East and a large amount of liquidity was supplied through the foreign sector. Beginning in 1979, however, the stock market fell into a long depression. The number of shareholders fell from 963,000 in 1978 to 772,000 in December 1985. In addition, during the same period, the number of firms listed on the Korean Stock Exchange fell from 356 to 342.[7] The value of funds raised through stock issues also decreased from 326.7 billion won to 294.6 billion won.

Encouraged by government support and the improved environment for securities investment resulting from strong growth and a current account surplus, the stock markets began to flourish again in 1986. The stock price index broke the 300 barrier (4 January 1980 = 100) that year and reached a record high of 1007.77 in 1989. The number of companies listed on the stock market increased from 342 at the end of 1985 to 626 at the end of 1989, and during the same period, total funds raised through the issue of stocks in one year leapt almost 50-fold from 294 billion won in 1985 to 14,669 billion won in 1989. In order to stimulate the development of the stock market, the government allowed the firms to sell new stocks at market value and privatized some large public enterprises. Owing to the ample liquidity due to the current account surplus and increased personal incomes, many individual investors participated in the stock market. In addition, price stability and the government's strict clampdown on speculation in real estate accelerated the hike of stock prices, which brought about a kind of "bubble" situation in which stock prices rose above their intrinsic value. However, as economic growth sharply declined and the current account deteriorated considerably, the

---

7. As of December 1985, there were 127 listed firms in Taiwan.

Korean stock market showed a long-lasting sluggishness thereafter; total market capitalization tumbled from 95.5 trillion won in December 1989 to 84.7 trillion won in December 1992 despite an increase in the number of listed companies from 626 to 688. The stock price index closed at 678 at the end of December 1992. As a result of the slump, many small individual investors experienced serious losses, and the government intervened in the market to stabilize stock prices. The government tried to support the stock market by loosening regulations on margin trading and inducing banks to supply credit for securities investment trust companies to buy stocks. But government intervention achieved at best only limited success in stabilizing stock prices and landed the securities investment trust companies in financial difficulties.

The size of the Korean stock market in terms of the total value of listed stocks is still small compared with other countries. At the end of 1992, the total market capitalization of listed stocks in Korea was only 4.6 percent of that of the Tokyo Stock Exchange, which exceeded $2.3 trillion.[8]

There are several reasons why the Korean stock market has been relatively small. First, Korean firms have preferred financing their operations through issuing debt rather than through equity instruments. They have been not only hesitant to share ownership with others but also afraid of disclosing their firms' financial conditions and other matters. In addition, the cost of debt has been quite cheap, especially in the 1970s and early 1980s. Korean tax laws also encourage debt over equity financing. While payment of interest on debt is exempt from taxation, dividends on shares are not. Moreover, once a firm offers stocks for public subscription, it feels compelled to pay a high dividend even if the profit rate was very low in order to "save face." In addition, government authorities frequently interfered in setting the dividend rate in order to attract more investors into the stock market.

Second, complying with the government policy of fostering heavy and chemical industries, large conglomerates invested extensively in government-supported investment projects. They found it more favorable to borrow from the banking system than to raise funds in the stock market because borrowing from banks enabled those firms to share risk with the government. The more they borrowed, the greater the degree of risk sharing became. Under normal circumstances, debt financing would be more risky for the entrepreneurs than equity financing, but the situation is reversed when the government is committed to the investment.

There are also disincentives from the stock investors' point of view. First, the purchase of stocks involves risk. This is also true in other countries, but in Korea the risk is more substantial. Above all, as stated ear-

---

8. The extent of going public by large firms in Korea is smaller than in Taiwan (Rowley 1987, 63).

lier, the supply of floating stocks is relatively small and is greatly influenced by "big customers" so that stock prices have been quite volatile. It is generally held that the extent of manipulation of stock prices by big customers is very large, so that small participants risk great losses.

Another factor contributing to the view that the stock market is dangerous for small participants is the presence of insider trading. Although insider trading is forbidden by law, it is doubtful if the law is well-observed (Rowley 1987, 74). Very few of such violations have been uncovered; in fact, few Koreans regard it as illegal.

Despite all of these difficulties and disincentives, the Korean capital market has been making significant progress in recent years, thanks to the effort of the government to promote it. But here again, it was the basic thrust of industrial policy during the 1970s that ran counter to development of the stock market, and the impediments mentioned above still persist.

The Korean bond market has been more agile than the stock market. From the second half of the 1970s to the first half of the 1980s, the issuance of corporate bonds increased sharply, and the balance amounted to nearly 35 trillion won as of December 1992, which is about 1.6 times the amount of corporate bills intermediated and discounted by investment and finance companies. This implies that the bond market has become an increasingly important source of long-term financing in Korea.

In Korea, however, the open market for bonds has been underdeveloped. First, as the bond yields in the primary markets have been regulated to levels far below those in the secondary markets, individual investors avoid absorbing newly issued bonds; bonds are mainly held by investment trust companies, trust accounts of banks, life insurance companies, and domestic branches of foreign banks. Second, most corporate bonds are issued under the guarantee of financial institutions; therefore the issue rates are uniform and do not reflect issuers' credit. Third, as secondary markets in bonds are not well-organized, bond transactions are inactive. In addition, maturities of the bonds are for the most part only two or three years. So far, they have been issued mostly to finance working capital; merely 10 percent of the total is devoted to equipment financing. This indicates that the increasing issuance of bonds in Korea is a second-best alternative, despite the high cost of bond financing, due to the lack of borrowing from banks (Hattori 1987, 147).

As mentioned earlier, the government has since the early 1970s been adopting the policy of developing nonbank financial institutions and the securities market with a view to replenishing bank financing. Owing to this policy, both the nonbank financial institutions and the capital market have developed rapidly.

The policy of fostering the capital market is certainly a worthy one, and it is encouraging that the capital market has made good progress in a short period. Here again, one has to note that the capital market cannot be a substitute for commercial banks, as will be seen below. It is important for Korea to have a well-operating stock market, but it is more important to have sound commercial banks.

The Curb-Loan Market

The size of the organized financial sector in Korea has been quite small relative to the real sector. Thus, the formal financial sector alone has been insufficient for financing investment. Institutional domestic finance has been supplemented by foreign capital imports from abroad and by the supply of short-term funds from the unorganized money market—known as the curb-loan market in modern terminology, or the "private finance" market.

Although institutional or modern finance was introduced a century ago and almost three decades have passed since the onset of rapid economic growth, the institutional financial sector of Korea has not yet completely absorbed the unorganized curb-loan market. Even now, the market is sizable.

The root cause of the large curb-loan market has been inflation, coupled with the control on bank interest rates. Owing to the low level of interest rates for loans and deposits, the banks were unable to absorb individual savings, the bulk of which flowed in the informal curb-loan market. There was perennial excess demand for bank loans, which the curb-loan market partially satisfied. Businesses that had little access to bank loans due to government credit control had to rely on this market. In particular, small and medium enterprises, which had difficulty in obtaining loans from formal financial institutions, had no other choice.

To a certain extent, the curb loan market serves as a safety valve—a channel of financing for firms that cannot borrow from the formal financial sector. It corrects, if only partially, for the inefficiencies of the organized financial sector. However, as the scale of the curb market grew, the financial structure of firms, especially of smaller ones, deteriorated due to their high debt-service burdens. In addition, the market has been serving the rentier class, who live on "unearned" income by taking advantage of the weak financial position of individuals and firms and of opportunities for tax evasion.

There are no credible data concerning the size of the curb-loan market in Korea. According to estimates of financial businessmen, in the early 1980s it was close to 40 percent of the size of the overall financial system (Scitovsky 1986, 183). But in recent years, the curb market seems to have diminished. Many indications suggest that it is now less than 10 percent of the total financial market. The main cause for this favorable turn of events is, among other things, price stability and resulting high interest rates in real terms in the organized financial market.

Financial Policy in the Future

Finance in Korea is far from developed, by any criterion. In terms of the variety of finance, few channels have been developed except for business finance. Finance for consumers is practically nonexistent. What is more important, the mortgage market is poorly developed, so that home buyers are unable to get loans, and in most cases houses must be paid for outright. Workers and others who save enough to buy houses invariably are frustrated to find that, by the time of purchase, the real value of their savings has eroded relative to house prices because of inflation. The underdevelopment of the financial system in Korea is due, among other factors, to the ways in which the development strategy pursued during the 1960s and 1970s was conceived and implemented. The financial sector was to serve business; it cares little about private financial saving. All other forms of finance, such as housing finance and consumer financing, were inconceivable during the extensive-growth days. This notion still pervades Korea today; for ordinary citizens, banks are places to keep deposits and not places from which to borrow.

Has the financial sector, then, succeeded in financing business effectively? In a sense, the answer to this question is yes, because the real sector has in fact expanded. But, from a long-run point of view, the answer has to be no, because the financial sector itself has become relatively atrophied in the course of financing business and is a major impediment to Korea's future development.

The financial industry is inefficient not only in mobilizing savings from surplus units but also in allocating them to deficit units such as firms. Needless to say, this is one of the side effects of the condensed economic growth of the last 30 years. The pursuit of the condensed-growth strategy rested upon preferential policy loans, which deprived financial institutions of incentives and the ability to innovate. One fallout of government control was the retarded and distorted growth of all financial institutions. Particularly hard hit are the banking institutions, which were and still are the most important financial institutions in Korea.

Officials gradually recognized during the 1970s that the distorted growth of banking institutions would, if left uncorrected, seriously impede the growth of the real sector. Thus, the government has been led, for the last two decades, to sponsor studies on the restructuring of financial institutions. Most of the studies have been done under the sponsorship of the Ministry of Finance by financial experts, economists, businessmen, and representatives of research institutes. Many of those studies recommended decontrol of banking and nonbanking institutions as the essential ingredient of financial reform. But these recommendations ran counter to the basic direction of development policy, which rested on close government control of banking institutions.

The Ministry of Finance also sponsored the Committee for Development of the Financial System with the aim of undertaking reforms, if only partial ones, within the overall framework of government control. Acting upon recommendations of this committee and of other studies, the government created various nonbanking financial institutions and took measures to foster the capital market, as described above. The banking institutions were left under strict government control, but the newly created nonbanking financial institutions were given some measure of freedom in conducting their business. In particular, short-term financing companies were given relatively greater freedom than banking institutions. This precipitated the decline in importance of banking institutions in the overall financial framework of Korea.

The government undertook some reforms in the 1980s. These reforms included denationalization of commercial banks, lowering of entry barriers in the banking business, liberalization of the foreign banking sector, introduction of new financial instruments, some decontrol of interest rates, and liberalization of the capital market. These reform measures gave rise to a great spurt of nonbanking financial institutions. But the banks were hardly normalized because government control on banks was hardly relaxed, despite the privatization of bank ownership. All in all, reforms since the early 1980s are more apparent than real. Despite the actions and measures taken by the government and the banks, banking practices have not significantly changed. Though the financial sector as a whole has grown tremendously, the anomaly in the operations of the banks, nonbanking financial institutions, and the capital market continues.

Decades of financial repression rendered the Korean banks incapable of adequately meeting businesses' need for loans. Even the biggest commercial banks, such as the "Big Five" city banks, can supply only a small portion of loan capital needed for carrying out conglomerates' major investment projects. The financial sector and banks in particular are simply too small and underdeveloped to accommodate the real sector requirement.

Under such circumstances, business will have to turn to foreign sources to obtain the capital to finance their investments. For the individual business, foreign banks are as good as domestic banks. But from the point of view of the economy as a whole, this is a sorry state of affairs because the economy is losing important financial business to overseas competitors. This is the price that the country has to pay for the lack of development in the banking sector. It is at best an anomaly for a country whose rate of saving is as high as 36 percent of GNP that it cannot adequately finance its own investments.

Indeed, should the anomaly be left uncorrected, it would be next to impossible for the financial sector to satisfactorily finance business investment, to say nothing of financing other activities. Moreover, the same anomaly, for reasons that will be explained later, would prevent the monetary authority from conducting monetary policy effectively. Furthermore, it would impede the international liberalization of the financial sector. Because of these and other reasons, the financial authority of Korea should take bold steps toward restructuring financial institutions and practices, even though time is growing short.

The Direction of Financial Reform

As mentioned earlier, there have been scores of studies sponsored by the financial authorities, but these studies have not produced any definitive results, partly because the purpose of the studies had been so closely circumscribed from the beginning and because the analyses were done based on inadequate data. Whatever reform measures the government may take, they must be preceded by good analysis. The government should encourage open discussion on the direction of future policy and, as much as is practicable, make information on finance available to the public as well as to the study teams. Without consensus on this matter, no action is likely to be taken.

The basic direction of financial reform should aim at creating an integrated financial market and having true entrepreneurs take charge of the financial industry. At present, the financial market in Korea is very much compartmented—whatever happens to one part does not affect other parts. This is the consequence of the policy loans and government control. The market is managed by administrators on administrative expediencies and not by financial entrepreneurs on financial principles. The basic problem is how to tear down the walls of the compartmented market and find good entrepreneurs.[9]

Banks

The root of the troubles besetting the Korean banks lies in the fact that they have not been operating on financial principles but on nonfinancial, administrative expedience. There has not been any entrepreneurship in the financial sector. Korean financial institutions have not been good resource allocators, as they were not allowed to play an active role in loan-making decisions. They have been poor saving mobilizers because most of the deposit rates have been held artificially low. Many bad loan decisions were made, especially in the 1970s, so that a number of so-called nonperforming assets were created. The poor investment deci-

---

9. A simple "liberalization" may create havoc, at least in the short run; it is related to the real sector of the economy, as will be seen later. Furthermore, the government wants to erect some safeguard against conglomerate domination of banks, a possibility if regulations on bank operations are lifted without any precautions being taken.

sions hurt the real sector of the economy, as described in relevant chapters in this book. The financial sector, of course, is not immune from the negative effects caused by the lack of autonomy in loan making; the accumulation of bad loans left some banks in a difficult situation. The banks, however, have had effective insurance against such contingencies: a practically unlimited guarantee—or so both the banks and the public believe—from the monetary authority.

Large borrowers have been unable or unwilling to repay the loans, but the banks do not dare declare them bad loans for fear of repercussions on the overall economy. The borrowers have tended to borrow more to finance "repayment" of earlier loans. The larger they are, the easier it is for them to borrow more.

Many suggestions have been made on how to normalize banking operations, especially regarding how to cope with assets that perform less than perfectly: the Bank of Korea should provide special loans to problem-ridden banks; loans should be swapped with borrowers' stocks; government debt should be issued to the general public to settle loan problems, with the understanding that bad loans originated from the economic development process from which almost all Koreans have benefited; and the banks should be granted autonomy in order to solve the bad loan problem.

The solution to the problem, whatever approach may be taken, is related to the government's management of the real sector of the economy, and therefore it goes beyond the realm of bank managers. Even if banks were allowed autonomy in making loans, it would be hard for them to exercise it in the case of policy loans—those made in the past as well as in the present.

Observers currently can witness the perennial excess demand for funds in the Korean banking sector. The money supply increases about 19 percent every year, and the nominal market rates of interest in 1991, both short and long, stayed in the vicinity of 19 percent; real interest rates are more or less "sticky" at a high 10 percent. In 1992, market interest rates declined from 19 percent at the beginning of the year to 14 percent by year's end. This fall was attributable largely to firms' sharply reduced demand for funds during the economic slowdown. Although the downward trend of nominal market rates has continued until recently, real rates are still high. With such high rates, few sound long-term investments are possible. Experience shows that even though the control on bank credits is relaxed and more credits are being made, interest rates do not fall significantly. Even at such high rates, there is a constant demand for more bank loans, from large enterprises as well as from the small and medium ones. This is in stark contrast to the case of Taiwan, where there is an excess supply of bank loans and consequently interest rates are very low. Korea's share of saving in GNP, as seen in chapter 2, is as high as that of Taiwan, and one would expect that business would have an easier time getting bank loans. Though good studies on the excess demand for bank loans are not available, the root cause of this phenomenon seems to be either or both of the following: first, the highly leveraged borrowers usually must renew borrowing, and second, there are many investments available for large borrowers who have easy access to bank loans, and the returns from these investments—in land, buildings, leisure facilities, as well as productive facilities—exceed the actual borrowing rates of 20 percent.

Unless and until borrowers use loans to finance for prescribed purposes and repay them within the prescribed time, normalization of banks will be impossible. Thus, the fundamental prerequisite for financial reform in Korea is a system that prevents the recurrent distress borrowing of unworthy firms. This would in turn require the government to establish a business environment in which delinquent borrowers pay appropriate penalties, including bankruptcy.

The anomaly in the Korean financial sector lies in the way in which the real sector has been managed. By virtue of the fact that the government and government-controlled banks shared risk with private investors, the banks have not been able to allow heavy borrowers to go bankrupt, even when the latter's performances clearly warranted it. This situation is rooted in the conventional belief that borrowers must be supported and that the purpose of the banks is to support business. But sound relations between banking institutions and borrowers should be based on the clear rule of financial operation—poor performers pay for their poor performance in the form of bankruptcy and are not rewarded by further access to loans. Korean banking institutions have not been playing by this rule and have abdicated exercise of their prerogative; those fortunate borrowers who were designated by the government for policy loans have been relieved of the discipline of the market. It is thus imperative for the Korean banking sector to regain its lost prerogative. But the banking sector, which is manned by people who are accustomed to the old way, is not likely to do so by itself. The government must help by abolishing or drastically reducing policy loans and by stemming the causes of chronic excess demand for loans through strengthened supervision of banks, allowing timely withdrawal of support from unworthy firms and introducing measures to reduce the attractiveness of investment in land, buildings, and leisure industries.

The perennial excess demand for loans has rendered monetary policy in Korea practically moribund. The Korean economy has been under constant inflationary pressure, but the monetary authority finds it very difficult to reduce the quantity of money, faced with the ceaseless outcry for increased lending. If a restrictive monetary policy is introduced, those who will feel the squeeze first are small and medium enterprises. On the other hand, it is very difficult to satisfy all requests for loans because this will intensify inflationary pressures. Furthermore, there is no guarantee that increased lending will be channeled toward productive uses and not for speculating in land and other properties. Monetary policy in Korea faces a dilemma; it can neither easily increase the money supply nor easily reduce it; it is caught in the middle, in a chasm of built-in inflation. In order to liberate the monetary authority from this dilemma, it is necessary to "normalize" the financial sector. Normalization of the financial sector requires determination of the government, which should be prepared to accept the short-term adjustment costs of imposing discipline on their borrowers.

Nonbanking Financial Institutions

As seen in the preceding sections, the nonbanking financial institutions have been growing much faster than banking institutions. This phenomenon is observable throughout the world; it is natural to observe the same tendency in Korea. What is unusual in Korea is the proliferation of investment and finance companies—at present, there are 24—created partly to substitute for banks. However, even though they complement the banks, they are a poor substitute for them because they perform, by their very nature, functions different from those of banks. Investment and finance companies were designed to absorb "underground" funds in the curb loan market so they could be channeled into investment. They absorb loan funds by issuing their own bonds and make short-term loans to businesses by discounting the firms' commercial paper at interest rates approaching those in the curb market. Attracted by higher rates, the savers purchased short-term securities issued by these companies, which attracted an enormous volume of funds from the curb market, as well as from banks. The investment and finance companies experienced incredible success, but partly at the expense of banks. The companies are limited to supplying only very short-term operating funds for those firms that meet qualifications set by the government; they cannot be expected to finance long-term capital investment. The retarded growth of the commercial banks cannot be corrected by adding nonbank financial institutions. Indeed, the proliferation of the nonbank financial institutions, to the extent that they have served as a substitute for commercial banks, has weakened rather than strengthened the structure of corporate finance; long-term investments are financed by rolling over short-term debts, and this has increased borrowers' risk and the cost of their investments.

It would seem, therefore, that when and if the banks were allowed to freely set interest rates, the sources of these companies' advantage would be modified. It seems, then, necessary to restructure these short-term finance companies, along with normalization of banks. One way to restructure is to allow some of the companies to become authentic banks and/or induce them to transform into real short-term financing companies worthy of their name—that is, real intermediaries for institutional borrowers and lenders.

As mentioned earlier, eight investment and finance companies were converted into banks or securities companies. The remaining companies are scheduled to reduce their deposit taking and lending business by June 1994. They are expected to act as short-term money market intermediaries for institutional borrowers and lenders and as dealing counterparts in open market operations with the central bank.

The Capital Market

The Korean stock market since the early 1970s has grown enormously with government encouragement. But, as observed earlier, the size of the stock market relative to the real sector of the economy is small compared with those of Japan or Taiwan. There has been a great increase in the number of participants in the market; however it has not yet fully developed into a sound and healthy one. There is much room for improvement.

First, the government has been encouraging the growth of the stock market, but at the same time it has on occasion been defeating its own purpose of promoting market development by exercising inconsistent control. For example, the government has occasionally manipulated stock prices to stabilize the market, but people's expectations in those cases reverberated back on the market, causing instability rather than stability.

Government policy has so far concentrated on increasing the supply of stocks; that is, the government has mainly been preoccupied with the issue market. The government, it would appear, has been concerned less with the demand side of the market—who purchases the stocks and based on what motives. This attitude reflects the traditional notion that the purpose of the financial market or institutions lies primarily in raising money for firms. As a consequence, the government has promulgated the merits of stock market participation by the public. With expectations swollen by bullish sentiment, the unsophisticated public has been led to participate in a market it does not understand well. Thus, the Korean market has come to be dominated by individual participants, and the proportion of institutional investors is comparatively very small, unlike the ratio in developed countries. This has made stock prices very volatile. It is necessary and strongly desirable that the government should help increase the participation of institutional investors and make more information available to individual participants with respect to the conditions and prospects of the listed companies.

Also, the government should strengthen its supervisory function, including prevention of insider trading and other irregular dealings, to protect the investors.

Internationalization of Domestic Finance and the Capital Market

In the early 1980s, the government announced that it was ready to proceed with internationalization of domestic finance, and it substantially accommodated pressures for market opening that major developed countries applied through the latter half of the 1980s. With the starting of the financial policy talks between Korea and the United States in 1990, the internationalization of the domestic financial market was further deepened.

The government tried to place foreign banks on an equal footing with domestic banks through the lifting of certain restrictions on their operations. Foreign bank branches were allowed to handle nonspecific money in trust in 1985, negotiable certificates of deposit in 1986, and specific money in trust in 1991. The government also permitted foreign bank branches to make use of the rediscount facilities of the Bank of Korea in 1986 and to borrow funds from the BOK as a means of financing a possible shortage in reserve requirements in 1988. Requirements for the establishment of multiple branches were abolished, and multiple branches were regarded as a single entity in 1991. In addition, foreign bank branches were allowed to join the Korea Federation of Banks and the Korea Financial Telecommunication and Clearing Institute as regular members in 1992.

As for the opening up of the life insurance market, foreign life insurance companies were first allowed access to the domestic market in 1987. At first, only branches were permitted, but subsequently the government allowed foreign life insurance companies to establish subsidiaries and joint ventures in 1989.

It is the Korean securities market in which foreigners show the greatest interest. Because the price/earnings ratio is still relatively low, foreigners are expecting a sharp rise in it. The great success of the Korea Fund, introduced in the New York Stock Exchange in 1984 as a prelude to internationalization, is due in part to this expectation. In 1981, the government announced that the Korean securities market would be globalized in four stages. In the first stage, international investment trusts were partially put into practice, and foreign and domestic security companies were allowed to do business with each other. For instance, the Korea Fund was listed at $100 million in the New York Stock Exchange. The second stage is to extend the opening of the domestic securities market through indirect methods, such as issuing convertible bonds (CBs) and increasing investment funds for foreigners in the foreign market, and allowing foreigners to do direct investment in the domestic securities market on a limited scale. The Korea Fund was increased to $150 million by 1989, and the $60 million Korea Europe Fund was introduced in the European market between 1987 and 1988. Domestic firms were permitted to issue CBs to foreigners in 1985, bonds with warrants (BWs) in 1987, and depositary receipts (DRs) in 1990. In a parallel with development, the government allowed foreign securities companies to own up to 10 percent of the paid-in capital of large domestic securities companies, subject to the provision that the total stake of foreign securities companies in a domestic securities company should not exceed 40 percent.

Three matching funds, which raise funds from domestic and foreign sources for investment in domestic and foreign securities, were established in 1990, with the size of each fund being $100 million. In November 1990, the Korean government announced guidelines for opening up the domestic securities market. The guidelines govern the terms and conditions under which foreign securities offices may conduct business in Korea's financial markets. Under these guidelines, foreign securities companies can establish either branch offices or joint ventures in Korea.

Foreign direct investment in Korean stocks was permitted in 1992, subject to certain limitations. Accordingly, substantial overseas capital flowed into the Korean stock market, especially after the fourth quarter of 1992. By the end of June 1993, net stock investment funds of $4.8 billion had flowed into the domestic stock market from abroad, and the share of foreign securities companies in the domestic stock market had increased gradually.

As for the remaining stages, the third stage is to allow foreigners unlimited access to domestic securities. Finally, the fourth stage is to completely liberalize capital transactions and to allow Korean citizens to invest in foreign securities. Steps for the third and fourth stages were incorporated into the revised medium-term capital-market opening plan in 1988.

At the request of the United States in the third round of financial policy talks between Korea and the United States, the government drew up a blueprint for financial liberalization and market opening (table 6.7). The first and second steps of the blueprint were announced at the end of March and June 1992, respectively. The third step of the plan was finalized as part of the "Five-Year Plan for a New Economy" in June 1993.

The Korean authority must cope with many problems in the course of implementing the liberalization policy. It has to clear up a variety of ambiguities in the guidelines in such a way as to not be too restrictive on foreign applicants and to live up to the spirit of market liberalization.

To the extent that international liberalization of the financial sector is necessary for sustained economic growth, the government should make serious efforts to expedite it. But, it is very important that the government do so with a clear rationale and with reasonable expectations as to the outcome of the liberalization. It will be disastrous to approach the problem in a haphazard way without a clear picture of the whole. Such an approach would make the market even more distorted, with the re-

Blueprint for liberalization and market opening, June 1993

͵ge and market	Major items
First stage (1993)	
Financial market	Introduce recommended BIS capital adequacy incrementally
	Completely liberalize operations of short-term money market
Capital market	Eliminate ceilings on foreigners' stock investment in companies with over 50% of equity held by foreigners
	Allow foreign investment trusts and investment consulting companies to participate in the equity of domestic investment trust firms
Foreign exchange market	Expand range of daily interbank foreign exchange rate fluctuations from 0.8% to 1.0%
	Allow nonresidents to open "free won accounts"
Second stage (1994–95)	
Financial market	Introduce ceilings on aggregate rediscounts gradually
	Diversify short-term financial products such as greater range of maturities of commercial paper
Capital market	Relax requirements for opening branches by foreign securities companies
	Raise direct stock investment ceilings for foreigners
	Allow international organizations to issue won-denominated bonds in the domestic market
	Permit establishment of domestic representative office of foreign credit-rating firms
	Raise ceilings on equity participation by foreign investment trust and investment consulting companies
Foreign exchange market	Completely lift restrictions on overseas portfolio investment by domestic institutional investors
	Raise ceiling on settlement in won for visible transactions
	Abolish ceiling on foreign currency deposits exempted from underlying documentation requirements
Third stage (1996–97)	
Financial market	Complete liberalization of interest rates excluding demand deposits
	Introduce financial products linked to market rates such as MMCs, MMFs
	Lower reserve requirement ratios gradually
Capital market	Permit foreign banks to establish subsidiaries
	Lower capital requirements for branches of foreign securities companies
	Continue to raise direct stock investment ceilings for foreigners
Foreign exchange market	Progressively permit full settlement in Korean won for visible and also invisible transactions
	Completely exempt normal transactions from underlying documentation requirements

BIS = Bank for International Settlements; MMC = money market certificates; MMF = money market funds.

sult that foreign investors will be as frustrated as domestic investors. The government first has to proceed with financial liberalization and market opening while also considering the evolution of macroeconomic variables, such as the balance of payments, price level, and the domestic-international interest rate gap. More importantly, institutional tools and policy instruments should be established in advance to attenuate the expected side effects. Second, domestic liberalization has to precede international liberalization. It is hoped that the financial authority's decision to internationalize financial markets will expedite the long-delayed domestic liberalization.

Central Bank

In this chapter, I have not discussed the position and function of the Bank of Korea, Korea's central bank. This omission is partly due to the fact that the Bank of Korea played little role in financial policy making over the last 30 years. The Bank of Korea has had to accommodate government policy. The primary duty of the Korean central bank is to check money supply and inflation, but an anti-inflationary stance was not among the primary aims of the government.

The Bank of Korea Law, enacted in June 1950, right before the Korean War broke out, stipulated that the Bank of Korea be largely independent, with a view toward pursuit of vigorous stabilization policy to combat rampant inflation. The law had established the seven-member Monetary Board, chaired by the governor of the Bank of Korea. The board members, designated by ministers of the government, represented various sectors of the economy.

The military government amended the law in 1961 to bring the Bank of Korea under government control. The amended law gave the minister of finance a broad range of authority in monetary and financial management, vesting him with the chairmanship of the Monetary Board. During subsequent decades, the Bank of Korea Law was amended four times, and the government steadily tightened its control on money and finance. As each of the new regulations regarding policy loans and new financial institutions came into being, the authority of the central bank was progressively weakened.

The "forced growth" policy adopted by the government during the 1960s and 1970s left the central bank with little elbow room. The Bank of Korea was made to automatically discount a certain proportion of the "policy loans" made by commercial banks, creating bank reserves at the Bank of Korea. The central bank lost control of the money supply. Interest rates were fixed by the government, subject to occasional alterations.

As the democratization movement swept the country in the middle 1980s and the popular clamor for price stability intensified, the need for greater independence of the central bank was recognized not only by the financial community but also by the populace. All presidential candidates pledged during the campaign in 1987 to amend the Bank of Korea Law to make the bank independent. It looked as if the independence of the Bank of Korea was all but guaranteed.

To the great disappointment of the Bank of Korea, however, this campaign promise was not fulfilled. After an intense legislative maneuver, the "independence" movement was defeated. The whole episode signified that Korea was not yet ready to have an independent central bank and that many still lacked understanding of the central bank's importance. Indeed, as long as the financial sector is so tightly controlled, it matters little whether power is vested in the Ministry of Finance or in the Bank of Korea. There is no guarantee that the Bank of Korea would do a better job than the Ministry of Finance because no matter who exercises direct control, it will produce substantially the same effects. The central bank can only be effective when it can control money and finance through indirect means. No wonder, then, that people, as well as the National Assembly, were only half-hearted in their support of central bank independence. In order for independence to be meaningful, the financial market has to be free from government control, and the price system has to prevail in the financial sector.

The financial sector, it appears, is finally being liberalized, although it comes late and its pace is still slow. The increasingly apparent inefficiency of financial repression and external pressure to open up financial markets are becoming overwhelming. In order for the financial sector to be liberalized, both domestically and internationally, a great many laws and regulations must be amended. The Bank of Korea Law should be amended as soon as practicable so as to effectively achieve monetary stabilization and expedite financial development in Korea. Financial liberalization and independence of the central bank are the two most important policy innovations the country needs in the 1990s.

7

Foreign Trade

In any economy, the external and domestic sectors are inextricably related, a fact that is becoming more and more conspicuous in today's world, with its increasing interdependence among nations. In the case of Korea, the link between external and domestic sectors is much closer than in most other countries. The pattern of Korea's external trade closely reflects the pattern of growth in industries, firms, industrial relations, and finance.

Recently, dramatic changes have been taking place in the international economic environment, especially in the Pacific region, in the form of rapid structural changes, emergence of common markets, and growing friction among trade partners of the region. These developments are forcing Korea to reevaluate its growth strategy from a new perspective. Korea must carefully evaluate where to anchor its international economic policy in the future and how to adjust itself to the new environment. The first half of this chapter is devoted to a review of the development of foreign trade and trade policy during the period under study. The second half will discuss the nature of Korea-US trade relations and offer suggestions for basic policy directions Korea should take.

Exports, Imports, and Trade Balance

In Korea, exports have grown at a much faster rate than GNP. In the early 1960s, exports amounted to less than 6 percent of GNP, but the continuous rapid annual growth of exports brought the figure close to 36 percent in 1987. Figure 7.1 shows the proportion of exports to GNP of

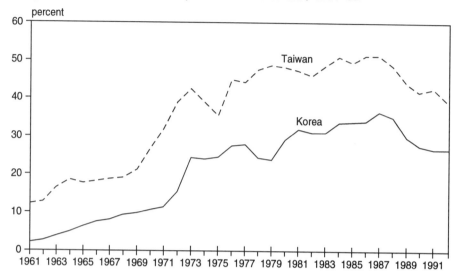

Figure 7.1   Korea, Taiwan: exports as a share of GNP, 1961–92

Sources: Bank of Korea, *Economic Statistics Yearbook,* various years, *National Accounts,* 1992; Council for Economic Planning and Development, *Taiwan Statistical Data Book,* various years; Director-General of Budget, Accounting and Statistics, Executive Yuan, *National Income in Taiwan Area of the Republic of China, 1992.*

both Korea and Taiwan. Both countries have become heavily dependent on exports to provide a substantial amount of income and employment. Naturally, resource-poor economies such as Korea and Taiwan can expand exports only through exporting manufactured goods. The proportion of exports of manufactured goods to total exports is shown in figure 7.2. More than 90 percent of the exports of both countries consist of manufactured goods. In the course of the last two decades, the export structures of these two countries have changed greatly. Exports of heavy-industry goods have become increasingly important while exports of light-industry products have shrunk as a share of total exports. Table 7.1 shows this change in Korea; the share of heavy-industry products now outweighs that of light-industry products. With somewhat different classifications, a roughly similar picture is presented for Taiwan in table 7.2.

Korean imports, summarized in table 7.3, consist mostly of grain, oil, capital goods, and raw materials, none of which is dispensable. Note the very small proportion of consumer goods in total imports. In 1992, for example, they constituted only 8 percent of total imports. Again, with somewhat different classifications, a roughly similar import structure for Taiwan is shown in table 7.4. It is apparent that the investment in export and import-substitution industries is inducing imports of capital goods and raw materials; most imports are directly related to exports and

Figure 7.2 Korea, Taiwan: exports of manufactured goods as a share of total exports

Source: Korea Foreign Trade Association, *The Statistics of Foreign Trade*, various years.

investment. As we saw in Figure 2.7, where the trade balances of the two countries are presented, both countries ran trade deficits in the 1960s, but Taiwan has been recording a surplus since 1970 (except for the two oil-shock years of 1974 and 1975), while Korea's balance worsened in the 1970s, due mainly to its large investments in heavy and chemical industries. During the 1980s, Korea's deficit has steadily narrowed, and in 1986, the trade balance showed a surplus for the first time in history. The trade surplus reached as high as $11.4 billion in 1988, but it shrank to $4.6 billion in 1989 and turned to a deficit of $2 billion in 1990. The deficit grew further to $7 billion in 1991. The deficit, however, was reduced to $2 billion in 1992 thanks to strong macroeconomic stabilization measures.

Export Policy

Export Policy in the 1960s

Aware of the shortage of foreign exchange in the 1950s, the government of Syngman Rhee adopted a variety of measures to facilitate exports. However, these merely helped to preserve the already-existing export flow, which consisted mostly of primary products. The government was aware of the importance of foreign exchange reserves in economic management, but the plight of the economy was such that it had not expected that substantial exports of manufactured goods would be possible.

Table 7.1 Korea: composition of exports, 1971–92 (percentages)

| Year | Manufactured goods | | Nonmanufactured goods |
	Light industry	Heavy industry	
1971	72.1	14.2	13.7
1972	66.6	21.3	12.1
1973	63.4	23.8	12.8
1974	54.1	32.5	13.4
1975	57.4	25.0	17.6
1976	59.0	29.2	11.8
1977	53.6	32.2	14.2
1978	54.5	34.7	10.8
1979	51.4	38.5	10.1
1980	49.4	41.5	9.1
1981	49.4	41.6	9.0
1982	45.0	46.9	8.1
1983	41.1	50.6	8.3
1984	39.5	52.5	8.0
1985	38.6	53.4	8.0
1986	44.0	48.4	7.6
1987	43.8	49.1	7.1
1988	41.8	52.1	6.1
1989	42.0	52.2	5.8
1990	41.1	53.6	5.3
1991	37.8	56.1	6.1
1992	32.4	60.4	7.2

Source: Korea Foreign Trade Association, *The Statistics of Foreign Trade,* various years.

The gradual but irreversible reduction of US aid in the early 1960s impelled the Korean government to promote exports, as specified by the first five-year development plan. Exports were deemed necessary to earn foreign exchange with which to finance imports. The government started to take a variety of aggressive export-promotion measures. In the course of the 1960s, the government introduced numerous measures to stimulate exports, such as fiscal incentives with respect to import duties and domestic taxes, preferential interest rates on loans, and a wastage allowance on imports of intermediate goods for export purposes. Furthermore, the government accorded successful exporters a variety of non-pecuniary rewards such as citations and decorations. These, in the context of the Korean economic and social environment, were no less important than pecuniary ones. The export promotion policy assumed a dominant place in economic policy. The president presided over the monthly export-promotion meetings, which began to identify export promotion with patriotism, thereby drumming up public support for exports.

The first five-year plan envisaged an average annual export growth rate of about 20 percent, with approximately half of the exports consisting of primary products. It turned out that actual export performance was much better than expected, with the average annual rate of export

Table 7.2 Taiwan: composition of exports, 1971–92 (percentages)

| Year | Manufactured goods | | Nonmanufactured goods |
	Light industry	Heavy industry	
1971	57.0	23.8	19.2
1972	55.6	29.2	15.2
1973	56.6	29.1	14.2
1974	52.9	32.8	14.3
1975	53.6	30.0	16.4
1976	56.0	31.6	12.5
1977	53.0	34.4	12.6
1978	52.3	36.8	10.9
1979	52.5	38.0	9.5
1980	53.0	37.8	9.2
1981	52.3	39.8	7.9
1982	51.7	40.6	7.7
1983	51.4	41.6	7.0
1984	50.3	43.5	6.2
1985	50.2	43.6	6.3
1986	49.4	44.0	6.6
1987	47.2	46.6	6.1
1988	43.5	50.9	5.6
1989	42.9	52.4	4.6
1990	42.9	52.8	4.3
1991	42.2	53.3	4.5
1992	41.1	54.8	4.1

Source: Department of Statistics, Ministry of Finance, *Monthly Statistics of Exports and Imports*, The Republic of China (Taiwan District), various issues.

growth reaching 44 percent, and there emerged a variety of major manufacturing export items, such as plywood, wigs, synthetic fabrics, and rubber tires. Moreover, more than two-thirds of the total exports in the final year of the plan consisted of manufactured goods, reflecting the better-than-expected pace of industrialization.

During the second five-year plan period, the average annual rate of increase of exports was 34 percent, and more than 70 percent of total exports consisted of labor-intensive manufactured goods. Again, export performance in that period far exceeded expectations. The people, as well as the government, were now increasingly confident about the future. The "can-do" spirit began to take root, and the mood of gloom and despair that had prevailed in the previous decade began to recede.

The export industries established during the 1960s consisted mostly of those firms that imported foreign capital goods along with half-finished products. In producing final goods to be exported or sold in the domestic market, the manufacturers processed the imported half-finished goods by making use of imported capital equipment and technology and by employing low-wage labor. Thus, the proportion of value added in merchandise exports was rather small. Since the government provided the exporters with all conceivable incentives, the effective rate of protection

Table 7.3 Korea: composition of imports, 1971–92 (percentages)

Year	Food and consumer goods		Industrial supplies		Capital goods	
	Total	Cereals	Total	Petroleum	Total	Nonelectric machinery
1971	21.0	12.0	50.6	7.3	28.4	14.6
1972	18.5	10.1	51.6	8.2	29.9	14.3
1973	18.3	9.0	55.0	6.5	26.7	12.9
1974	15.4	7.5	57.7	14.1	27.0	10.6
1975	16.2	7.9	57.2	17.5	26.5	11.7
1976	12.0	5.1	60.5	18.4	27.5	12.0
1977	10.9	4.1	61.4	17.9	27.7	14.0
1978	10.6	3.1	55.6	14.6	33.8	17.2
1979	11.5	3.6	57.5	15.3	31.1	16.6
1980	12.1	4.8	65.0	25.3	23.0	10.4
1981	14.2	7.4	62.2	24.4	23.6	9.7
1982	10.2	3.4	64.1	25.2	25.7	10.2
1983	10.7	3.7	59.5	21.3	29.8	10.4
1984	9.5	3.0	57.5	18.9	33.0	10.7
1985	8.5	2.8	55.9	17.9	35.6	11.5
1986	9.8	2.5	54.2	10.7	36.0	15.6
1987	9.7	2.1	54.8	9.1	35.5	15.9
1988	9.8	2.2	53.5	7.1	36.8	15.6
1989	10.2	2.1	53.3	8.0	36.4	17.2
1990	10.0	1.8	53.6	9.1	36.5	17.7
1991	11.2	1.5	52.2	9.9	36.6	17.8
1992p	10.5	2.2	52.1	11.7	37.4	16.2

Source: Korea Foreign Trade Association, *The Statistics of Foreign Trade,* various years.

of the meager value-added portion of export goods was extremely high. This gave rise to an extension of exporting activities to all possible manufacturing areas, and the import content of exports tended steadily to increase, whereas the net earnings per dollar of exports steadily decreased. Excessive investments were made in a whole range of light industries producing consumption goods. Despite the great increase in exports, the balance of payments showed hardly any improvement. Toward the end of the 1960s, it became clear that the so-called export and import substitution of light consumption goods was more or less complete, and the export promotion effort began to be overtaken by diminishing returns; export incentives became increasingly less fruitful. The economic planners in the government began to hold the view that "enhancement" of the industrial structure—that is, establishment of heavy and chemical industries—was needed to further increase exports.

Export Policy in the 1970s

With the launching of the ambitious program of developing heavy and chemical industries in the early 1970s, trade policy began to depart sig-

Table 7.4 Taiwan: composition of imports, 1971–92 (percentages)

| Year | Capital goods | Agricultural and industrial raw materials | | Consumption goods |
		Total	Fuels and oils	
1971	32.0	62.9	4.8	5.1
1972	31.1	63.2	8.2	5.7
1973	28.6	65.8	3.9	5.6
1974	30.7	62.4	12.3	6.9
1975	30.6	62.6	13.2	6.8
1976	29.1	64.7	16.7	6.2
1977	25.8	66.4	18.1	7.8
1978	24.7	68.5	16.8	6.8
1979	24.6	69.0	16.5	6.4
1980	23.4	70.8	24.1	5.8
1981	16.2	76.9	23.0	6.9
1982	16.3	75.5	21.2	8.2
1983	13.9	78.3	21.4	7.8
1984	13.6	78.6	19.1	7.8
1985	14.1	76.9	21.5	9.0
1986	15.0	75.6	12.9	9.4
1987	16.0	74.1	10.5	9.9
1988	14.9	73.7	7.9	11.4
1989	16.4	72.1	8.4	11.5
1990	17.5	70.5	10.9	12.0
1991	16.7	72.4	9.3	10.9
1992	17.8	69.3	7.8	12.9

Source: Council for Economic Planning and Development, Taiwan Statistical Data Book, The Republic of China, 1992.

nificantly from the established trend of the 1960s. First, many of the export promotion measures adopted in the 1960s were toned down. For example, the wastage allowance was reduced, and the reduction of income or corporate tax of up to 50 percent of export earnings was abolished in 1973. In 1975, tariff reduction and exemption on imports for export purposes were replaced by a system of tariff drawbacks, significantly reducing the incentive to import for reexport. Furthermore, from 1975, exporters were charged higher prices for government-operated public utilities such as electricity.

The scaling down of export incentives, however, did not mean a deemphasis on exports. It merely reflected the government's awareness that export promotion in the 1960s had been excessive and that exports of light-industry goods would not suffer from reduced incentives.

One may ask if the new objective of developing heavy and chemical industries in the early 1970s was consistent with the more traditional objective of export promotion. As far as the government was concerned, there was no inconsistency between the two objectives. The government promoted heavy and chemical industries with a view toward promoting exports from the very beginning,[1] maintaining that the comparative advantage of Korea was shifting away from labor-intensive to capital-intensive industries. Without these industries, so the government envisaged, plan targets for total exports of $10 billion and a per capita income of $1,000 by the end of the decade could not be attained. With a view toward achieving these objectives, the government set forth long-term goals such as a production capacity of 10 million tons of steel, 5 million tons of shipbuilding capacity, 940 thousand barrels of oil refining, and half a million units of automobiles (The Heavy and Chemical Industry Planning Council 1974).[2] The program rested on the anticipated increase in exports; the capacity envisaged far exceeded what the domestic market warranted. The argument advanced by the government was that both Japan and West Germany had developed their heavy and chemical industries when they were in comparable stages of development.

Along with heavy and chemical industry promotion, export promotion remained unwaveringly the prime policy objective; the government intensified its export promotion efforts by strengthening moral suasion and employing nonpecuniary means of inducement. The annual export targets set forth by the development plan were singled out to be the most important of all, to be attained at any cost. In 1975, the government established general trading companies, each of which was given its own export target. Knowing that the destiny of their companies depended on government favor, the trading companies complied with government exhortations with maximum fidelity.

One may sympathize with the government's vision that the country needed to start building "upstream" industries. The ratio of value added in light industries, which processed semifinished goods imported from abroad, was diminishing; they needed import substitutions of half-finished products, as well as of some of the heavy industries. However, the government, impelled by the urge to accomplish the goal in a minimum span of time, took over the entrepreneurial function from private investors by designating individual companies to invest and thereby ushered in many long-term sources of inefficiency.[3] Furthermore, the assumption that Korea's comparative advantage in the 1970s was rapidly shifting from light industries to heavy and chemical industries proved to be over-

---

1. The heavy and chemical industries were partly promoted on national defense grounds—there was concern on the part of the policymakers that US forces would withdraw from Korea and that the threat from North Korea would then increase, particularly in view of the deteriorating military situation in Vietnam. However, export promotion was the most important factor in heavy and chemical industry planning.

2. No explanations as to how these targets were selected are given in the document.

3. This was discussed in chapter 3; the significance of this practice from the point of view of institutions will be elaborated upon in chapter 8.

stated, as subsequent export performance attests. At this point, the heavy and chemical industries had yet to become export industries and rather resembled import-substitution industries. By the end of 1975, as much as 93 percent of total priority loans outstanding were directed toward heavy and chemical industries, and as much as 40 percent of the total corporate tax for heavy and chemical industries was exempted, as compared with only 8 percent for light industries. What the economy gained out of all this was not a great surge of exports but redundant investment and excess capacities, which in turn generated great inflationary pressure, a large increase in wage rates, a depreciation of the won, large deficits in the balance of payments, swelling of external debts, and tightening of government control—a set of phenomena reminiscent of the results of an import-substitution program in many developing countries.

It is true that during the third five-year plan period (1972–76) exports did increase at a rapid pace, but the increase in exports during this period—and for that matter during the fourth plan period (1977–81)—was almost entirely due to the good performance of labor-intensive industries. Furthermore, the general trading companies contributed much to achieving the export targets of the government. Knowing that the achievement of export targets was more important than profits from exports, the trading companies made an all-out effort to fulfill the export volume assigned to them, even though the profit margin from exports was very narrow.

One particular aspect of export promotion deserves special emphasis: export value added, upon which monetary, fiscal, and other promotion incentives were calculated, was expressed in gross rather than net terms.[4] Furthermore, imports of raw materials for reexport were given wastage allowances, while imports of final consumption goods were tightly controlled. These policies, in effect, gave exporters tremendous incentives to import and process semifinished intermediate goods, using economies of scale. There were few incentives to produce intermediate goods themselves. When an exporting company exhausted the source of profit in one industry, it moved on to another industry so that, in the end, the technologies developed were concentrated on those related to assembling and processing of semifinished goods. As seen in chapter 4, large firms in Korea are those that most successfully exploited economies of scale by taking advantage of the system of export incentives in the 1960s and 1970s. The export strategy in the 1960s and 1970s thus contributed to the emergence of conglomerates, with detrimental effects on small and medium enterprises.

---

4. For example, when an exporter imports semifinished goods at the cost of $900,000, adds to them a value of $100,000, and exports them at $1 million, the amount of export loans he is entitled to is $1 million rather than $100,000.

Export Policy from the 1980s to the Present

During the 1980s, government policy shifted its focus to the correction of the excesses and imbalances of the previous decades. Restructuring of industries, market mechanisms, private initiatives, and price stability, not maximizing growth, now were the goals of economic policy. In line with this general policy direction, export promotion policy shifted from maximizing export growth to strengthening competitiveness through improvements of export structure. On the whole, the export promotion measures of the 1980s were more mature than those of previous decades. Exports still enjoyed a central position in economic policy, but they were no longer given the sole priority. To be sure, old habits, nurtured through decades of practice, still persisted. For example, the Korean Ministry of Trade and Industry still routinely monitors export figures. The government, as well as the people, are now sophisticated enough to know that maximizing export figures is not always a good policy. This change in direction has been amply rewarded—the price level stabilized, and the balance of payments improved, recording a long-awaited surplus in 1986. The emergence of a surplus owes much to the appreciation of the yen vis-à-vis the dollar, but the trend in the balance of payments was such that the surplus would have appeared even in the absence of the change in the exchange rate. The balance of payments began to improve in 1981, and the exchange rate realignment merely accelerated what appeared to be inevitable.

The current account surplus in 1986 was $4.6 billion, but it increased to $9.9 billion in 1987 and to $14.2 billion in 1988. The rapid increase in the surplus, along with the natural trend that could be observed in the early 1980s, was caused by the great appreciation of the Japanese yen and other major currencies against the dollar after the Group of Five (G-5) agreement in September 1985 and the very small appreciation of the Korean won against the dollar during the same period. Thanks to this currency realignment, the Korean won depreciated vis-à-vis the Japanese yen and German mark by about 43 and 38 percent, respectively, between September 1985 and the end of 1987. This gave Korean exporters great competitive advantage in international markets. The ensuing export boom brought sizable profits to exporters and gave rise to an annual increase of real GNP of about 12 percent during 1986–88. The boom, by its very nature both exogenous and temporary, proved to be a mixed blessing. Exporters concentrated on maximizing exports, and the business community as a whole was imbued with optimism and was easily swayed by the popular demand of the workers for higher wages. On the other hand, the Korean won began to appreciate considerably in 1988, but not enough to deter the rapidly growing Korea-bashing mood emerging in the United States and Western Europe. Domestically, the rapid rise in profits gave rise to much speculation in land and real estate, and the rapid rise in wages resulted in an increase in consumption spending, which in turn caused an increase in imports.

This state of affairs could not continue, and in 1989 the country faced a severe downturn. Real GNP growth decreased from 12.4 percent in 1988 to 6.8 percent in 1989 due mainly to the slowdown in exports, which increased only 3.0 percent compared with 29 percent in 1988. The current account surplus dropped from $14.2 billion to $5.1 billion in 1989 and reversed to a deficit from 1990 on. The shift of the current account from surplus to deficit was to be expected because of the nature of the Korean industrial structure as well as prolonged recession in most developed countries. This unfavorable turn of events also may be attributed to many other factors, such as the loss of international competitiveness due to the belated appreciation of the won, eruptions of labor disputes and wage increases, and increased imports due to import liberalization.

Import Policy

During the 1950s, the volume of Korean imports was determined by the volume of aid from the United States. There was no import policy worthy of its name, except for the policy of maximizing US aid. Since the early 1960s, import policy had been constrained by the perennial current account deficit and by the need to foster export industries and import-substitution industries. Import policy during the entire period under study can be roughly characterized as follows: extremely "liberal" with respect to raw materials for the use of exports, somewhat less liberal with respect to goods for domestic industries, and restrictive with respect to consumer goods. The basic thrust of all industrial policy prevalent in that period was emphasis on exports and export industries, and secondary consideration was given to import-substitution industries.

Import Liberalization in the 1960s

As noted in chapter 3, the Korean government in 1964 adopted a unitary fluctuating exchange rate system, putting an end to the multiple exchange rate system that had been maintained since the 1950s. The 1964 exchange rate readjustment signaled the advent of partial liberalization of imports. Significant import liberalization does seem to have taken place between 1965 and 1967. The import license system became less strict as so-called automatically approved items increased in number from 1,948 in 1965 to 3,760 in 1967 (Luedde-Neurath 1986, 67–68). However, this figure does not accurately denote the real extent of liberalization during this period because, despite the doubling of automatically approved items, many import barriers persisted, such as restriction by special laws, allocation of foreign exchange, export obligations, advance deposits, and overall import quotas. Import liberalization measures taken during this period were designed mainly to encourage imports of capital goods, raw materials, and semifinished goods for export and import-substitution industries and to discourage imports of consumer goods.

The government adopted a major import liberalization policy in 1967[5] by adopting the negative list system, under which all items not listed could be freely imported. This policy is regarded as a major step toward import liberalization even though the objective was not to encourage the whole range of imports but to liberalize certain kinds. The volume of actual imports did not increase significantly, suggesting that import liberalization brought about by the negative list system was not as great as expected. According to a calculation made by the Korean Ministry of Trade and Industry, the value of the increase of imports attributable to liberalization of imports was $22 million in 1967 and $68 million in 1968, or only 4.6 percent of total imports in both years (Luedde-Neurath 1986, 78).

The Setback of Import Liberalization in the 1970s

In the 1970s, as Korea launched an ambitious program to foster heavy and chemical industries, the import liberalization policy encountered a great setback. As the number of priority imports was enlarged to serve the heavy and chemical industries, imports of nonpriority items were more severely restricted than they had been in the 1960s.

Analyses of the trend of Korea's import policies customarily refer to what is known as the import liberalization ratio, which is the number of freely importable items as a proportion of the total number of potentially importable items. The restricted items listed in table 7.5 are those permitted for import, subject to the approval of government ministries including the Korean Ministry of Trade and Industry and/or private organizations such as producers' associations.

The minister of trade and industry annually announces items whose imports will be restricted from 1 July to 30 June of the following year. Then other responsible ministries, government agencies, and private associations authorize or reject inclusion of these items on the list. Table 7.5 shows the import liberalization ratio between 1976 and 1992. The automatically approved items refer to those items that are freely importable. As one can see from the table, the import liberalization ratio increased steadily from 1976 through 1992. In 1976, the import liberalization ratio was only 51.0 percent; it reached 69.4 percent in 1980.

---

5. The first year of the second five-year plan period was 1967. As noted in chapter 2, major policy innovations in Korea were made usually in the initial year of each five-year plan.

Table 7.5 Import liberalization, 1976–92

Year	Total number of items	Automatic approval (AA) items	Restricted items	Prohibited items	Liberalization ratio (share of AA items)
1976	1,312	669	579	64	51.0[a]
1977	1,312	691	560	61	52.7[a]
1978	1,097	712	385	0	64.9[b]
1979	1,010	683	327	0	67.6[b]
1980	7,465	5,183	2,282	0	69.4[c]
1981	7,465	5,579	1,886	0	74.7[c]
1982	7,560	5,791	1,769	0	76.6[c]
1983	7,560	6,078	1,482	0	80.4[c]
1984	7,915	6,712	1,203	0	84.8[c]
1985	7,915	6,944	971	0	87.7[c]
1986	7,915	7,252	663	0	91.6[c]
1987	7,915	7,426	489	0	93.8[c]
1988	7,915	7,553	362	0	95.4[c]
1989	10,241	9,776	465	0	95.5[d]
1990	10,274	9,898	376	0	96.3[d]
1991	10,321	10,036	285	0	97.2[d]
1992	10,321	10,079	242	0	97.7[d]

a. Based on 4-digit level under Standard Industrial Trade Classification.
b. Based on 4-digit level under Customs Cooperation Council Nomenclature.
c. Based on 8-digit level under Customs Cooperation Council Nomenclature.
d. Based on 10-digit level under Harmonized Commodity Description and Coding System.

Source: Ministry of Trade and Industry, Korea.

While some liberalization did in fact take place in the second half of the 1970s, all available indications show that in absolute terms there was no significant trade liberalization before 1981. This is shown by table 7.6. The table shows the total value of imports in 1981 and the amount of duties levied.

Three important features of the Korean import system emerge. One is the fact that approximately 63 percent of total imports were entirely duty-free. These imports included petroleum and semifinished and intermediate goods for reexport, which accounted for about 50 percent of total imports. Other duty-free items included those used in "important industries." The second feature is the relatively small amount of imports of consumption goods (4 percent of the total). However, consumption goods accounted for as much as 17 percent of total import duties levied. The third is the fact that capital goods were relatively lightly taxed while raw materials and intermediate goods were relatively heavily taxed.

It is customary for observers of Korea's economic development to maintain that Korea's economic policy in general and its foreign trade in particular succeeded because the government's policy consistently relied on market mechanisms. Ideologically, it is true that Korea adopted the free enterprise system, but it is not entirely true to say that its policies

Table 7.6 Customs duties levied on imports by type of good during 1981

Type of good	Tariff rate (percent-ages)	Imports		Import duties	
		Billions of dollars	Percentage of total	Billions of won	Percentage of total
Duty-free goods	0.0	16.1	62.6	n.a.	n.a.
Raw materials for export	0.0	6.3	24.5	n.a.	n.a.
Crude oil	0.0	6.4	24.9	n.a.	n.a.
Other	0.0	3.4	13.2	n.a.	n.a.
Goods subject to tariff		9.6	37.4		
Raw materials and intermediate goods	17.0	3.4	13.2	411.5	46.2
Capital goods	9.9	4.3	16.7	291.3	32.7
Grains	5.6	1.0	3.9	38.3	4.3
Consumption goods	24.3	0.9	3.5	149.6	16.8
Total		25.7	100.0	890.7	100.0

n.a. = not applicable.

Source: Soo-gil Yang et al., *Basic Problems of Industrial Policies and Remodelling Direction of Support Policies,* Korea Development Institute, 1987.

have always been consistent with free market principles. The government certainly was aware of the importance of the price mechanism, but in many instances the government substituted a nonprice system to allocate resources. We saw in the proceeding chapter that financial policy was significantly removed from market mechanisms, and we have just seen that the Korean government, in conducting its trade policy, exercised extensive controls on both exports and imports. Korea's trade policy did exploit the principle of comparative advantage to some extent, but it also departed significantly from it to the extent that it relied on the visible hand of government.

On the whole, Korea's trade policy in the 1960s and 1970s smacked of mercantilism, in that it encouraged export promotion on the one hand and import restrictions on the other. The basic thrust of the policy was fundamentally reasonable, in view of the infancy of its manufacturing industries and the substantial foreign-exchange constraints under which trade and industrialization policies were conducted. The government could not afford to forgo export promotion and fully liberalize imports.

Granted that the generally restrictive nature of Korean trade policy during the 1960s and 1970s was unavoidable, the fact remains that the policy had many flaws, one of the most important of which was that it was too restrictive on imports of consumption goods and too lenient on imports of intermediate goods so that effective rates of protection for low value-added products at the final stage of the production process were extremely high. This situation has been modified since 1978, but the basic tendency persisted for a very long time. In effect, the policy indiscriminately protected all industries as infant industries, with some more heavily protected than others. The system of protection with respect to heavy and chemical industries in the 1970s reveals a variety of undesirable aspects. Import of machines began to be restricted to encourage import substitution of them. In the 1970s, the government announced targets for the proportion of domestically produced components in industrial equipment used by major industries. In order to enlarge this proportion, the government granted import licenses on machines only when domestic products were unavailable. These local-content requirements were imposed particularly strenuously on the automobile industry. According to a reliable study, these requirements resulted in high production costs for the automobile industry, as average prices of domestically produced automobile parts and components were much higher than import prices (Balassa 1985, 376).

Import Liberalization Since the Early 1980s

As discussed above, Korea's import policy was fairly restrictive until the end of the 1970s, but it has since become more liberal, and this liberalization has accelerated since 1984. The government took a major step in 1989 to hasten import liberalization: it reduced import restrictions, reduced tariffs, removed many nontariff barriers, and substantially liberalized agricultural imports. As shown in table 7.5, the import liberalization ratio was 80.4 percent in 1983, but the figure increased to 95.5 percent in 1989, meaning that import restrictions in that year were applied to only 0.5 percent of all industrial product classes. The corresponding percentage was as much as 23 percent in 1982. Most of the restricted items were those that used agricultural products as inputs. However, the government has also been taking measures to liberalize many of these items as well.

Yet the import liberalization ratios do not tell the whole story. One has to first consider tariffs to get a clearer picture. Even if imports are liberalized, the tariff rate may be too high to permit effective importation. Therefore, in order for an import liberalization policy to take effect, tariff rates must be lowered. Korea's tariff rates, as shown in table 7.7, have been lowered since the early 1980s. In 1982, the average level of tariffs stood at 23.7 percent, but by 1989, tariffs decreased to 12.7 percent. Second, there are barriers other than those taken into consideration by the Korean Ministry of Trade and Industry in calculating the import liberalization ratio. Some of the imports are subject to special laws such as the Grain Management Act, Fertilizer Management Act,

Table 7.7 Average tariff rates,
1980–92 (percentages)

Year	Average tariff rates
1980	24.9
1981	24.9
1982	23.7
1983	23.7
1984	21.9
1985	21.3
1986	19.9
1987	19.3
1988	18.1
1989	12.7
1990	11.4
1991	11.4
1992	10.1

Source: The Office of Customs Administration.

Pharmaceutical Act, and others. These laws restrict imports of a variety of products for such domestic policy objectives as consumer protection, public health, and national security. They call for inspection and approval of import items by administrative units or boards, often represented by domestic interest groups. To cope with the problem, the Korean government since 1987 has reformed these laws to minimize the burden on imports. In 1989, the government appointed an interministerial task force to review their effects on imports, and based on the findings of the task force, the government adopted a package of measures to simplify or eliminate import regulations.

Furthermore, Korea has intensified its import liberalization policy in the 1990s, especially regarding agricultural products. In March 1991, Korea announced a new three-year import liberalization program for 1992–94. Under this program, Korea will liberalize 133 products (agricultural products account for 131 of these), or 47 percent of the total 283 products whose import is still restricted: 43 products in 1992, 45 products in 1993, and the other 45 products in 1994. The US government sent Korea its own list requesting the liberalization of 93 products through the General Agreement on Tariffs and Trade, and Korea has conscientiously taken care to include as many of these products as possible. By 1994 Korea's import liberalization ratio will reach 98.5 percent (agricultural products making up 91.9 percent) up from 97.2 percent in 1991 (84.7 percent in agricultural products).

Hereafter, Korea will draft and offer a new three-year import liberalization program for 1995–97 for 150 products covered under the balance of payment provisions of the GATT, or otherwise bring them into conformity with GATT rules.

Moreover, Korea has also implemented a tariff reduction policy pursuant to the five-year tariff reduction program (1989–93) announced in 1988 in connection with the import liberalization program. This tariff reduction program will reduce average tariff rates from 11.4 percent in 1991 to 7.9 percent in 1994. Average tariff rates on industrial products will be reduced from 9.4 percent in 1991 to 6.2 percent in 1994, and the ratio for agricultural products will drop from 19.9 percent in 1991 to 16.6 percent in 1994.

In addition to import liberalization and tariff reductions, Korean authorities adopted a three-phase liberalization and market opening plan in June 1993. According to the plan in 1993, all foreign direct investment (FDI) in Korea will be shifted to a notification-based system for entry into Korea. Also in 1994–95, sectors eligible for FDI in Korea will be expanded and listed in advance under an open investment plan. Moreover, procedures for FDI will be further simplified.

Korea in the Global Economy

The nature of the condensed growth Korea has achieved during the last several decades are discussed elsewhere (chapters 1 and 8); there is no need to dwell upon it here. One thing that is relevant to this chapter is the fact that a small economy that was isolated three decades ago has since become a middle-income country whose economy has become integrated with the rest of the world. At the beginning of this process, the world was not very much affected by what Korea did and therefore treated it with benign neglect. Korea, now standing at the forefront of middle-income countries, has become the 12th-largest trading nation in the world. Gone is the comfort of being unimportant: Korea is no longer free to do whatever it wants; it must play roles commensurate with the economic status it has achieved.

What, then, is the position of the country from the global point of view, and what kind of role is it expected to play?

In recent years Koreans have discussed whether the country has to internationalize its economy; "Korea in the world economy" has become a fashionable topic. The Koreans are now concerned about what to do and where to go from here. Yes, the Korean economy needs to be internationalized. But what does this mean? Misunderstanding of the term is prevalent. For many Koreans it simply means more exports, or more imports, or both. But internationalization of an economy should mean something more than that; otherwise, the Korean economy could be considered to have "gone global" in the early 1960s. For others, internationalization means subjection to intensive pressure from strong foreign countries that the country finds hard to accommodate. But this is a very negative and narrow perspective, and one the country certainly cannot welcome.

Rather, internationalization of the economy should mean that economic agents, including the government, business, and the people, should be aware of the place or position of the economy in the global context, be prepared to play roles commensurate with that position, and thereby contribute to the prosperity of the global economy. From this point of view, the Korean people must shed the old nationalistic perspective and adopt a broader, international, more "enlightened" perspective.

Looking at the Korean economy from a global point of view, one is led to have two conflicting images. One image is that Korea, charged with a historical destiny, is an important country—much more important than most Koreans think. Its importance transcends physical and even economic size, for reasons to be subsequently explained. Since Korea has become a very important country in the world, the Koreans have to assume responsibilities commensurate with the historical role thrust upon them. There is a cost, and it is incumbent on Korea to shoulder it—even more so for Korea than comparable countries.

The other image is that Korea is in a vulnerable position in many important respects, both politically and psychologically as well as economically. The ability of the country to cope with this mission has yet to be proved. Korea's problems appear overwhelming: achievement of democracy, restructuring of its economic structure, and achievement of unification—all these call for herculean effort. The country has to overcome these difficult problems before it can assume its global role. To these problems let us now turn.

Global Responsibility

From a global point of view, Korea is a front-runner among developing countries. Korean success owes much to the postwar international economic system, as discussed in chapter 1. The country has prospered on an export-led growth strategy, and even though the current situation is vastly different from the period just after World War II, the development of the country will continue to depend on a free trade system. The country, therefore, is called upon to make its own contribution to maintaining the international system; this means it has to accept the cost of abiding by internationally accepted rules of conduct.

Viewed from this angle, Korea has made great strides in the last decade or so in liberalizing its mercantile trade regime, in liberalizing its regulations on investment, and in protecting international property rights. To pursue these policies, Korea has paid short-run "costs," such as reduced growth of exports due to elimination of export subsidies and increased imports due to liberalization of imports. Fortunately, abiding by the international rules of the game will produce more benefits than costs. Democratization of the economy and liberalization of the trade regime constitute a policy package likely to strengthen the new sources of growth. There is little long-run conflict between playing by international rules and providing the economy with these sources of growth.

Each and every country has its own idiosyncrasy with respect to the institutions and structure that circumscribes its adjustment path. Korea is no exception. As we have so far seen in this book, the economy of Korea has a number of weak points. The country has had only a short time to adjust its thinking and behavior to the changing environment. The inadequate time, together with the overestimate abroad of the strength of the Korean economy, has courted suspicion and criticism from abroad on its behavior in conducting its foreign economic policy. Korea has to cope with all this misunderstanding and misconception while still trying to live up to the world's expectations.

Korea as Mediator in Asia

Korea has a special place in the community of Pacific Basin countries. One may legitimately doubt if there is such a "community" because of the diversity of the nations it purports to encompass. Indeed, there are not yet any economic blocs there as big as the European Union. But, the Asia-Pacific nations do display vitality and energy, with or without the presence of a new, overarching international community. Korea is fortunate in being surrounded by these countries.

The United States and Japan, economic superpowers, are the central Pacific Basin countries. There are newly industrializing economies (NIEs), and more will appear shortly. Korea, though small and not so powerful as the United States or Japan, will have a special place in that it will be an important factor in determining the future direction of the region, as a "mediator" between the United States and Japan, and as a front-runner of NIEs. Depending upon how it plays these roles, the country can contribute, as much as the superpowers, to the prosperity of the region and the rest of the world.

Korea's Role Among Asian NIEs

Korea is currently in a leading position among the developing countries in the North and Southeast Asia. The ASEAN countries are expected to have their own condensed-growth periods in the near future; already, Thailand, Malaysia, and Indonesia are very close behind Korea. All these countries are eager to attract capital and technology from developed countries. Korean firms have started making investments in Malaysia, Thailand, and Indonesia. The presence of the United States in this region has not changed much in recent years, while Japan has emerged as the dominant country there in terms of the trade and investment. Asia-

Pacific developing countries have shown interest in the Korean experience and welcome Korean investment. The economic capability of Korea is limited compared with the United States and Japan, but it still should cultivate relations with these countries to the best of its ability.

Strategic Crossroads

Korea occupies a very strategic area of Northeast Asia. The Korean Peninsula is located at the contact point of four major world powers: the United States, Japan, China, and Russia. All major wars in Northeast Asia during the last century or so have been fought largely over political and military hegemony on the Korean peninsula. The struggle among the major powers gave rise to the division of the country; Korea is now the only divided country in the world. Korea certainly should not permit itself to be a pawn in the struggles of the great powers. The country should be the master of its own destiny. The struggle between South and North Korea is expected to end in such a way as to benefit South Korea in the economic sphere, but this fact cannot be a source of comfort for South Korea because the economic difficulties of North Korea may eventually become South Korea's problem. China and Russia have both been showing interest in the Korean experience as a possible model for their own development. Recently, Korea has established diplomatic relations with almost all former socialist countries, including Russia and the People's Republic of China.

During recent years, Korea's economic relations with China and Russia have developed at a rapid pace. In 1992, Korea's exports to China recorded $4.5 billion, 5.9 percent of the total, and imports from China amounted to $3.7 billion, 4.6 percent of the total. During each year in the 1988–92 period, exports to China have grown at 29 percent, and imports from China have swelled by 28 percent on an annual average basis. Korea's direct investment in China has also grown very quickly, recording $141 million—13.4 percent of total overseas direct investment—in 1992. Most of the investment has centered on projects in electric and electronic products, textiles, and footwear, which have steadily lost competitiveness in their home base in recent years.

Korea's trade with Russia has increased fast, recording an export value of $365 million and an import value of $495 million in 1992. In 1991 Korea also provided Russia with $3 billion in loans to promote the expansion of economic relations on a mutually beneficial and peaceful basis.

Korea is now in a special position in this region. If the country continues to do well, it can certainly contribute decisively to the peace and prosperity of this otherwise crisis-prone region. In this sense, the success of Korea will be significant not only for Korea but also for the entire region.

Unification

Korea has to achieve unification. For the last several years, the world has witnessed tremendous changes: East and West Germany have been united, and the East European countries have been democratized. The Persian Gulf War has formally ended, and the communist system of the Soviet Union has collapsed. The Cold War is now a thing of the past. But there is still a small-scale cold war on the Korean peninsula; an Iron Curtain still screens off North Korea. The eyes and ears of the world are trained on the Korean Peninsula, and there is a dense atmosphere of uncertainty over it. One thing that has become obvious is that the Korean question has become an internal one; unification depends upon the Korean people, just as German unification has been achieved through German initiative. It is important that South Korea encourage, with all available means, North Korean liberalization, domestic as well as international. Also, peace must be preserved between the two Koreas. The German experience affords Korea one lesson; the economic and political burdens that unification will impose on South Korea will be great, and they are likely to be much greater than those West Germany has faced. Although unification is first and foremost the problem of the Korean people, all major powers of the world have an important stake in it because the peace of the region depends upon how it proceeds. Korea now should have a vision for achieving unification and for what happens beyond unification. The country is charged with a historical mission, as important a one as at any other time in her history.

In order for Korea to play these roles well, the domestic economy has to be properly managed—economic and social institutions have to be so arranged as to maintain balanced development and harmonious social relations.

There is no substitute for good domestic economic management, which is the foundation of sound unification policy and of good management of international relations. Maintenance of vital domestic institutions is easier said than done in Korea today. It requires extraordinary vision, intelligence, and courage on the part of the people.

Korean-US Trade Relations

The remainder of this chapter summarizes the highlights of trade relations between Korea and the United States. There are two reasons for singling out the bilateral relationship between the two countries here. First, the United States has been and will continue to be the most important trade partner of Korea, and Korea has every incentive to maintain frictionless relations with the United States. Second, the United States has been and will continue to be the leader of the international system,

Table 7.8   Korea: trade balance with the United States, 1970–92 (millions of dollars)

Year	Exports	Imports	Trade balance
1970	395	585	−190
1971	532	678	−146
1972	759	647	112
1973	1,021	1,202	−181
1974	1,492	1,701	−209
1975	1,536	1,881	−345
1976	2,493	1,963	530
1977	3,119	2,447	672
1978	4,058	3,043	1,015
1979	4,374	4,603	−229
1980	4,607	4,890	−283
1981	5,661	6,050	−389
1982	6,243	5,956	287
1983	8,245	6,274	1,971
1984	10,479	6,876	3,603
1985	10,754	6,489	4,265
1986	13,880	6,545	7,335
1987	18,311	8,758	9,553
1988	21,404	12,757	8,647
1989	20,639	15,911	4,728
1990	19,360	16,943	2,417
1991	18,559	18,894	−335
1992	18,090	18,287	−197

Source: Korea Foreign Trade Association, *Statistics of Foreign Trade,* various years.

and the pattern of trade relations with the United States—with or without friction—will be duplicated by that with other parts of the world.

Development of Trade Friction

The two most conspicuous aspects of Korea's foreign trade are high export dependence on the United States and high import dependence on Japan. As shown in table 7.8, Korea had trade deficits with the United States until 1981, but since then the deficits have turned into surpluses that reached $4.3 billion in 1985, and there has been a robust increase in exports. This trend accelerated from 1986 to 1988. The proportion of total exports that went to the United States also increased from 27.4 percent in 1981 to 39.6 percent in 1987. As the bilateral trade surplus with the United States rapidly increased, so did the deficit with Japan. In 1981, the trade deficit with Japan was $2.9 billion, but it swelled to $5.2 billion in 1987 (table 7.9).

The main reason exports to the United States increased so rapidly from 1986 to 1988 is that the Japanese yen appreciated vis-à-vis the dollar largely in the same period, giving Korean exporters great competitive advantage

Table 7.9   Korea: trade balance with Japan, 1970–92
(millions of dollars)

Year	Exports	Imports	Trade balance
1970	236	813	−577
1971	263	962	−699
1972	408	1,031	−623
1973	1,242	1,727	−485
1974	1,380	2,621	−1,241
1975	1,293	2,434	−1,141
1976	1,802	3,099	−1,297
1977	2,148	3,927	−1,779
1978	2,627	5,981	−3,354
1979	3,355	6,657	−3,302
1980	3,039	5,858	−2,819
1981	3,503	6,373	−2,870
1982	3,388	5,305	−1,917
1983	3,404	6,238	−2,834
1984	4,602	7,640	−3,038
1985	4,543	7,560	−3,017
1986	5,426	10,869	−5,443
1987	8,437	13,657	−5,210
1988	12,004	15,929	−3,925
1989	13,457	17,449	−3,992
1990	12,638	18,574	−5,936
1991	12,356	21,120	−8,764
1992	11,600	19,458	−7,858

Source: Korea Foreign Trade Association, *Statistics of Foreign Trade,* various years.

over Japanese exporters in the US market. On the other hand, Korea's imports from the United States did not increase very rapidly because approximately 40 percent of Korea's imports from the United States consist of primary products, for which demand is somewhat inelastic with respect to both price and income. As for the deficit with Japan, it has been increasing quickly because the parts and components used for Korea's export products, particularly the technology-intensive products, have been imported from Japan. Consequently, an increase of Korean exports, no matter where they are destined to go, automatically increases imports of these goods from Japan. Thus, Korea's exports to the rest of the world other than Japan automatically increase Japan's exports to the rest of the world. Korea's exports to Japan did not significantly increase, partly because Korea's industrial structure is similar to that of Japan and Korea's exports consist of those items in which Japan enjoys comparative advantage. It is noteworthy that during 1989, when Korea's current account surplus registered a great reduction, imports from Japan increased tremendously, though exports to both Japan and the United States decreased noticeably. During 1988 and 1989, the trade deficit with Japan decreased mainly due to yen appreciation, import market diversification, and increase in the domestic substitution of intermediate capital goods from

Japan. However, since 1990, the trade deficit with Japan has increased, mainly due to the rapid decrease in exports to Japan. The decrease has been caused by weaker price competitiveness of Korean exporting goods compared with those of other developing countries such as China, Taiwan, and Singapore. Korea's deficit with Japan in 1991 amounted to $8.8 billion, which exceeded by far Korea's total deficit with the rest of the world.

The structure of Korea's exports to the United States and that of imports from the United States are listed in table 7.10 and table 7.11, respectively. In 1992 Korea exported to the United States 22 percent of its total textile exports, about one-quarter of its other light-industry products, including footwear, dolls, and toys, and about one-third of its total machinery exports, including electronics and automobiles. Thus the United States is Korea's preponderant exports market. In the same year, about 30 percent of total imports of food and consumer goods, and 30 percent of capital goods came from the United States.

During the 1970s and 1980s, the United States imposed a variety of import restriction measures on Korea's exports: MFA (Multi-Fiber Agreement) quotas on textiles in 1974 (renewed in 1986 with more stringent conditions), an orderly marketing arrangement (OMA) on footwear between July 1977 and June 1981, an OMA on color television sets between December 1978 and June 1980, a voluntary export restraint (VER) on steel in 1984, antidumping duties of 64.8 percent on photo albums and 13.9 percent on color television sets, countervailing duties of 25 percent on oil-drilling rigs, and a property rights charge on semiconductor chips in 1987. Moreover, recent years have witnessed an increasing number of petitions and affirmative rulings in cases on infringement of intellectual property rights, and in January 1988 the United States decided to withdraw Generalized System of Preferences (GSP) privileges for Korean exporters. During 1988–91, several items, including plastic bags, erasable programmable read-only memory (EPROM) chips, acrylic sweaters, and polyester film, have been added to US import regulations via mechanisms such as import prohibition orders and antidumping duties (table 7.12). In addition to these moves, US trade authorities are under heavy pressure from various US exporters to press the Korean government to take further action to liberalize imports.

During the second half of 1980s, the United States requested that Korea reduce tariff rates; remove import restrictions not only on manufactured goods but also on agricultural products; lift entry barriers to service industries, including finance, insurance, and advertising; appreciate the won; and expand the domestic market to absorb the deflationary impact of exchange rate revaluation. Since the beginning of 1990s, the pressure has been turned up, with a focus on areas in which the United States expects to be competitive. It has asked Korea to phase out restrictions on agricultural products at the earliest date, protect intellectual property rights, and completely open the service industries. To encourage

Table 7.10 Composition of Korea's exports to the United States, 1981–92 (percentages)

Export commodity	1981	1982	1983	1984	1985	1986	1987	1988	1989	1990	1991	1992
Total	26.6	28.6	33.7	35.8	35.5	40.0	38.7	35.3	33.1	29.8	25.8	23.6
Food and direct consumption	12.0	11.7	12.4	13.5	12.3	13.2	16.0	11.4	9.9	9.1	7.9	7.4
Crude materials and fuels	10.3	18.4	12.5	11.9	20.1	17.7	15.1	14.2	11.6	6.3	4.2	5.0
Light industry products	28.8	34.4	39.9	43.6	45.1	42.6	39.0	35.6	35.3	34.1	28.7	26.4
Textiles	24.9	28.1	33.1	37.7	37.9	35.0	31.7	28.5	29.0	27.7	23.4	22.2
Footwear	54.5	67.6	70.1	68.7	74.1	72.2	65.6	64.9	66.9	62.3	52.9	48.4
Heavy industry products	27.7	25.9	32.8	34.1	34.8	41.9	42.1	37.8	34.2	29.2	26.5	24.2
Metal goods	30.9	22.5	31.5	37.4	36.2	34.1	30.7	25.6	21.1	22.6	19.0	16.3
Machinery and equipment	30.0	36.8	37.6	45.9	46.0	48.0	45.9	41.3	44.8	39.0	35.9	34.1
Electronic products	45.8	51.0	61.7	60.2	54.6	52.0	41.2	36.6	35.7	29.4	29.4	29.3
Motor vehicles	1.3	0.1	0.1	11.0	0.4	71.2	83.2	83.5	66.2	57.6	43.4	25.3

Source: Bank of Korea, Monthly Balance of Payments, various issues.

167

Table 7.11 Composition of Korea's imports from the United States, 1981–92 (percentages)

Import commodity	1981	1982	1983	1984	1985	1986	1987	1988	1989	1990	1991	1992
Total	23.2	24.6	24.0	22.4	20.8	20.7	21.4	24.6	25.9	24.3	23.2	22.4
Food and consumer goods	47.4	49.6	50.4	42.8	36.8	30.9	33.8	36.3	37.2	34.7	29.1	29.8
Cereals	72.1	92.5	90.2	71.8	56.4	45.1	62.8	58.4	63.5	65.0	32.0	30.0
Direct consumer goods	23.4	27.7	32.1	36.8	33.4	31.2	29.1	31.7	28.7	21.2	29.8	32.6
Consumer durable goods	14.0	19.2	17.2	17.1	17.0	17.7	15.3	16.8	20.2	20.5	25.8	28.2
Industrial materials and fuels	16.1	17.7	17.0	17.3	17.2	18.5	18.8	20.7	20.4	19.9	17.5	15.7
Producer goods for light industry	43.0	46.3	44.3	46.3	47.4	44.1	45.9	46.7	47.3	47.6	41.7	41.7
Capital	18.7	31.6	28.3	25.4	22.8	21.4	22.0	27.4	30.9	27.9	29.7	29.5
Machinery and equipment	18.6	30.5	29.0	26.1	24.5	16.7	19.2	23.6	28.2	26.8	24.7	27.0
Electric and electronic machinery	14.8	44.2	41.1	35.9	33.6	25.3	23.4	25.7	27.6	25.2	31.7	27.7
Transport equipment	21.5	17.2	13.3	15.2	13.3	33.7	34.6	56.7	67.6	46.3	56.5	52.2

Source: Bank of Korea, *Monthly Balance of Payments*, various issues.

Table 7.12 Chronology of Korea-US trade friction

Regulated period	Types of regulation	Items
July 1974–June 1980	MFA quotas	Textiles
July 1977–June 1981	OMA	Footwear
1976–June 1982	Countervailing duties	Leather handbags
December 1978–June 1980	OMA	Color TV sets
January 1979–January 1984	Countervailing duties	Tires, tubes
1984–March 1992	VRA	Steel
1986–present	MFA quotas	Textiles
1987–present	Antidumping duties	Albums, color TV sets
January 1988	Withdrawal of GSP	
April 1988–present	Import prohibition order	Plastic bags
March 1989–present	Import prohibition order	EPROMs
June 1990–present	Antidumping duties	Acrylic sweaters
May 1991–present	Antidumping duties	Polyester films
December 1992–present	Antidumping duties	Welded stainless steel pipes and tubes
February 1993–present	Antidumping duties	Stainless steel pipe fittings
March 1993–present	Antidumping duties	Wire rope
April 1993–present	Antidumping duties	DRAMs
July 1993–present	Antidumping and countervailing duties	Flat-rolled steel products

MFA = Multi-Fiber Agreement; OMA = orderly marketing arrangement; VRA = voluntary restraint agreement; GSP = Generalized System of Preferences; EPROM = erasable programmable read-only memory; DRAM = dynamic random-access memory.

accession, the United States has adopted various means to restrict imports from Korea, including the invocation of the Super 301 provisions of the 1988 Omnibus Trade and Competitiveness Act.

In response, the Korean government has been trying to comply as much as possible. It has reduced average tariff rates from 25 percent in 1981 to 10.1 percent in 1992. The reduction of tariffs is more pronounced with respect to manufacturing goods than agricultural goods. The average tariff rates of Korea are still higher than the United States' 7 percent level, but they are scheduled to lower to a similar level, 7.9 percent, by 1994.

The United States has been showing great interest in opening up Korea's agricultural and service markets. In 1991, 243 agricultural and fishery products, including 62 US priority items, were fully liberalized. Since 1987, negotiations have been conducted concerning national treatment of foreign banks, protection of intellectual property rights, and opening of the insurance, motion picture, and advertising markets. The Korean and American governments have reached agreement on most of these issues. National treatment of US banks has been granted by allowing them access to rediscounts from the Bank of Korea and the privilege of issuing certificates of deposit. The establishment of US firms in the insurance industry has been permitted with a slight restriction in 1986. Agreements have been reached with respect to the importation of motion pictures and the opening of the advertisement market in late 1988. Furthermore, the Korean government has prepared and has been carrying out two five-year plans on the protection of intellectual property rights. The Unfair Competition Law was amended to extend protection to trade secrets in 1991, and the Semiconductor Mask Works Law was enacted in 1992.

In addition, under pressure from the United States, Korea revalued its currency by about 8.7 percent in 1987 and 15.8 percent in 1988. In 1989, the exchange rate was maintained at a steady level, reflecting the opinion of some economists, both Korean and American, that the Korean won had appreciated to an appropriate equilibrium level. On 2 March 1990, a market average exchange rate system was introduced to enhance the market mechanism's ability to determine the exchange rate. Since the adoption of the system, the Korean won has tended to depreciate, reflecting the current account deficit.

Differences in Korean and US Perspectives

The sentiment of the American public toward Korea over the last several years has had its ups and downs. As its basic undercurrent mirrors (albeit not perfectly) the attitude toward Japan, a brief account of what I perceive to be the gist of American sentiment toward Japan might be in order. The unfavorable side of American perceptions concerning Japan might be summarized as follows: Japan's economic success owes heavily to industrial targeting and mercantilistic commercial policies, which have been pursued in the postwar international systems under the aegis of the United States. It has shown little interest in fulfilling its responsibility as an economic superpower, even though it has been a major beneficiary of the postwar free trading system. Japan has been relegating the burden for their own and others' security to the United States and has been concentrating on economic buildup to undercut the US competitive advantage. It is employing all conceivable unfair practices in promoting exports and restricting imports, while paying lip service to the free trading system. Japan, after all, cannot be trusted.[6]

---

6. But, on the other hand, there are some favorable sides as well. Knowledgeable Americans do appreciate the effort of the Japanese government to "internationalize" its economy and to expand the domestic market, as exemplified by the Maekawa Report. They are aware that Japan cannot be entirely blamed for the large current account surplus with the United States and that the inflow of Japanese money to the United States has been an essential element in financing the US deficit. They maintain that close economic ties between the United States and Japan is a cornerstone of healthy international economic relations. Furthermore, there have emerged in the US strong antiprotectionist groups, which are strongly against restricting imports from Japan. A fair number of US manufacturers depend upon imports of intermediate goods from Japan, and in Washington and elsewhere there are lobbying groups whose interests lie in maintaining import flows from Japan.

Since the early 1980s, and particularly since 1989, the Korean government has been making a great effort to liberalize its rigid import regime, to liberalize restrictions in foreign investment, and to protect intellectual property rights. The motive behind these policies has been to achieve a structural transformation of the economy, as well as to improve economic relations with the United States and other trading partners. The US Trade Representative Office was also very sympathetic to the Korean efforts and helped avert an invocation of Super 301. Yet, the United States identified Korea as a priority watch list country in 1992 and 1993, reflecting the belief of US intellectual property rights owners that the Korean government did not efficiently implement IPR laws. Nevertheless, the two governments' fostering of amicable relations through cooperative efforts, coupled with the resolution of the trade imbalance after 1989, is expected to soften the friction.

However, basic differences in perspective persist. In the United States, Korea is often singled out as an unfair trader. Such comments frequently appear in leading newspapers and political statements. The progress of trade liberalization in Korea appears too slow to Americans; to them, Koreans are paying lip service to the principle of free trade and adopting delaying tactics. The Americans are annoyed at the eruption in Korea of an "antiexcessive consumption campaign" in 1990, interpreting this as inspired by the government to reduce imports. This perception has reinforced US impatience, unleashed in recent negotiations, and widened the gulf of misunderstanding. To many Americans, Korea's trade and industrial policy, its industrial and trade structure, and the style of conducting business strongly resemble those of Japan. The laws and regulations on trade and foreign investment are not transparent; they are subject to arbitrary interpretation by bureaucrats and are used to the disadvantage of foreigners. Korea was heavily responsible for the US trade deficit, they believe. Furthermore, Korea undermined the principles of the GATT during Uruguay Round negotiations in Brussels by joining the positions of the European Community and Japan, despite the fact that it is the greatest beneficiary of the GATT system. All in all, the sentiment seems to be that Korea is a "second Japan" and cannot be trusted. Korea has to show in deeds, not by words, that it will live up to the spirit of free trade.

These perceptions have been reinforced by several economic and noneconomic factors, some of which are of Korea's own making. First, Korea's exports to the United States are concentrated in two major sectors. One is the labor-intensive sector, with products such as textiles, apparel, and footwear, for which the import-penetration ratio of the US market is high. The other is the capital- and technology-intensive sector, in which the US has been enjoying a comparative advantage: automobiles, electronics, and machinery. This concentration has made Korea's exports much more visible to the Americans than would otherwise be the case.[7] Second, Korea's surplus has grown too dramatically in the last few years, thanks to what was hailed in Korea as the "three lows" prevailing in the international economy: low oil prices, low international interest rates, and low exchange rates (that is, the depreciation of the won vis-à-vis the yen). The dramatic increase of Korean exports during 1986–88, although based on temporary factors, led the American people to have an exaggerated view of the strength of Korean exports, and drew an unduly harsh reaction.

The Korean perspective on bilateral trade is very different from the US perspective. Koreans were somewhat bewildered by the impatience with which the United States pressed Korea on trade matters when Korea achieved current account surpluses during 1986–89. For the Koreans, who had experienced a lifelong current account deficit, the surplus itself was looked upon as a symbol, not only of export success but also of economic independence. The Koreans tend to regard their surplus as fragile, and they regard American pressure to reduce it as unfriendly and domineering, particularly in view of the fact that their country is still a very large debtor country. They are dismayed by the fact that the pressure did not abate, even when the Korean surplus with the United States disappeared after 1990. Korean exports to the United States cannot be expected to increase explosively for the time being, and Korea's imports from the United States are expected to outpace exports. The Korean economy is experiencing a great structural transformation, whose impact on trade will be more significant than is generally recognized. Korea's growth once was led by exports, but since 1989 it increasingly has been led by domestic demand, particularly by consumers, and growth slowed in 1992 as domestic demand shrank in response to efforts to tighten control of it. The extent to which this transformation is taking place may be too excessive, but the large increase in wages and other income has been powerfully shifting—prematurely, in my opinion—the comparative advantage of Korea from labor-intensive industries to technology-intensive industries. Unless and until Korea's technology and other innovative activities enhance productivity as much as wages increase, Korea's exports cannot be expected to grow rapidly. On the other hand, the great increase in nominal income, coupled with imports liberalization, has been inducing a powerful increase in imports, as demonstrated by recent developments.

Furthermore, the American perception that Korea is a small Japan is surprising and even annoying to the Koreans. True, Korea in the past emulated some Japanese practices: industrial targeting in the 1970s, the

---

7. Compared with this, Taiwan's exports to the United States are much more diverse in terms of the variety of goods and consequently much less visible than the Korean exports, despite the fact that total exports of Taiwan to the United States exceed those of Korea.

establishment of general trading companies in 197: tices in exports, among others. But to the Koreans, tl different from Japan: theirs is still a poor country, income is about one-fifth of Japan's, it is still sufferii burden of servicing external debt, and the surplus payments is extremely fragile (and actually turned to in 1991). Korea's industrial capacity is certainly no m, though it is vastly exaggerated in the United States. Ko automobiles and electronic products in the United State   . many of the components and parts used in major Korean exports are those imported from Japan.

As trade negotiations between Korea and the United States become increasingly product-specific, Koreans tend to regard the negotiations as promoting the interests of particular industrial groups rather than promoting the principles of free trade. The US position appears to the Koreans to be departing from GATT principles to promote its own interests under the guise of free and multilateral trade. Suspicious of their government's traditional "softness" toward foreigners, Koreans tend to believe their government is making unilateral concessions too easily, and they resent the Americans who elicit these concessions.

Policy Directions

Korea needs to review the basic direction of its foreign economic policy, in view of the fact that the economy is fundamentally changing. There are short- and long-run problems in need of reappraisal. The short-run problems do not seem to merit discussion in this book because of the rapidity with which change is occurring in the international arena; whatever stop-gap measure Korea takes now in response to external pressure, for better or for worse, will quickly be a thing of the past. Seen in this light, what the country needs is an appropriate long-run policy outlook upon which short-run policy should be conceived.

Complementary Foreign and Domestic Policy

Foreign economic policy cannot be separated from domestic economic policy; the former is but an extension of the latter to an international arena. Hence, they cannot have two different standards. For example, it is impossible to maintain a liberal international economic policy on the basis of an illiberal domestic economic policy, and vice versa. Just as Korea needs extensive liberalization in its international economic relations to fulfill its responsibilities, enumerated above, it needs to renovate its domestic institutions.

mate goal of an economic policy is to enhance the material
being of people and to contribute to the prosperity of the world
onomy. That is why I advocate a Korean economic policy today to
foster what I call long-run growth potential. Foreign economic policy, as
part and parcel of economic policy, should serve the same purpose; it
should extend and strengthen domestic policy to achieve this end. In
order to do so, the country needs to develop a global focus, to maintain
a liberal international trading system, and to play by the international
rules of the game.

One prerequisite for pursuing a liberal international trading system is
to undergo domestic liberalization by bringing down the web of controls
imposed on firms and financial institutions. Domestic liberalization should
precede external liberalization. The mercantilistic system in both the real
and financial sectors has to be replaced by a free and competitive one.
This basic direction is necessary for Korea because it, and only it, can
improve the efficiency of its economy and promote growth in the long
run, and not because it is forced to do so by a foreign country. This
basic policy line will enable the country to fulfill its global responsibilities. As emphasized above, Korea should be aware of its own importance in the world while being ready to pay the price for it.

Trade Negotiations

Korea needs to establish the fundamentals of its international economic
policy, based on the course set forth above, and maintain it consistently.
The country should improve its channels of communication with trade
partners and make greater efforts to increase their understanding of Korean
policy. There is no substitute for understanding—though it may not always be accompanied by mutual sympathy—in international trade diplomacy. It is a mistake to think that Korea can maintain amicable trade
relations with her trade partners simply by making concessions. Of course,
concessions can be made, and indeed, must be made; they are a necessary ingredient of international diplomacy. But when they are made,
they should be made within the boundaries of the basic policy direction.

Regulatory Transparency

Trade friction cannot be resolved once and for all by some magic wand.
Friction will always be there, even among friendly trade partners. Interests collide, and perspectives differ. For example, both sides may believe
they are abiding by the "golden rule" and still disagree: Americans want
Koreans to do to them in Korea just as they think they do to Koreans in
America, and the Koreans hold that they are doing to Americans just as
they are doing to themselves. But if the basic rules of the game can be

established, friction can be kept within bounds. Laws, regulations, and other institutions should be made as transparent as possible. The lack of transparency, which calls for arbitrary interpretation by bureaucrats, is a fertile source of friction. Until this changes, Korea will be on the defensive against ceaseless complaints, which will eventually require concessions.

Sensitivity to Indicators

In order for Korea to have a mature and enlightened long-run economic policy, the government as well as the people must take their trade figures and other macroeconomic indicators—current account surplus or deficit, the rate of growth, and so forth—with equanimity. After all, these figures can change in Korea as much as in other countries. There is no need to rejoice at a surplus or lament a deficit unless these figures reflect some long-term disequilibria. Short-run, ad hoc measures to deal with the temporary phenomena are poor substitutes for sound long-run policy direction.

Export Diversity

It is risky for Korea to concentrate on exporting a small number of items. Korea might have been too enthusiastic in expanding their market shares in a few products—automobiles, machinery, semiconductors—and not innovative enough in less visible and more traditional labor-intensive items.

Korea and Japan

The lopsided nature of trade between Korea and Japan and the one-way dependence of Korea on Japan in industrial technology suggest that Korea ought to reassess its trade and industrial strategy. The Koreans have been asking the Japanese to transfer industrial technologies to Korea in order to help reduce the huge Japanese trade surplus with Korea. To this request, the Japanese routinely answer that it is private business rather than the government that holds the technologies, and the government cannot force them to comply with Korean requests. Furthermore, the Japanese hold the view that Korea should welcome rather than lament its trade deficit with Japan because it is the very source of its industrial growth.

Aside from the question of which position is more logically founded, it seems clear by now that requests for technology transfer will not bear fruit. Korea should try harder to reduce its technological dependence upon Japan. Korea's trade deficit with Japan originates fundamentally from its technological deficit with Japan, which in turn originates from its emulation of Japanese industrial policy. It is no coincidence that the major export industries of Korea—automobiles, electronics, and machinery, which are dependent upon Japanese technology—coincide with major Japanese export industries. One can see why it is not easy to elicit Japanese "concessions" on technological transfer. Korea simply has to try harder to invest more time and resources to develop its own technology. This would help achieve a horizontal division of labor with Japan with regard to technological development.

Korea is different from Japan in one fundamental aspect, which militates against adherence to the Japanese model in the future. It is that Korea's domestic market is too small to allow it to maintain an industrial structure identical to that of Japan. The extent to which it is exposed to overseas influences is much greater for Korea than for Japan. At present, Korean exports constitute as much as 30 percent of its GNP; the same figure for Japan two decades ago was around 10 percent. The size of a country is inversely related to its degree of international specialization.

Agricultural Sector Liberalization

Korea faces intractable problems with respect to liberalization of the agricultural and financial sectors.[8] The Korean agricultural sector still holds as much as 16 percent of the total employed, much higher than the 6.4 percent in Japan. Should the imports of still more agricultural products be liberalized without heed to the still massive population in the rural economy, which is already heavily indebted, it will be difficult to assuage the farmers' discontent. Nonagricultural sources of income for Korean farmers amount to only 30 percent of their total income, so import liberalization of agricultural products strikes at the very heart of the farmers' livelihood. The only way to cope with this situation is to facilitate absorption of the rural population into the urban-industrial sector. But this, from now on, will be a slow process and cannot be done quickly. The government should devise appropriate measures to deal with this situation with patience and a long-run perspective. The trade problem has always been everywhere as much a domestic as an international problem, and it would prove disastrous to Korea if agricultural exporting countries were to extort from Korea what the country cannot afford to yield.

---

8. The second problem that the country has to face is the problem of liberalization of the financial sector. I have discussed this problem at length in chapter 6.

8

New Perspectives and Policy Directions

The preceding discussion requires little in-depth recapitulation. However, it might be useful for me to briefly summarize the strands of thought that run through the book. Specifically, I will summarize my views on characteristics of Korean economic development over the last three decades, briefly discuss the roles played by the agents of economic development, summarize the nature of the great transition period in which the economy finds itself, set forth my views on the need for and the contents of new perspectives on economic development, and discuss desirable policy directions.

Thirty Years of Korean Economic Development

I have characterized Korea's economic growth as a prime example of a latecomer's high-rate growth, which "condenses" the longer development process of developed countries. The economic history of industrialization has been replete with cases of very fast growth in backward countries. The most important source of growth in such economies was the technological backlog they could take over from advanced countries. A developing country with appropriate resource endowments could appropriate the low-level industrial technology used for producing those goods that had passed the peak of their life cycle. The developing country could also modernize its own institutions and even ideologies by imitating those of advanced countries. Modernization invariably has taken this form, and the more backward the country, the more rapid has been the pace of industrialization.

Thus far, Korea has achieved its high rate of growth by adopting an export-led growth strategy, which has allowed the country to make fullest possible use of its substantial endowment of human resources and to compensate for the shortage of poorly endowed natural resources. The export-led growth strategy was implemented by an energetic government in collaboration with business and labor.

One exogenous but no less important factor has to be added: the favorable international environment surrounding Korea during the postwar period, which featured US economic aid in the 1950s, a stable and global free-trade regime prevailing among nations, and strong demand for labor-intensive products in advanced countries. These have been very conducive to exploiting the latecomer's advantage. If Korea had developed in an international environment similar to that of, say, a century ago, when the flow of goods, capital, and technology was limited to advanced countries, development would have been well-nigh impossible, even with the positive roles played by the agents of development.

Roles of the Economic Agents

The three agents of development—government, entrepreneurs, and workers—were united to form a sort of "Korea Inc." during the 1960s and 1970s and played their roles more or less well. This unity was responsible for the initial success of the export-led growth strategy.

Role of the Government

Until the early 1960s, the Korean economy did not achieve noticeable growth; the country subsisted on US economic aid. However, some notable preparations for later growth were made during the presidency of Syngman Rhee between August 1948 and April 1960. Progress was made in developing education and in providing the basis for import substitution in light industries. After a brief and unsuccessful attempt at democracy between April 1960 and May 1961, the country was ruled by the late President Park Chung Hee until his assassination in October 1979. It was during this period that the Korean economy achieved its condensed growth, and the role of the government was a major factor in bringing it about and in molding the present economic structure.

The Korean government during the period under discussion consisted of two groups of individuals performing different functions. One group comprised top elites in the executive branch, who set up national economic priorities, made important decisions, and gave out orders. Virtually all important powers were concentrated in their hands. The other group consisted of the technocrat-bureaucrats, who devised the means to carry out priorities set by the elite.

When the priorities and the means were both appropriate, the policy succeeded. On some occasions, the policy failed because of flaws in the means, even though the priorities themselves were broadly appropriate. However, when the priorities were inappropriate, the policy almost invariably ended in failure because the means devised for carrying out the priorities merely magnified the error.

In setting priorities and implementing them, the government made a number of innovations with respect to its institutional framework and to its operation. The success of the government during the 1960s was due largely to these innovations. First, the government elites perceived popular consensus on the desirability of economic development and in 1962 launched the first five-year economic development plan, which was revised in the following year, incorporating in it timely policy innovations. Furthermore, the government made innovations regarding the agents implementing the plan. The establishment of the Economic Planning Board, headed by the deputy prime minister, who is in charge of national economic planning and coordination of those policies, was an organizational innovation. Formal and informal agencies, including the Korea Development Institute, were also founded to assist the Economic Planning Board, and the Professors' Committee on Plan Evaluation was established to evaluate the implementation and effects of the plan.

The success of the Korean economy during the 1960s has to do with the characteristic ways in which priorities were conceived and implemented; the government made an all-out effort to achieve industrialization. Virtually all policy measures at the disposal of the government were directed toward assisting business; not only traditional monetary and fiscal measures, but also policies on labor, foreign trade, agriculture, and finance were geared directly or indirectly toward assisting business.

During the 1960s, the priority set by the elite was to maximize exports, employment, and investment. The means devised to carry out this priority included exchange rate changes, foreign capital inducement, and monetary and fiscal reforms, in such a way as to conform the economy to the workings of the market. The export-led growth strategy succeeded because priorities and means combined to induce investment in labor-intensive industries in which Korea had comparative advantage. The initial success of the policy kindled a "can-do" spirit among the people, who followed the policy with great enthusiasm and bred a series of successes throughout the decade.

Furthermore, the government provided the economy with appropriate infrastructure. Roads, ports, and communication systems were established, often ahead of the demand for them. The government also established basic institutional frameworks to carry out the plan, such as laws and regulations regarding inducement of foreign capital and investment, the labor market, and the capital market.

The government, after the constitutional amendment in 1972, intensified its development effort, partly to legitimate the forcible constitutional amendment, which concentrated all powers, political and economic, to the incumbent president by guaranteeing lifetime tenure. The government set heavy and chemical industries' establishment as a priority, along with the goal of maximizing exports and income. The targeting of heavy and chemical industries in iron and steel, shipbuilding, nonferrous metals, machinery, electronics, and petrochemicals was designed partly to foster defense industries and partly to strengthen and deepen the industrial structure by establishing upstream industries.

The motives behind the new set of priorities were understandable, and the economic rationale was not illogical, to the extent that the country did need upstream industries. Troubles, however, arose from two sources. One was from the scale of the projects; they exceeded by far what the country could accommodate. The other was the government's assumption of the entrepreneurial function. Instead of leaving the initiative to private investors, the government took over major decision making.[1] In order to muster needed financial resources, the government exercised total control on money, credit, interest rates, and loans to specific projects. The incipient import liberalization policy was rescinded. The labor movement was suppressed, and controls on prices became widespread.

The government introduced innovations regarding organizations in charge of the heavy and chemical industrialization programs; in 1976 it established in the Presidential Office the Heavy and Chemical Industry Planning Council, which operated more or less independently of the Economic Planning Board. It also modified program implementation, including a wide variety of direct controls on bank loans and other resources. Many of these innovations ran counter to the price mechanism and economic principles. The results were waste and distortions in resource use, inflationary pressure, the emergence of immense conglomerates, and widening inequality in the distribution of income and wealth. Some would say that there were instances of success: some of the industries built during the 1970s—automobiles, shipbuilding, and electronics— became major export industries in the 1980s. But there were many more instances of excessive or redundant investments in the absence of a solid foundation of technology, skill, managerial ability, financial basis, and marketing prospects. Both the objective and the means adopted during

---

1. These two sources of trouble originate from the political motives behind the investment program: a large-scale success was needed to justify the forcible amendment of the Constitution. Thus, the government elite was impelled to take measures that substituted arbitrary decisions based on noneconomic considerations for market mechanisms. Organizational and other "innovations" that the government instituted during this period are discussed below.

the 1970s defied fundamental economic principles such as financial prudence and comparative advantage. Because it could not be sustained, heavy and chemical industrialization was phased out by 1979. The economy was rescued by the better performance of the light industries established during the previous decade.

During the 1980s, the priority changed from maximization of exports and heavy and chemical industrialization to price stabilization, and the means adopted were fiscal restraints, direct control of wages, and restructuring of industries. Partly aided by the reduction in the prices of imports including oil, the government succeeded in arresting inflation. But the anti-inflationary policy measures included strong doses of fiscal contraction, and in the face of growing demand for public services such as environmental protection and social welfare, the proportion of government spending in GNP declined until 1989.

Furthermore, the government introduced various measures for liberalizing the economy. The industrial targeting policy was discarded, the banks were denationalized, and trade was partly liberalized. But, industrial restructuring achieved little; economic concentration continued unabated, and imbalances wrought during the 1970s were hardly effectively addressed.

Throughout the postwar period, the government played the leading role in Korea's economic development, leaving a mixed record of successes and failures. It played its most successful role during the 1960s: in motivating the people, in establishing export-led growth, and in making a number of important innovations with respect to the operations of the government. During the 1970s, however, it played an even stronger role in trying to forcibly establish heavy and chemical industries. But it failed to achieve desired goals and left in its wake an unbalanced industrial structure, along with a built-in system of inflation. This is due largely to the fact that the objectives and means it employed departed widely from the institutions of the market. The government during the 1980s tried to correct the excesses and distortions of the previous decades, with some measure of success in moderating inflation, but at best marginal achievements in industrial restructuring.

Role of Entrepreneurs

The second most important agents of development in Korea were Korean entrepreneurs, who led the economy's industrial takeoff. Korea witnessed the emergence of vigorous entrepreneurship in the 1960s, and the quality of Korean entrepreneurship was quite excellent, both in terms of drive and business sense of the entrepreneurs. Some may have been surprised by this burst of entrepreneurial energy in Korea during the high-growth period because the country had little entrepreneurial tradition. However, it can be easily accounted for. At the initial stage of development, capital and technology could be easily imported from abroad, and the cost of labor and capital was low so that prospects for profit were exceedingly bright. Furthermore, the strong government supported entrepreneurs with monetary, fiscal, and other means, reducing the risk of their investments.

The heavy and chemical industrialization program in the 1970s, coupled with the general trading company, gave rise to great conglomerates. The government sought to achieve the twin priorities of its economic policy through aid to those large businesses that invested in priority areas and showed satisfactory export performance. Consequently, economic growth during the 1970s essentially was a story of the expansion of conglomerates.

This expansion involved an opportunity cost: the retarded growth of small and medium enterprises. Though the government tried to aid small and medium enterprises, the attempt was thwarted by the main thrust of the industrial policy, which has been to aid big business. The lack of satisfactory growth of small and medium enterprises, which are a reservoir of entrepreneurship, poses a major problem for the future development of the economy.

The most outstanding and persistent characteristic of Korean entrepreneurial behavior, especially that of the conglomerates, is their strong preference for expansion. The leading entrepreneurs demonstrated their willingness to expand investment, even in those industries in which they had little experience or knowledge. Expansion was achieved primarily through use of technologies and capital imported from abroad and through domestic finance made available by the government.

The internal organization of Korean businesses is also expansion-oriented. Ownership and operation of these conglomerates are concentrated in the hands of the single owners, who wield extraordinary power. The hierarchical system and the monolithic line of command have been conducive to swift and bold decision making, which often succeeded by committing the future in all-or-nothing gambits rather than in marginal ways.

Korean entrepreneurs certainly have played the key role in achieving condensed growth. They displayed fearless expansion, riding on a business environment characterized by government's assumption of major entrepreneurial functions.[2] The business environment during the 1970s in particular, created by the exclusive emphasis on heavy and chemical industries, was not conducive to stimulating small innovations by small and medium enterprises.

---

2. Depending upon the system of reward and incentives, the type of entrepreneurship that develops is different; when expansion is rewarded, entrepreneurs will do their best in demonstrating their ability to expand. This was clearly manifested during the 1970s.

Role of the Workers

The other important agents of development in Korea are
not just those employed by modern firms, but all other ꞵ
During the period under study, they simply worked ꞵ
under what might appear to others to be impossible conditions.
high growth of Korea was sustained by an abundant supply of labor,
low wages, and a high increase in labor productivity.

It has been the workers' nose-to-the-grindstone propensity that enabled the economy to withstand forces working against development.
The quality of the workers has been excellent in terms of their ability to
learn and adapt to the industrial environment. This has been buttressed
by the high level of education of Korean workers, which is higher than
in most countries in a comparable stage of development. And the productivity of labor has been increasing very rapidly.

Contrary to the widespread impression that wage rates in Korea have
been very low and have lagged seriously behind the increase in productivity, the share of labor in GNP has been increasing considerably; the
total real wage bill for workers has been rising as much as other income.
It is true, however, that the workers have been underpaid, considering
that the average Korean worker has been subject to long working hours
and unsafe conditions. Over the last several years, nominal wage rates
have increased greatly to compensate for the wage gap.

The labor disputes that swept the country on the wing of the democratic movement beginning in 1987 reflect the "underdog" psychology
instilled in the minds of the Korean workers. Recently, labor disputes
have subsided, and it is a testimony to the workers' ability to adjust to
changing economic conditions.

The Great Transition

The Korean economy continued to do reasonably well in the first half of
the 1980s, although the rate of increase of exports and income decelerated
somewhat. The balance of payments improved, alleviating the pressure of
foreign debt service. Inflationary pressure was arrested by tightening fiscal
spending and through favorable international developments. It was no
mean achievement for an economy that had experienced chronic inflation
for decades. But one source of inflation, perennial excess demand for bank
loans, remained intact; the contracted budget was inadequate to support
the necessary infrastructural investment, and this exacerbated the situation. The favorable performance of the economy merely postponed solution of manifold problems. The polarization of the industrial structure,
with giant conglomerates on the one hand and small and medium enterprises on the other, was accompanied by the premature decline of labor-

ensive export industries and bred inefficiency as well as inequity. Labor disputes, though suppressed, increased both in number and in intensity. The demand for democracy became widespread, and a sense of deprivation and distrust of the government began to emerge. The economy was facing a turning point, though it was buried under the surface. The system and functions of the government, the industrial structure, and labor relations, among others, needed rejuvenation.

As if to refute this view, the Korean economy benefited from international developments in the mid-1980s. The Asian Games in 1986 and the Olympic Games in 1988 instilled a renewed sense of national pride. The Plaza Agreement in September 1985 and the spectacular realignment of major currencies, which led to rapid depreciation of the Korean won vis-à-vis major currencies, gave rise to a tremendous increase in Korean exports, which in turn produced a sizable current account surplus and a growth rate exceeding 12 percent per annum for three consecutive years.

The surplus and the high growth rates, however, were a mixed blessing; they exceeded economic potential by far and as such could not be sustained in the long run. However, wishful thinking and short memory, which attended the fortuitous growth of exports and income, made people think the economy was stronger than it really was and deprived government and business of the chance to take seriously the problems inherited from the 1970s. Furthermore, the increase in profit and income gave rise to a great speculative fever, pulling up prices of land and other real estate to the great woe of small savers who had worked hard to be able to afford houses. Furthermore, Korean firms were much more enthusiastic about investments for expanding production capacity and real estate rather than in the rationalization of the production process and R&D expenditures, which would be indispensable to overcome increasing international competition and high wage rates. As a result, the structural weaknesses of the Korean economy became more evident than those of Japan or Taiwan as the bubbles in the economy began to burst in the early 1990s.

After the major currencies were realigned and the Japanese industries regained their competitiveness, Korea's export volume began to decrease, especially in advanced countries' markets, notably the United States and Japan. The surplus in the trade account, which amounted in 1988 to $11.4 billion, decreased to $5.0 billion in 1989 and was followed by a deficit of $2.0 billion in 1990. In 1991 the trade account deficit further expanded to $7.0 billion. Despite this lackluster trade performance, the economy has shown high growth rates during the last several years.[3] As a result of this GNP growth, primarily buttressed by surging domestic consumption and construction activity, the Korean economy was again

---

3. Growth rates for 1990 and 1991 were 9.3 and 8.4 percent, respectively.

severely battered by almost double-digit inflation and a record deficit in the trade balance in 1991.

Recognizing that the Korean economy urgently needs to improve its balance of payments position and to stem surging inflationary pressure, the government has since 1992 shifted to a macroeconomic stabilization policy, together with a policy for microeconomic structural transformation. To implement these policies, the government restrained construction activities, induced a mild increase in wage rates, and tightened money supply growth to below 18.5 percent, though the strong demand for funds persists.

In 1992, thanks to these policies, the current account deficit was reduced to $4.4 billion, a much greater improvement than expected, and consumer price increases stabilized at 4.5 percent. However, the GNP growth rate tumbled to below 5 percent, showing a sharp downward trend throughout the year.

Many people, especially those in the business community, argue that the sharp drop of the GNP growth rate in 1992 would eventually lead the Korean economy into severe stagnation and that the economy now needs monetary stimuli to regain high growth rates and equipment investment expansion. However, these arguments tend to overlook the fact that the Korean economy has not yet completely escaped from the dangerous trap of the bubble economy, which has undermined its long-run growth potential. This point will be elaborated in more detail in the next section of this chapter.

The high 1990 and 1991 growth rates themselves should not be cause for rejoicing because they were not a sign that adjustment was taking place in the desired direction. Rather, they indicated that the sources of growth were shifting from overseas demand to domestic demand. One might argue that the shift was more or less expected and was not entirely unwelcome. What was unwelcome was the abruptness and the speed with which the shift took place; just as the dramatic increase in exports during 1986–88 was overdone, the increase in consumption and construction in 1990 and 1991 by far overshot the appropriate level. If this state of affairs were to continue, the economy would have to suffer from either or both of the two phenomena: inflation and the greater balance of payments deficit.[4] Obviously, this state of affairs cannot be sustained long; the growth rate of the economy must eventually settle to a normal growth path[5] in order to reduce inflation and the balance of payments deficit.

---

4. The balance of payments deficit per se should not be a matter of much concern because Korea, as a developing country, should still be a capital-importing country. But the capital imported should preferably finance investment rather than consumption.

5. By normal growth path, I mean the rate of growth commensurate with potential growth rates. During the initial phase of the adjustment, the rate of growth may have to be even lower than the normal growth path.

Added to these difficulties, originating partly from the cyclical downturn and partly from weaknesses in the economic structure, was the great democratic movement that swept the country during 1987–90. All economic agents began to demand a larger share in the national income. Labor demanded higher wages, farmers demanded higher prices for agricultural products, the urban poor demanded better housing and social services, and the business class demanded more government assistance. The propertied classes were naturally less vocal, but their relative reticence did not imply their willingness to yield any part of their vested interest.

In this atmosphere, the old sources of growth, such as low wages, high productivity of labor, and a high propensity of business to invest, have largely disappeared. Wage rates increased during 1987–89 by about 70 percent, and in many manufacturing industries they more than doubled. The high rate of increase of real wages continues to this day. The high productivity of labor has declined, and so has the willingness to work long hours.

The propensity of businessmen to invest has also sagged, particularly in manufacturing. With frontiers of extensive investment largely exhausted and government assistance reduced, some businessmen have retreated to speculation in land and other real estate to make up for the loss of profit in their manufacturing industries. The technological backlog can no longer be readily exploited, as industries produce more products whose life cycles have not yet peaked. Firms have to rely more on homegrown technology and innovations. This in turn will require restructuring of organizations and business operations. Furthermore, the government can no longer devote all its attention to business; it has to attend to many new problems such as environmental protection, social welfare, and the less privileged.

These developments have precipitated the need for restructuring, which began to be felt toward the end of the 1970s but has been largely ignored for the last 10 years. The public still longs for a reinstated growth-promotion policy. It would be unfortunate, however, if more years are wasted and only mediocre performance can be expected in the future.

New Perspectives on Korea's Development

A prevailing perspective on Korean economy is that Korea's remarkable achievements continue unabated and that the Korean economy is very robust and strong. There are essentially no serious problems for the Korean economy, in this view. Even though there are some structural weaknesses—industrial imbalances and distributive inequities—they should not be exaggerated; they will eventually disappear with some minor policy adjustments. It is essential to maintain a high growth rate because no problems will be solved without growth. With a growth-oriented policy emphasizing technological progress, the economy will in due time restore its old growth path.

This perspective appears innocuous enough; its optimism comforts those holding the conventional view. But whatever merit this view might have had in the past, it is disappearing fast. Even though one may agree, as I do, with the view that the economy does have its own basic strengths, one also has to note its weaknesses, which have important bearing on future performance and should be addressed seriously. Growth based on an unbalanced structure and weak financial sector creates problems as well as solves them. Furthermore, growth can no longer be generated by a growth policy like that of the past; such a policy will only spur inflation and aggravate structural imbalances.[6]

Economic policy in the future should rest upon a new perspective—that is, the Korean economy is experiencing a great transition; the period of extensive growth is being phased out, and a period of intensive growth has set in.[7] The country is facing an extraordinary challenge, which calls for a new set of policies based on a new vision. Unless the country responds to the challenge, the growth momentum of the past will be lost.

The first fundamental point of the new perspective is that Korea's existing institutional framework, marked by the web of mercantilistic control on both financial and real sectors coupled with chronic inflationary pressure, will seriously impede future growth if allowed to persist in its present form. Economic development, in Korea as well as in other countries, depends upon people, who conform their activities in accordance with systems of rewards and penalties. Otherwise identical people will perform completely differently when confronted with different incentives and disincentives. The most important determinants of economic development, therefore, are the socioeconomic institutions governing these incentives.[8] Economic theory usually holds that institutions are given

---

6. Professor Tibor Scitovsky (1986) characterized Korea's economic growth during the period under study as a "forced" growth. If growth was so forced as to be accompanied by destruction of the whole range of the institutional framework, which, as will be discussed shortly, is the fundamental determinant of long-term growth, the country paid a very high price for it. Good institutions are hard to establish but easily destroyed. Bad institutions usually outlive their usefulness.

7. Not only the Korean economy but also Korean society as a whole is experiencing a historical transition. The authoritarian government has been replaced by a democratic government. The country has to achieve its own democracy; otherwise, neither social stability nor economic development will be possible.

8. Here, institution should be broadly interpreted to include not only the legal, administrative, and regulatory systems, but also the prevailing beliefs, values, and patterns of behavior.

and unchanging, and analyses are usually restricted to economic variables. But, what is far more relevant than economic variables to the problems of economic development—which is by definition a long-term process—are just such institutions. If they restrict economic activities, only some people are rewarded and others are discriminated against. Where incentive systems are unfair, the performance of the economy will fall short of its potential.

Korea has not yet established a firm institutional basis on which capitalism can soundly flourish. Mercantilist institutions persist, breeding inefficiency and corruption. Korea needs to establish a free and competitive system. To improve the institutional framework is never easy but should be urgently pressed.

One might think that institutions created by man can always be changed by him too. This is, of course, true. But, institutions are parameters of a society; people create institutions, but at the same time their activities are bound by them. Most people are myopic: they rarely perceive that institutions need change, and even when the need is perceived, they try to adjust to suit the institution before changing the institution itself. Even the most absurd of human institutions have lives of their own, especially when they are fortified with age and buttressed by strong interest groups that thrive on them. The most important responsibility of those in charge of the economic management of a developing country is to establish institutions that conform economic activity to the long-term development of the country.

The institutional strengths and weaknesses of the Korean economy have become manifest. In the early stages of industrialization, the Korean people responded very positively to more or less appropriate incentive systems, contributing decisively to good economic performance.

However, the economic and social institutions of Korea became distorted during the 1970s. In the economic sphere, the system of rewards significantly departed from the more appropriate ones established during the previous decade and spawned an unbalanced economy. The system of rewards established during the industrial targeting of the 1970s was an administrative system supported by mercantilistic policy, as opposed to a competitive price system—the former being a system of allocating resources through arbitrary decision making by an administrator, and the latter being the system of allocation through an impersonal and monopoly-free price mechanism. In the context of the Korean economy in the 1970s, the administrative system rewarded specified areas of activity—namely, exports and heavy and chemical industries, at the expense of other activities. An industrial structure, whatever may have shaped it, has a way of outliving its cause; the unbalanced industrial structure still shows little sign of abating more than a decade after industrial targeting was discarded. The rigged price system persists, as is exemplified in financial operations.

The second fundamental point of the new perspective is the necessity for fostering long-run growth potential, rather than to promote short-run growth. As already explained, economic growth cannot be engineered permanently by government. The old ways in which growth and exports are forcibly promoted are acceptable only when the economy is simple and small. Now these old ways had better be done away with. This is not to say that growth and exports are now less important than in the past. Nor does it imply that the role of the government in growth is necessarily lessened. It does mean that a short-run growth promotion policy in the 1990s will be self-defeating; it will bring only inflation and aggravate the existing structural imbalance—the very sources of growth deterrence. The short-run behavior of the macroeconomic variables—rates of growth of income and exports, saving and investment—are less relevant to long-run growth than is restructuring socioeconomic institutions. Only the latter can eventually pull up by the root the high-cost and low-efficiency economic structure.

The third point to be stressed is that the transition should be viewed from social and historical as well as economic viewpoints. From the social point of view, it is surprising and frustrating to witness the frequent outbursts of dissatisfied people in a country that supposedly has made such great strides. Considering that Korea is an extremely homogeneous country in terms of race and culture, one is led to construe the dissatisfaction as the result of an extraordinarily strong centrifugal force working against Korea's naturally cohesive society. This force is the perception that even though the people's economic well-being has improved, they have been unfairly treated. These complaints ought to serve as a reminder that it is the purpose of development to serve people rather than people serving development.

This new perspective of development is, by its nature, a historical one. One need not be a historical determinist to discern a variant of dialectics frequently at work in the process of economic development; even if a particular institutional arrangement works well for a certain period, it is bound, during the course of development, to serve those forces that in due course work in the opposite direction. The Korean economy has been managed by an authoritarian government for four decades, with a set of institutional arrangements that, for better or worse, have given a unique cast to the development of the country. With the authoritarian government gone and the system worn out, it is time for a new system.

A truly "strong government" should be defined as the government that succeeds in maximizing the nation's potential by deriving a broad national consensus through a rational and democratic procedure. Only a government of this type can successfully accomplish its historical mission, diminishing sociopolitical unrest among the people and satisfying the economic agents who faithfully observe agreed-upon norms.

The fourth and last point to be emphasized is the need for a new look at the relationship between Korea and the rest of the world. Korea, as a poor developing country intent on mobilizing all available resources for industrialization, has until recently been adopting a kind of mercantilist policy regarding trade, investment, and industrial policies. This policy was justified in the initial stages of development, and it served its purpose rather well.

But now that the stage of extensive growth is over, the country needs a much more liberal approach with respect to international trade and investment. The Korean people should be aware that their country has become an important one—more important than they realize. This importance transcends the economic size of the country and its per capita income. Korea is heir to several missions: as a country at the forefront of the newly industrializing countries, as a part of the Pacific Basin community, as a strategic location in Northeast Asia, and as the last country faced with eventual unification with the last of all Stalinist regimes. Korea has to excel in fulfilling these missions, which it can do by firmly adhering to the principles of the free and multilateral trading system. The country needs extraordinary vision, endurance, and courage to do so.

Korea is now exposed to international competition, and the only good way to survive in it is to compete with other countries, playing by international rules of the game. Korea has faced this competition only since the end of the Korean War, and nationalist sentiment has been very strong. But let no one be a prisoner of nationalism but use it constructively, and not destructively, for the good of the country. Needless to say, it will be inconvenient and costly to compete head-on with the world, but the country has to pay the price to receive the benefits.

From the international perspective, all Asian newly industrializing economies, including Korea, are in transition. They have all grown to what they are today on the wings of free trade prevailing during the postwar period. Korea's competitive advantage in labor-intensive manufactured goods is being eroded by rising wage rates, a diminishing rate of improvement in productivity, and increasing difficulties in achieving technological breakthrough. The technological gap with advanced countries is not being narrowed, while the gap with later-developing countries—notably, the countries of the Association of Southeast Asian Nations—is being closed. There is no room for complacency, and the best way to confront the future is to take risks by internationalizing.

The problems related to unification will loom increasingly larger during the remainder of this decade and beyond. Wishful thinking has it that unification will be forthright—achieved as soon as there is a major change in leadership in the North. Unfortunately, South Koreans' knowledge of North Korea is limited, and there is absolutely no predicting what will happen or how soon. In any case, the North should be induced to adopt an open-door and reform policy, and the channels of communication between North and South should be enlarged so as to establish a thread of mutual trust on which any discussion of unification must be based if it is to be grounded in realism. Under these circumstances, the best preparation South Korea can make will be to strengthen the fundamentals of socioeconomic development, based upon the perspective advocated here.

There have been, and will be, formidable changes in the domestic socioeconomic situation and international environments. Unless the people and the system adapt themselves to these changes, the sources of inefficiency will take firmer root, and economic performance will suffer accordingly. The sources of dynamic growth in the past—low wage rates, abundance of labor, high labor-productivity growth, a high rate of investment, the commitment of an authoritarian government to economic development, and a favorable international environment—have been substantially exhausted, without being adequately replenished by new sources of growth, such as a more rapid rise of labor productivity, innovations in technology and management, innovations in government, and social discipline and stability.

Policy Directions

Reorientation of the Role of Government— Innovations in Its Operation

One may broadly summarize the direction of economic policy in the future as macroeconomic stability with microeconomic liberalization. These policies are two sides of the same coin: price stability cannot be achieved without liberalization of government controls, and government controls cannot be liberalized if price stability is not achieved. In order to achieve the goal of price stability and structural reform, the government will need to maintain a key role. Just as it provided the general tenor of development in the past, so also will it provide the initiative for normalizing growth patterns for the future. The tasks ahead are now much heavier and more difficult. In the past, the targets were simple to define and the means of achieving them were straightforward; today, target-oriented policies are fast becoming counterproductive, the same policy instruments are not readily available, and the policies are less effective.

It is ironic that the people expect so much more from the government with democratization. The Korean people, who nursed their grievances quietly under authoritarian rule, now demand that the government redress them immediately. Yet the reach of government power has been significantly reduced. The instruments of direct control[9] in the economic policy arsenal of the government have ceased to be effective, and those of indirect control have in most cases never been very well-developed. During the authoritarian days, the government relied mostly on direct controls in its exercise of economic policy. Remnants of direct controls still remain, but no one now seriously expects them to promote the sound operation of the economy. On the other hand, indirect controls, which are supposed to work through the market, still do not work; the market mechanism has not been developed very well in areas where direct controls used to operate.

The Korean government has a reservoir of very capable people, but their outlook can easily become too obsolete to meet future needs. It would be easy for them to give in to the forces of inertia and to behave as if nothing had changed, despite the policy vacuum created by the departure from direct controls.

What the Korean economy most badly needs is reassessment of government's role. The structure of the government today, formed during the early days of economic planning, was suited for achieving selected targets, and the framework of economic planning conducted by the Economic Planning Board was one of setting targets and mobilizing all available means to achieve them. These are all out of date; the target-oriented economic planning and economic policy tools geared toward achieving economic targets no longer generate long-term growth because they are not very relevant to improvement in the system of resource utilization.

The system of target-oriented economic planning and the tenor of economic policy based upon it should be overhauled and discarded. This will require the government to change its structure and organization. As mentioned earlier, Koreans believe the government can and must do everything and that the government should be held responsible for solving all problems. It appears as if the government itself is not completely free from this illusion; it has been promising the people to do so many things that are beyond its ability. But as unkept promises and disappointed expectations pile up, so does distrust in government. As distrust deepens, complaints grow. No government, authoritarian or democratic, can be effective in such an environment.

---

9. The policy instruments the central government exercises consist of direct and indirect controls. Direct control means the alteration of economic variables or institutional operations through government order without intermediation of market mechanisms. Taking an example from monetary policy, the direct control on the money supply would take the form of the government's order to a bank to allocate a specific amount of bank credit to specific borrowers. Indirect control means the attempt of the government to alter economic variables through change of a policy instrument, which, through the market mechanism, is supposed to bring about the desired change.

The government has to establish its credibility among the people, ridding itself of the exaggerated view of its own abilities. The government has to unload the old and imaginary burden and take up new and realistic responsibilities to promote long-run growth. The general areas of new responsibility should be to establish institutions in such a way as to establish a free and competitive price system, restore balance in the economic structure by encouraging small and medium enterprises, provide greater equality of opportunity, help conglomerates gain clearer focus in their operations through specialization, establish a harmonious industrial culture, and to improve the educational system in order to help develop human resources.

In implementing economic policy, it is important to persuade the people of its soundness. During the authoritarian days, the government simply put into practice whatever policy measures it wanted. But this procedure has become quite inadequate. The Korean government has its own share of bureaucratic practices, along with conventions accumulated during the authoritarian days. It has been a poor communicator; its policies and actions have often courted public suspicion by virtue of the ways in which policies were formulated and implemented. Now the government ought to democratize the process of implementing policies and reduce its distance from the people.

Stabilization

It is highly desirable for Korea to achieve price stabilization. Those who have elementary acquaintance with the Korean economic scene know that inflationary pressure has become a semipermanent feature. The growth promotion policy gives a "go" signal to monetary and fiscal policy. The money supply increases, and the price level is pushed up. Price inflation gives rise to wage inflation, which in turn pushes up exchange rates and interest rates, and the government is forced to allow price rises in the public utilities it administers. The money supply increases again, pushing up the price level a second time. The economy is thus caught in successive prices rises.

Some prices—namely, of land, houses, and other durable goods—rise faster than prices of other goods, as people buy in the present to avoid the consequences of future inflation. Intense speculation on land and equities ensues, creating bubbles in the markets of these assets. The stabilization policy gives the "stop" signal, often belatedly. The bubble eventually bursts, and those who happen to own those assets suffer capital losses.

The most desirable policy direction to improve the high-cost *cum* low-efficiency structure of the Korean economy seems to be to abandon the stop-go type of macroeconomic management. Korea, for the last decade or so, has witnessed several cycles of this stop-go policy. When growth promotion pushes up prices, the government reverts to a tight-money policy, and when the fiscal and monetary tightening slows down the economy, the government eases up. This policy has progressively weakened the economy's efficiency.

It is impossible for Korean authorities to adopt a very stringent anti-inflationary policy because it will instantly cause great liquidity problems for the heavily leveraged firms. But it is highly desirable to take a reasonably visible stabilization policy stance consistently over several years, along with the liberalization policy discussed in the preceding section. If this is done, one may be sure that economic performance will greatly improve. Korea needs this combination of price stability and financial liberalization.

A note of caution is in order: this policy "mix" will cause many difficulties for the government because it will not immediately produce the desired effects. Many people want development without cost. They prefer an easy path to growth: inflation. The impatient public and opponents of an anti-inflationary policy will step up criticism against any anti-inflationary policy stance. Therefore, unless the government is confident that this policy mix is the right one, consistent implementation will be difficult. The government will find it easy to succumb and revert to the old stop-go policy.

Normalization of Financial Operations

Since the early 1980s, the controls of the government have been reduced. Controls on prices and wages have been reduced; international trade has been liberalized. The targeting of industries has been rescinded, and the government no longer interferes in business operations as extensively as in the past. However, the legacy of government interference in the past is manifest in important fields of the economy today, notably in the operation of the financial sector. Ownership of the commercial banks has since the early 1980s been privatized, but their operations are still not free from government aegis.

The financial system retains the remnants of the noncompetitive price system; it embodies the structural weaknesses originating from the distorted system of incentives of the past. No effort of the government to promote potential growth will be effective unless the financial sector operation is normalized through establishment of a competitive price system. Normalization of financial operations is a necessary, though not a sufficient, condition for establishing a competitive market-price system in Korea. The anomaly of Korean financial operations is exemplified by the perennial excess demand for bank loans, caused among other factors by the excessively leveraged financial structure of busi-

nesses.[10] The businesses have made maximum use of a[ll]
channels of finance—internal and external, formal and info[r-mal to fi-]
nance their expansion. They have had incentives to expand be[cause the]
return from expansion has been greater than the return from othe[r kinds]
of business activities. As long as highly leveraged businesses continue[to]
depend on bank loans, a great proportion of the loans will be reserve[d]
for these purposes, leaving bank loans for other businesses in perennial
shortage. There is a glut of bank loans for highly leveraged firms, while
there is only anemic help for new businesses and for those firms that
have tried to maintain financial prudence. The shortage of bank loans in
turn discourages innovation.

Korea needs to liberalize its financial system as soon as is practicable.
The third- and fourth-stage liberalization programs should be expedited
and carried out ahead of schedule. "Policy loans" should be phased out
as quickly as possible, and rates of interest should be liberalized. Banks
and nonbank financial institutions should be allowed to make their own
decisions regarding business operations, and extensive window guidance
should be rescinded. These liberalization policies will, of course, encoun-
ter problems, but these difficulties should not deter liberalization. If the
policies are carried out consistently, along with price stability policies,
one may be sure that financial saving will increase, interest rates will be
brought down, and the supply of loanable funds at commercial banks
will increase. This will relieve the small and medium-sized firms that
suffer from the perennial shortage of bank loans.

As liberalization proceeds and financial markets are integrated, monetary management and financial policy will have to be conducted by those
hands with knowledge and experience. The central bank is the natural
repository of such expertise, and it should be made more independent
of the government in its conduct of monetary policy through amendment to the Bank of Korea Act. When the Bank of Korea assumes authority to conduct monetary policy independently, it should pursue a
consistently anti-inflationary policy in order to dispel inflationary expectations because the Bank of Korea would be in a better position than the
government to end the vicious "stop-go" cycle that has characterized
Korean monetary policy in recent decades.

Other Policies to Strengthen the Bases of Sustained Growth

I have stressed the importance of strengthening the bases for continued
growth. Policies for promoting them, along with those discussed in the

---

10. The heavy indebtedness of Korean businesses has been caused by excessive expansion, which in turn has been caused by the business perception that the return from
expansion is greater than the return from technical and managerial innovations. The
tautly expanded businesses are viable only as long as business conditions are favorable;
otherwise, they will suffer losses and have to borrow more to service their debts.

the available
rmal—to fi-
ause the
types
to

. be those on education, labor, health, science
mental protection, and other infrastructure. Pol-
ugh not discussed in this book, are very impor-
litical as well as economic viewpoints. These ar-
due regard in the past, causing many serious
begun to be felt increasingly acutely in recent
some aspects of these problems throughout this
esist the temptation to dwell upon them further

Conclusion

Korea is regarded as a most promising candidate to join the club of advanced nations by the end of this century. In fact, if the present rate of growth continues throughout the 1990s, real per capita income will reach $10,000 by the end of 1996, as is envisaged by the Economic Planning Board. While this may be possible, the Korean economy will face a variety of challenges during the decade.

When the Korean economy experienced a precipitous downturn in 1989, accompanied by a series of violent labor disputes, a ripple of fear that the economy was in a crisis spread throughout the country. The rate of growth in that year was a mere 6.8 percent, and a crisis of confidence seemed to have seized the country. The performance of the economy in terms of macroeconomic indicators, to the extent that they reflected the cyclical downturn and structural maladjustment of the economy, were more or less expected. It was on these grounds that some people maintained that the situation was normal and that the "crisis" was nothing but a false alarm. There were, on the other hand, those who viewed the situation as a potential crisis; they pointed to the deterioration in the competitiveness of Korean exports in the international market and the deterioration of incentives in investment, urging the government to take appropriate policy actions to cope with the situation. When growth fell to 4.7 percent in 1992, after marking around 9 percent per annum in 1990–91, there was again much talk of a crisis.

Whether or not the word "crisis" is a correct expression of the present situation is beside the point. The real issue, perhaps missed by both contenders, is whether Koreans have awakened to the nature of the coming transition and are motivated to make concerted efforts to adjust to it before inertia takes root. Several years have passed since the democratization process was set in motion, and it is encouraging that improvements in many areas are being made, even though one wishes that the progress could have been faster.

Korea can be optimistic about the abundant growth potential of the country. The many good scientists educated abroad can enhance the level of science and technology. There are many good, experienced administrators who can establish order and discipline. And above all, there are people who still work very hard. The Korean people are now, as ever before, demonstrating exuberant energy in their pursuit of economic gain. As long as these motives are guiding economic life, a significant slowdown in economic activity is unthinkable, and the growth of the economy is assured.

However, the drive to prosper by itself does not guarantee achievement of a place among high-level industrial countries. In fact, it may do harm if it is not backed up by sound social ethos. The profit motive has to be channeled into productive uses. On the individual level, behavior has to be guided by professionalism and checked by a law-abiding spirit and sense of social responsibility. On the social level, it has to be bound by fair social institutions, broadly interpreted to include laws, regulations, conventions, and customs. The "invisible hand" can only bring social wealth when it operates within a proper institutional framework. If an acquisitive nature is let loose in a vacuum created by the lack of such an institutional framework, it could end up in a nationwide, zero-sum or negative-sum game.

Economic development, after the initial phase of extensive growth is over, has to proceed under the rubric of a proper institutional framework. Korea needs to establish this framework, to ensure a fair return for honest work, to eliminate the sources of unearned windfall gains, and to encourage fair and effective competition. "Turning calamity to blessing" is a venerable piece of oriental wisdom, and this can be achieved only by those who perceive change and adjust accordingly.

Appendix

Table A.1 Interest rates on deposits and loans at depository banks, 1961–92 (percentages)

| Year | Deposit rates | | Loan rates | | |
	Time deposit (1 year)	Installment savings (1 year)	Discount on commercial bills	General loans	Overdrafts
1961	15.00	5.00	13.87	17.52	18.25
1962	15.00	10.00	13.87	15.70	18.25
1963	15.00	10.00	14.00	15.70	18.25
1964	15.00	10.00	14.00	16.00	18.50
1965	26.40	23.00	24.00	26.00	26.00
1966	26.40	23.00	24.00	26.00	26.00
1967	26.40	23.00	24.00	26.00	28.00
1968	25.20	21.00	26.00	25.20	28.00
1969	22.80	19.00	24.00	24.00	26.00
1970	22.80	19.00	24.00	24.00	26.00
1971	20.40	17.00	22.00	22.00	24.00
1972	12.00	10.00	15.50	15.50	17.50
1973	12.00	10.00	15.50	15.50	17.50
1974	15.00	11.20	15.50	15.50	17.50
1975	15.00	11.20	15.50	15.50	17.50
1976	16.20	12.20	18.00	18.00	19.00
1977	14.40	12.20	19.00	16.00	18.00
1978	18.60	13.20	19.00	19.00	21.00
1979	18.60	16.20	19.00	19.00	21.00
1980	19.50	15.10	20.00	20.00	22.00
1981	16.20	13.80	17.00	17.00	17.00
1982	8.00	7.60	10.00	10.00	10.00
1983	8.00	7.60	10.00	10.00	10.00
1984	10.00	10.00	10.00–11.50	10.00–11.50	10.00–11.50
1985	10.00	10.00	10.00–11.50	10.00–11.50	10.00–11.50
1986	10.00	10.00	10.00–11.50	10.00–11.50	10.00–11.50
1987	10.00	10.00	10.00–11.50	10.00–11.50	10.00–11.50
1988	10.00	10.00	11.00–13.00	11.00–13.00	11.00–13.00
1989	10.00	10.00	10.00–12.50	10.00–12.50	10.00–12.50
1990	10.00	10.00	10.00–12.50	10.00–12.50	10.00–12.50
1991	10.00	10.00	10.00–15.00	10.00–12.50	12.00–15.00
1992	10.00	10.00	10.00–14.00	10.00–12.50	11.00–14.00

Source: Bank of Korea.

Table A.2 Korea: Interest rates and ratio of savings deposits and M2 to GNP, 1961–92[a] (percentages)

Year	Interest rates		CPI rate of increase	Ratio of M2 to GNP	Ratio of time and savings deposits to GNP
	Time deposits[b]	General loans			
1961	15.00	17.52	8.1	14.0	1.8
1962	15.00	15.70	6.6	14.5	3.4
1963	15.00	15.70	20.7	11.0	2.5
1964	15.00	16.00	29.5	8.9	2.0
1965	26.40	26.00	13.6	12.1	3.8
1966	26.40	26.00	11.8	15.1	6.8
1967	26.40	26.00	10.5	19.8	10.1
1968	25.20	25.20	10.7	26.4	15.5
1969	22.80	24.00	11.8	32.7	20.9
1970	22.80	24.00	16.3	32.2	20.7
1971	20.40	22.00	13.2	31.8	20.7
1972	12.00	15.50	11.7	34.6	21.7
1973	12.00	15.50	3.3	36.8	22.7
1974	15.00	15.50	24.7	32.3	19.4
1975	15.00	15.50	24.9	31.1	19.2
1976	16.20	18.00	15.4	30.2	18.8
1977	14.40	16.00	10.2	33.0	20.2
1978	18.60	19.00	14.4	33.0	21.4
1979	18.60	19.00	18.2	32.1	21.2
1980	19.50	20.00	28.8	34.1	23.3
1981	16.20	17.00	21.5	34.4	25.3
1982	8.00	10.00	7.1	38.1	26.2
1983	8.00	10.00	3.4	37.2	25.4
1984	10.00	10.00–11.50	2.3	35.3	24.7
1985	10.00	10.00–11.50	2.4	39.2	25.9
1986	10.00	10.00–11.50	2.7	37.3	27.1
1987	10.00	10.00–11.50	3.0	38.0	28.0
1988	10.00	11.00–13.00	7.1	38.8	28.9
1989	10.00	10.00–12.50	5.7	41.4	30.9
1990	10.00	10.00–12.50	8.6	40.1	30.6
1991	10.00	10.00–12.50	9.3	40.5	29.5
1992	10.00	10.00–12.50	6.2	41.9	30.8

CPI = consumer price index.

a. Figures for M2, total deposits, and time and savings deposits are all on an end-of-year basis.

b. Time deposit interest rate with a maturity of one year or less.

Source: Bank of Korea, *Monthly Bulletin.*

Table A.3 Taiwan: interest rates and ratio of savings deposits and M2 to GNP, 1961–92[a] (percentages)

Year	Interest rates Deposits[b]	Loans[c]	CPI rate of increase	Ratio of M2 to GNP	Ratio of time and savings deposits[d] to GNP
1961	10.80	18.72	7.8	23.9	12.9
1962	9.72	18.72	2.3	24.7	14.3
1963	9.00	16.56	2.2	28.5	16.6
1964	8.40	15.48	−0.2	31.7	18.0
1965	8.40	15.48	−0.1	33.3	18.9
1966	9.00	14.76	2.0	35.4	21.0
1967	8.40	14.04	3.3	37.7	21.4
1968	8.40	14.04	7.9	36.4	21.1
1969	9.00	14.04	5.0	38.2	23.6
1970	8.76	13.20	3.6	40.9	26.8
1971	8.25	12.50	2.8	45.3	30.1
1972	7.75	11.75	3.0	50.0	32.6
1973	9.50	13.75	8.2	50.0	29.9
1974	11.50	15.50	47.5	46.6	30.6
1975	12.00	13.75–14.00	5.2	55.9	36.8
1976	10.75	12.50–12.75	2.5	58.8	39.2
1977	9.50	11.25–11.50	7.1	66.2	44.6
1978	9.50	11.25–11.50	5.8	72.2	48.1
1979	12.50	14.75–15.25	9.8	65.4	44.1
1980	12.50	14.25–16.20	19.0	64.0	43.5
1981	13.00	13.00–15.25	16.3	64.1	45.3
1982	9.00	9.00–10.75	3.0	74.0	55.5
1983	8.50	8.50–10.25	1.4	84.5	65.3
1984	8.00	8.00–10.00	0.0	90.1	72.0
1985	6.25	6.25– 9.50	−0.2	104.7	86.3
1986	6.25	5.00– 9.00	0.7	112.8	89.7
1987	6.25	5.00– 9.00	0.5	126.9	99.8
1988	6.25	5.00– 9.00	1.4	137.2	106.5
1989[e]	(9.50)	(10.00)	4.4	142.9	110.2
1990	(9.50)	(10.00)	4.1	144.0	116.8
1991	(8.27)	(8.62)	3.6	154.2	128.1
1992	(7.75)	(8.30)	4.5	167.0	141.4

CPI = consumer price index.

a. Figures for M2, total deposit, and time and savings deposits are all on an end-of-year basis.

b. Time deposit rates are for a maturity of six months in 1961–65, nine months in 1966–74, and one year since 1975.

c. Unsecured loan rates of banks.

d. M2 minus M1A.

e. The ceilings and floors on deposit and lending rates were completely abolished on 19 July 1989. Figures in parentheses are deposit or lending rates offered or charged by First Commercial Bank.

Source: Central Bank of China, *Financial Statistics Monthly Taiwan District.*

Table A.4 Japan: interest rates and ratio of savings deposits and M2 to GNP, 1961-92[a] (percentages)

Year	Interest rates Deposits[b]	Loans[c]	CPI rate of increase	M2 as a share of GNP	Time and savings deposit as a share of GNP
1961	5.50	8.20	5.3	64.9	28.7
1962	5.50	8.09	6.8	71.1	31.0
1963	5.50	7.67	7.6	75.5	31.8
1964	5.50	7.99	3.9	75.3	31.8
1965	5.50	7.61	6.6	75.4	32.0
1966	5.50	7.37	5.1	74.6	32.3
1967	5.50	7.35	4.0	73.6	31.9
1968	5.50	7.38	5.3	71.5	31.7
1969	5.50	7.61	5.2	71.5	30.9
1970	5.25	7.69	7.7	72.2	30.7
1971	5.75	7.46	6.1	81.4	34.4
1972	5.25	6.72	4.5	87.1	37.5
1973	6.25	7.93	11.7	84.2	34.7
1974	7.75	7.37	24.5	79.3	31.7
1975	6.75	8.51	11.8	82.3	33.4
1976	5.25	8.18	9.3	83.1	33.9
1977	5.25	6.81	8.1	83.2	34.8
1978	4.50	5.95	4.2	85.6	35.8
1979	6.00	7.06	3.7	86.5	36.5
1980	6.25	8.27	7.7	85.2	37.3
1981	5.75	7.56	4.9	89.1	39.0
1982	5.75	7.15	2.8	91.6	39.9
1983	5.50	6.81	1.9	93.9	41.9
1984	5.50	6.57	2.3	94.8	41.9
1985	5.50	6.47	2.0	96.8	43.7
1986	3.76	5.51	0.6	101.2	46.4
1987	3.39	4.94	0.1	106.9	51.6
1988	3.39	4.93	0.7	110.7	54.2
1989	4.32	5.78	2.3	115.8	68.5
1990	6.08	7.70	3.1	116.0	68.6
1991	5.25	6.99	3.3	112.6	64.1
1992	3.82[d]	5.62	1.7	109.5	61.5

CPI = consumer price index.

a. Figure for M2, total deposits, time and savings deposits are all on an end-of-year basis.
b. Time deposit interest rates with a maturity of one year or less.
c. Average contract interest rates on loans and discounts of all banks.
d. Deposit interest rate on Small Money Market Certificates. Ceiling rates based on Temporary Interest Rates Adjustment Law.

Source: Bank of Japan, *Economic Statistics Annual.*

References

Balassa, Bela. 1985. *The Newly Industrializing Country in the World Economy*. New York: Permagon Press.

Balassa, Bela, and John Williamson. 1987. *Adjustment to Success: Balance of Payments Policy in the East Asian NUCs*. Washington: Institute for International Economics.

Bank of Korea. 1982. *The Korean Economy: Performance and Prospect*. Seoul.

Bank of Korea. 1990. *The 40-Year History of the Bank of Korea*. Seoul (in Korean).

Bank of Korea. 1993. *The Korean Economy—Past Performance and Current Issues*. Seoul.

Bloomfield, Arthur I., and John P. Jensen. 1967. *Reports and Recommendations on Monetary Policy and Banking in Korea*. Seoul: Bank of Korea.

Cho, Dong Sung. 1987. *The General Trading Company—Concepts and Strategy*. Lexington, MA: Lexington Books.

Cho, Soon. 1979. "A Study on Medium-Term and Long-Term Development Strategy. A report submitted to the Korean Government." Mimeo (in Korean).

Cho, Soon. 1987. "Economic Development and Social Development in the Process of Modernization." *Kyong Je Hak Yon Gu* 35: 215–25. Seoul (in Korean).

Cho, Soon. 1988. "Equity Problem in Korea." Paper presented at the Third International Meeting of the Korean Economists. Seoul: Korean Economic Association (in Korean).

Cho, Soon. 1990. "Economic Development in Korea: Some Characteristics and Problems during the Past Four Decades." *Seoul Journal of Economics* 3, no. 1: 101–26.

Cho, Soon. 1991. "Development Strategy of the Korean Economy." *Korean Economic Journal* 30, no. 3: 231–51. Seoul (in Korean).

Cho, Yoon Je. 1988. "The Effect of Financial Liberalization on the Efficiency of Credit Allocation—Some Evidence from Korea." *Journal of Development Economics* 29, no. 1: 101–10.

Choo, Hak-Joong. 1979. *Income Distribution and Its Determining Factors in Korea* 1. Seoul: Korea Institute of Development (in Korean).

Choo, Hak-Joong. 1982. *Income Distribution and Its Determining Factors in Korea* 2. Seoul: Korea Institute of Development (in Korean).

Chung, Un-Chan. 1982. "Korean Finance at the Crossroads." *Korean Economic Journal* 21, no. 4: 427–64. Seoul (in Korean).

Chung, Un-Chan. 1987. "Economic Growth and Financial Development in Korea, 1962–1982." Paper presented at Conference on Economic Development of Japan and Korea. Honolulu: East-West Center.

Cole, David C., and Yung Chul Park. 1983. *Financial Development in Korea 1945–78*. Cambridge, MA: Harvard University Press.

Dornbusch, Rudiger, and Yung Chul Park. 1987. "Korean Economic Policy." *Brookings Paper on Economic Activity* 2: 389–444. Washington: Brookings Institution.

East Rock Institute. 1988. *The Dynamics of US-Korea Trade Relations: Economic, Political, Legal, and Cultural*. New Haven: Whitney Humanities Center, Yale University.

Eucken, Walter. 1952. *Principles of Economic Policy*. Translated into Japanese by Tadao Ohno. Tokyo: Keiso Shobo (in Japanese).

Federation of Korean Industries. 1986. *The 40-Year History of Korean Economic Policy*. Seoul (in Korean).

Gerschenkron, Alexander. 1962. *Economic Backwardness in Historical Perspective*. New York: Frederick A. Praeger.

Gurley, John G., Hugh T. Patrick, and E. S. Shaw. 1965. "The Financial Structure of Korea." Seoul: Agency for International Development. Mimeo.

Hattori, Tamio. 1987. *The Industrial Development of Korea*. Tokyo: Institute of Developing Economies (in Japanese).

Heavy and Chemical Industry Planning Council. 1974. *The Heavy and Chemical Industry Plan Objectives*. Seoul: Heavy and Chemical Industry Planning Council. Mimeo (in Korean).

Hong, Won Tack. 1976. *Factor Supply and Factor Intensity of Trade in Korea*. Seoul: Korea Development Institute.

Hong, Won Tack. 1979. *Trade, Distortions, and Employment Growth in Korea*. Seoul: Korea Development Institute.

Hou, Chi-ming. 1987. "Strategy for Industrial Development." Conference on Economic Development in the Republic of China on Taiwan. Taipei: Chung-Hua Institution for Economic Research.

Ito, Teiichi, ed. 1984. *Business Leadership in Developing Countries*. Tokyo: Asia Keizai Kenkyonjo (in Japanese).

Jones, Homer. 1968. *Korean Financial Problems*. Prepared under the auspices of Agency for International Development. United States Operations Mission to Korea. Mimeo.

Jones, Leroy P., and Il SaKong. 1980. *Government, Business, and Entrepreneurship in Economic Development: The Korean Case*. Cambridge, MA: Harvard University Press.

Jwa, Sung-Hee. 1988. "The Political Economy of Market-Opening Pressure and Response: Theory and Evidence for the Case of Korea and the U.S." *Seoul Journal of Economics* 1, no. 4: 387–415.

Kim, Chojng Woong. 1986. "Industrial Development and Policy Loans." *Korea Development Review* 8, no. 1: 43–76. Seoul (in Korean).

Kim, Choongsoo. 1991a. *Wage Policy and Labor Market Development of Korea*. NIESI Working Paper 9101. Seoul: National Institute for Economic Systems and Information.

Kim, Choongsoo. 1991b. *The Role of Government in a Transition to a Market Economy-Lessons From Korea's Economic Development Experiences*. NIESI Working Paper 9105. Seoul: National Institute for Economic Systems and Information.

Kim, Kwang Suk, and Michael Roemer. 1979. *Growth and Structural Transformation*. Cambridge, MA: Harvard University Press.

Kirschen, E. S. and Associates. 1964. *Economic Policy in Our Time* (volumes 1, 2, and 3). Amsterdam: North-Holland Publishing Company.

Korea Development Finance Corporation. 1970. *Money and Capital Markets in Korea and the Potential for Their Improvement*. Seoul: Korea Development Finance Corporation. Mimeo (in Korean).

Krause, Lawrence B. 1982. *US Economic Policy Toward the Association of Southeast Asian Nations: Meeting the Japanese Challenge*. Washington: Brookings Institution.

Krueger, Anne O. 1979. *The Developmental Role of the Foreign Sector and Aid.* Cambridge, MA: Harvard University Press.

Kuznets, Simon. 1966. *Modern Economic Growth.* New Haven: Yale University Press.

Kwack, Sung Y. 1986. "The Role of Financial Policies and Institutions in Korea's Economic Development and Un-Chan Chung Process." In H. Cheng, *Financial Policies and Reforms in Pacific Basin Countries.* Lexington, MA: Lexington Books.

Kwack, Sung Y. 1988. "Korea's Exchange Rate Policy in a Changing Economic Environment." *World Development* 16, no. 1: 169–83.

Kwack, Sung Y. 1989. "Growth and Distribution in Korean Economy." *Kyong Je Hak Yon Gu* 37: 145–67. In Korean.

Kwon, Jene K. 1986. "Capital Utilization, Economies of Scale, and Technical Change in the Growth of Total Factor Productivity." *Journal of Development Economics* 24: 75–89.

Kwon, Jene K., ed. 1990. *Korean Economic Development.* New York: Greenwood Press.

Leamer, Edward E. 1984. *Sources of International Comparative Advantage.* Cambridge, MA: MIT Press.

Lee, Hyo-Soo. 1988. "A Comparative Analysis of Industrial Relations: Korea and Japan." *The Korean Economic Review* 4, no. 1: 227–56.

Lee, Joung Woo. 1983. "Economic Development and Wage Inequality in South Korea." Ph.D. dissertation at Harvard University, Cambridge, MA.

Lee, Kyu-Uck. 1985. *Mergers and Economic Concentration.* Seoul: Korea Research Institute (in Korean).

Lee, Kyu-Uck, and Sung-Soon Lee. 1985. *Business Integration and Economic Power.* Seoul: Korea Development Institute (in Korean).

Lee, T. H., and Kuo-shu Liang. 1982. "Taiwan." In Bela Balassa and Associates, *Development Strategies for Semi-Industrial Economies.* Baltimore: Johns Hopkins University Press.

Lewis, W. A. 1955. *The Theory of Economic Growth.* London: George Allen and Unwin.

Lim, Jongchul. 1982. "Basic Nature and Achievements of Korean Foreign Trade (1962–81)." *Korean Economic Journal* 21, no. 4: 471–528. Seoul (in Korean).

Lim, Jongchul. 1991. "Growth and Structural Change." *Korean Economic Journal* 30, no. 3: 257–86.

Luedde-Neurath, Richard. 1986. *Import Control and Export-Oriented Development.* London: Westview Press.

Mason, Edward S. et al. 1980. *The Economic and Social Modernization of the Republic of Korea.* Cambridge, MA: Harvard University Press.

McKinnon, Ronald I. 1983. *Money and Capital in Economic Development.* Washington: Brookings Institution.

Ministry of Labor. 1986. "The Report on the Survey of the Wage Situation by Occupation." Seoul: Ministry of Labor. In Korean.

Musgrave, R. A. 1965. *Revenue Policy for Korea's Economic Development.* A report submitted to Robert R. Nathan Associates. Seoul (mimeo).

Nam, Chong-Hwan. 1988. "Growth Pattern and Policy Regime." *Korean Economic Journal* 27, no. 4: 463–80.

Noland, Marcus. 1990. *Pacific Basin Developing Countries: Prospects for the Future.* Washington: Institute for International Economics.

Ohkawa, Kazushi. 1970. *Economic Development and Experiences of Japan.* Tokyo: Daimei-do (in Japanese).

Okimoto, Daniel I. 1989. *Between MITI and the Market-Japanese Industrial Policy for High Technology.* Stanford, CA: Stanford University Press.

Pack, Howard, and Larry E. Westphal. 1986. "Industrial Strategy and Technological Change." *Journal of Development Economics* 22: 87–128.

Park, Chong Kee. 1975. *Social Security in Korea—an Approach to Socio-Economic Development.* Seoul: Korea Development Institute.

Park, Fun-Koo, and Se-Il Park. 1984. *Wage Structure of Korea.* Seoul: Korea Development Institute.

Park, Yung Chul. 1989. *Essays on Trade and Development in Asia Pacific.* Seoul: Korea Research Institute for Human Settlements (in Korean).

Park, Yung Chul. 1989. *Essays on Trade and Development of Financial Industry in Korea.* Seoul: Korea Development Institute (in Korean).

Rowley, Anthony. 1987. *Asian Stock Market: The Inside Story.* Homewood: Dow-Jones-Irwin.

Scitovsky, Tibor. 1986. "Economic Development in Taiwan and South Korea, 1965–81." In Lawrence H. Lau, *Model of Development.* San Francisco: Institute of Contemporary Studies Press.

Shinohara, Myohei. 1961. *The Growth and Cycles of the Japanese Economy.* Tokyo: Sobunsha (in Japanese).

Smith, Adam. 1950 [1776]. *An Inquiry into the Nature and Causes of the Wealth of Nations.* London: Methuen.

Steinberg, David I. 1985. *Foreign Aid and the Development of the Republic of Korea: the Effectiveness of Concessional Assistance.* Washington: US Agency for International Development.

Suzuki, Yoshio. 1985. *Financial Deregulation and Financial Policy.* Tokyo: Toyo Keizai Shinposha (in Japanese).

Westphal, Larry E., Yung W. Rhee, and Garry Purcell. 1981. *Korean Industrial Competence: Where it Came From.* World Bank Staff Working Paper no. 469. Washington: World Bank.

World Bank. 1979. *Korea: Policy Issues for Long-Term Development.* Washington: World Bank.

World Bank. 1987. *Korea: Managing Industrial Transition.* Washington: World Bank.

Yonekawa, Shinichi, and Hideki Yoshihara, eds. 1987. *Business History of General Trading Companies.* Tokyo: University of Tokyo Press (in Japanese).

Yoo, Jung-Ho. October 1990. *The Industrial Policy of the 1970s and the Evolution of the Manufacturing Sector in Korea.* KSI Working Paper no. 9017. Seoul: Korea Development Institute.

Young, Soo-gil. 1989. *Trade Policy Problems of the Republic of Korea and the Uruguay Round.* KDI Working Paper no. 8913. Seoul: Korea Development Institute.

Young, Soo-gil. 1983. *Basic Problems of Industrial Policies and Remodeling Direction of Support Policies.* Seoul: Korea Development Institute (in Korean).

Index

Chemical industries, buildup of, 38–44, 150, 150n, 180–181
China, relations with Korea, 162
Chun Doo Hwan regime
  export policy, 152–153
  fifth five-year plan, 47–50
  financial policy, 119–121, 132, 138
  sixth five-year plan, 50–56
Citizens National Bank, 112
Clerical workers, wages for, 93–95, 94t
Commercial banks
  denationalization of, 120
  loan management regulation, 77
Committee for Development of the Financial System, 131–132
Commodities
  market-dominating, number of, 66–67, 67t
  from noncompetitive manufacturers, 67, 68t
Communication effect, 65
Communist nations, trade with, 55
Comprehensive Stabilization Program, 40
Conglomerates, 62–64, 63n
  behavioral characteristics of, 71–72
  dominance and significance of, 67–68, 68n
  efficiency of, 72–74, 74n
  expansion of, 65–66, 182
  macroeconomic aspects of, 66–68
  microeconomic aspects of, 68–69
  prototype of, 69n
  shares in manufacturing shipments and employment, 68, 69t
  specialization of, 77
Constitution of the Republic of Korea
  amended, November 1954, 13
  first, 13, 102
  Yushin (Revitalization), 38
Counterpart Fund, 14
Creative destruction, 78
Curb loan market, 130
Currency. See also Exchange rates
  depreciation of, 170, 184
  revaluation of, 170
Current account deficit, 185
Customs duties, by type of good, 155, 156t

Democratic Justice Party, 50
Democratic Party government. See also Park Chung Hee regime
  during 1960–61, 33
  economic policy, 32
Democratization, demand for, 52–53
Depository banks, interest rates on deposits and loans at, 201t
Deregulation, of interest rates, 120n, 120–121, 122t–123t
Development. See Economic development
Domestic finance, internationalization of, 138–141
Domestic policy, foreign policy and, 173–174

Economic development. See also Growth; Industrialization
  big-push model of, 6
  five-year plans, 27–59
  history of, 177–178
  new perspectives on, 186–191
  in 1950s and 1960s, 11–26
  recent, 58–59
  role of entrepreneurs in, 181–182
  role of government in, 7–9, 36, 42, 178–181
  reorientation of, 191–193
  role of workers in, 183
Economic hardware, 8
Economic planning, target-oriented, 192
Economic Planning Board (EPB), 41, 54, 179
  establishment of, 33
Economic policy. See also Industrial policy; specific policy
  directions, 191–197
  of first five-year plan, 29–31
  future, 187
  goal of, 174
  in 1950s, 11–16
  to strengthen bases of sustained growth, 195–196
Economic software, 8
Economy
  degree of concentration, 65–66
  efficiency of, 72–74
  global, Korea in, 159–163
  institutional framework, 188
  present situation, 196–197
  restructuring of
    during fifth plan period, 48–50
    future, 76–79
    past, 74–76
    since early 1960s, 20–21
  3D syndrome, 100
  transition of, 183–186
    social and historical viewpoints, 189
Education, policy emphasis on, 101n, 101
Electrical Industry Promotion Act (1969), 36
Emergency Decree on Economic Stabilization and Growth, 42
Emergency Monetary Measure, 28
Employment. See Labor; Unemployment
Entrepreneurs
  behavioral characteristics of, 71–72
  encouraging, 78–79
  role in development, 181–182
Entrepreneurship, 182, 182n
  and industrial structure, 61–66
EPB. See Economic Planning Board
Equity, 74n
  during second plan period, 37–38
  during sixth plan period, 54–55
  social, regulation to ensure, 81–82
  during third plan period, 44
Exchange rates, 55, 55n
  international adjustment, 39

Other Publications from the
Institute for International Economics

POLICY ANALYSES IN INTERNATIONAL ECONOMICS Series

BOOKS

Economic Sanctions Reconsidered (in two volumes)
  Economic Sanctions Reconsidered: Supplemental Case Histories
  Gary Clyde Hufbauer, Jeffrey J. Schott, and Kimberly Ann Elliott/*1985, 2d ed.*
    December 1990
                        ISBN cloth 0-88132-115-X   928 pp.
                        ISBN paper 0-88132-105-2   928 pp.

  Economic Sanctions Reconsidered: History and Current Policy
  Gary Clyde Hufbauer, Jeffrey J. Schott, and Kimberly Ann Elliott/*December 1990*
                        ISBN cloth 0-88132-136-2   288 pp.
                        ISBN paper 0-88132-140-0   288 pp.

Pacific Basin Developing Countries: Prospects for the Future
Marcus Noland/*January 1991*
                        ISBN cloth 0-88132-141-9   250 pp.
                        ISBN paper 0-88132-081-1   250 pp.

Currency Convertibility in Eastern Europe
John Williamson, editor/*October 1991*
                        ISBN cloth 0-88132-144-3   396 pp.
                        ISBN paper 0-88132-128-1   396 pp.

Foreign Direct Investment in the United States
Edward M. Graham and Paul R. Krugman/*1989, 2d ed. October 1991*
                        ISBN paper 0-88132-139-7   200 pp.

International Adjustment and Financing: The Lessons of 1985-1991
C. Fred Bergsten, editor/*January 1992*
                        ISBN paper 0-88132-112-5   336 pp.

North American Free Trade: Issues and Recommendations
Gary Clyde Hufbauer and Jeffrey J. Schott/*April 1992*
                        ISBN cloth 0-88132-145-1   392 pp.
                        ISBN paper 0-88132-120-6   392 pp.

American Trade Politics
I. M. Destler/*1986, 2d ed. June 1992*
                        ISBN cloth 0-88132-164-8   400 pp.
                        ISBN paper 0-88132-188-5   400 pp.

Narrowing the U.S. Current Account Deficit
Allen J. Lenz/*June 1992*
                        ISBN cloth 0-88132-148-6   640 pp.
                        ISBN paper 0-88132-103-6   640 pp.

The Economics of Global Warming
William R. Cline/*June 1992*
                        ISBN cloth 0-88132-150-8   416 pp.
                        ISBN paper 0-88132-132-X   416 pp.

U.S. Taxation of International Income: Blueprint for Reform
Gary Clyde Hufbauer, assisted by Joanna M. van Rooij/*October 1992*
                        ISBN cloth 0-88132-178-8   304 pp.
                        ISBN paper 0-88132-134-6   304 pp.

Who's Bashing Whom? Trade Conflict in High-Technology Industries
Laura D'Andrea Tyson/*November 1992*
                        ISBN cloth 0-88132-151-6   352 pp.
                        ISBN paper 0-88132-106-0   352 pp.

SPECIAL REPORTS

FORGHCOMING

For orders outside the US and Canada please contact:

Longman Group UK Ltd.
PO Box 88
Harlow, Essex CM 19 5SR
UK

Telephone Orders: 0279 623925
Fax: 0279 453450
Telex: 817484